Program Development in UNIX®

Program Development in UNIX®

Case Study Approach

J. T. Shen

Prentice Hall PTR
Upper Saddle River, NJ 07458
http://www.prenhall.com

Library of Congress Cataloging-in-Publication Data

```
Shen, J. T.
      Program development in UNIX : case study approach / J. T. Shen.
      p.  cm.
      Includes bibliographical references and index.
      ISBN 0-13-237397-1 (pbk.)
         1. Computer software—Development. 2. UNIX (Computer file)
      I. Title.
   QA76.76.D47S489  1997
   005.1—dc20                                    96-42338
                                                    CIP
```


Editorial/production supervision: *BooksCraft, Inc., Indianapolis, IN*
Cover design director: *Jerry Votta*
Cover design: *Design Source*
Acquisitions editor: *Mike Meehan*
Manufacturing manager: *Alexis R. Heydt*

© 1997 by Prentice Hall PTR
Prentice-Hall, Inc.
A Simon & Schuster Company
Upper Saddle River, NJ 07458

The publisher offers discounts on this book when ordered in bulk quantities.
For more information, contact:

Corporate Sales Department
Prentice Hall PTR
One Lake Street
Upper Saddle River, NJ 07458
Phone: 800-382-3419   Fax: 201-236-7141
E-mail: corpsales@prenhall.com.

All product names mentioned herein are the trademarks of their respective owners.

Printed in the United States of America

10 9 8 7 6 5 4 3 2 1

ISBN: 0-13-237397-1

Prentice-Hall International (UK) Limited, *London*
Prentice-Hall of Australia Pty. Limited, *Sydney*
Prentice-Hall Canada Inc., *Toronto*
Prentice-Hall Hispanoamericana, S.A., *Mexico*
Prentice-Hall of India Private Limited, *New Delhi*
Prentice-Hall of Japan, Inc., *Tokyo*
Simon & Schuster Asia Pte. Ltd., *Singapore*
Editora Prentice-Hall do Brasil, Ltda., *Rio de Janeiro*

Table of Contents

Preface

This book was written as a result of my experiences in UNIX programming over the past 10 years. This UNIX program development book provides a handful of useful tools you may use effectively to become more productive in your work. This book takes the case study approach. There are a total of seven programming projects, in addition to examples shown in each chapter. Major projects included in this book are a FORTRAN-like language parser, a source code manager, a memory manager, a client-server application based on sockets, a text editor, a drawing editor, and a table editor.

The text is divided into three groups with each group dedicated to a specific area of programming: program development, UNIX programming, and graphical user interface. The topics for program development include source code management (SCM), an object library building tool (MAKE), an automatic parser generator (LEX/YACC), a source code debugging tool (DBX), and shell script-writing skills. The UNIX programming topics include programming with various UNIX system resources such as FIFOs, signals, time/timer, lock, memory, sockets, and remote procedure calls (RPC). The graphical user interface includes sample programs to create pulldown menus, scrolled windows, and drawing areas. It also shows how to use the file selection box, set a watch cursor, how to emulate a table using the Motif widget, and rubber band techniques.

Chapter 1 provides a brief introduction to a shell and to shell script-writing. The material covered in this chapter paves the road for Chapter 3.

No UNIX programmer can get away with the makefile in his or her work. Chapter 2 tries to solve the mysteries of dynamic macros and the suffix rules.

Chapter 3 is a case study by itself. This chapter demonstrates the power of UNIX shell scripts by using them to implement an SCM.

Chapter 4 introduces the UNIX lexical analyzer, LEX, and Chapter 5 introduces the UNIX syntax checker, YACC. LEX and YACC are tied closely together in writing a parser for a language. Few people have problems with LEX, but many people find it difficult to understand and to use effectively. So this book presents a step-by-step procedure to write a parser using LEX/YACC.

Chapter 6 is a small chapter. It shows the reader how to set up the .dbxinit file, how to set breakpoints, how to print the variable and/or the structure contents, and how to perform a memory dump in various data formats. The most important section of this chapter is the explanation of how to debug a separate process.

Chapter 7 deals with seven useful UNIX resources (i.e., signal, FIFO, time/timer, lock, dynamic memory, socket, and RPC) and gives examples showing how to program with each of these resources effectively.

Chapter 8 consists of three case studies: a text editor, a drawing editor, and a table editor. These three editors then are combined into one application. The main program starts the main window, which consists of the text editor. From the main window menu, it can start the drawing editor or the table editor. In all three editors, you easily can select the colors and fonts you want to make the program more colorful.

This book is intended for programmers who want to increase their productivity through programming tools and examples. The case study approach allows me to skip the details and focus only on those issues considered key in the program development task. The examples shown can be applied easily to real projects. You will find it easy to dig out part of the code from this book and plug it into your own applications.

This book is suitable for UNIX programmers who have at least one year of experience in UNIX and C programming and have some exposure to the X window system.

My biggest thanks go to my wife, Susan, who has constantly encouraged me during this long writing period. Thanks are also given to my colleague, Scott Bolen, who has inspired me in some of the material covered in both UNIX and X/Motif programming. Special thanks are given to the people at BooksCraft, Inc., who edited and formatted the book to a good shape. Finally, my sincere thanks go to God, who makes all things possible.

Shell Scripts

1.1 INTRODUCTION

This chapter familiarizes you with script-writing skills and paves the way for chapter 3, which implements a source code control system based heavily on scripts.

When you log on to a machine, the operating system automatically runs a program that allows you to communicate with the computer by entering commands and receiving responses. This program is called a "shell" in UNIX jargon, and a number of UNIX shells are available today. The three most popular ones are Bourne shell, C shell, and Korn shell. Since the shell's job is to handle the communication between the computer and the user, a shell acts as an interactive command interpreter. But a shell is also a language interpreter. You can combine shell commands with the control structures to form a reusable procedure, then execute it by invoking the shell. The file containing a sequence of shell commands that the shell can read and execute is called the "shell script."

The first shell that runs immediately after a user logs on is called the "login shell." The login shell is predetermined in the /etc/passwd file. Every system user has a corresponding entry in this password file. At the end of the line for each entry is a field that specifies which shell to run after that user has successfully logged on to the system. Later, the user can change the shell whenever he or she wants. To determine your login shell, type

```
echo    $SHELL
```

To determine which kind of shell you are currently using, type

```
ps      $$
```

1.2 DIFFERENCES BETWEEN THE SHELLS

A different developer created each shell. For example, the Bourne shell was developed by S. R. Bourne at AT&T, the C shell was developed by Bill Joy and others at the University of California at Berkeley, and the Korn shell was developed by David Korn at AT&T. Because the Bourne shell runs much faster than the C shell, it is recommended that you write the shell script in the Bourne shell. On the other hand, because C shell has features such as history and aliases, most users like to use it as the login shell. The Korn shell is a successor to the Bourne shell, and it includes most of the C shell's good features plus a few new features of its own.

The login and logout actions are different. If the Korn or Bourne shell is the shell when a user logs on, the script in .profile is executed and nothing is executed when a user logs out. If C shell is the login shell, when a user logs on, the script in .login is executed, and if the script .logout exists, it is executed when a user logs off. In addition, whenever a new C shell is created, the .cshrc script is executed.

The scopes for variables are different, also. All variables in the Bourne and Korn shells are local unless they are exported. All variables in C shell are local, and environment variables are global.

By convention, built-in shell variables for the Bourne and Korn shells have names in all capital letters, while the C shell's built-in shell variables have names in all lowercase letters. For example, the built-in shell variable for the command search path is PATH for Bourne and Korn shells and path for C shell.

The syntax for variable assignment are different. In both Bourne and Korn shells, use the following syntax for variable assignment

```
name=value
```

Note that there is no space on either side of the equal sign. Here are examples of how to set the PATH variable in Bourne and Korn shells:

```
PATH=/usr/bin:/etc:/bin
PATH=$PATH:$HOME/bin
```

The first assignment sets the value of PATH so that the shell searches the directories /usr/bin, /etc, and /bin in that order for command. The second assignment adds the $HOME/bin directory to the end of the search path.

In C shell, use the following syntax for regular variable assignment:

```
set name  =   value
```

Note that spaces are allowed on either side of the equal sign. Here are examples of how to set the path variable in C shell:

```
set path = (/usr/bin  /etc  /bin)
set path = ($path  $home/bin)
```

The first assignment sets the value of path so that the shell searches the directories /usr/bin, /etc, and /bin in that order for command. The second assignment adds the $home/bin directory to the end of the search path.

Use the following syntax for environment variable assignment:

```
setenv  name  value
```

For example, the following command sets the environment variable DISPLAY to the terminal number 0 of an X server whose Internet address is 123.456.789.25:

```
setenv  DISPLAY  123.456.789.25:0
```

In the Bourne or Korn shells, you can execute a shell script by the . (dot) command, and use the source command in C shell to execute a script.

1.3 WORKING WITH THE BOURNE SHELL

This section examines the aspects of using the Bourne shell such as invoking, exiting from the shell, and using the shell metacharacters and special shell variables.

1.3.1 Invoking the Bourne Shell

You can invoke the Bourne shell in either interactive or batch mode. To invoke the Bourne shell in interactive mode, type

```
sh
```

You then can execute any shell command after the $ prompt. To invoke the Bourne shell in batch mode, type

```
sh  [-x]  file
```

or

```
chmod +x file;  file
```

or

```
. file
```

where file is the script filename.

1.3.2 Exiting from a Shell

To exit from a shell in interactive mode, simply type

```
^d
```

where ^ is the metakey Ctrl.

When a script terminates with an exit statement in the batch mode operation, it automatically exits from the shell.

1.3.3 Shell Metacharacters

The Bourne shell accepts the wildcard representation of filenames in the command line it receives. It achieves this function through special characters called "metacharacters" that allow automatic substitution of characters in the filenames. These metacharacters are

*   matches any string of characters (including NULL string)

?   matches any single character

[]   matches any single character within the brackets

For example, if you want to list all C program files in the current directory, use

```
ls   *.c
```

1.3.4 Special Shell Variables

Table 1.1 lists some of the most often-used special shell variables:

Table 1.1 Special Shell Variables

Shell Variable	Meaning
$#	the number of positional parameters
$*	the list of command line arguments
$n	if n = 0 it means command name if n = 1 it means the first argument and so forth
$-	the shell options
$?	the exit status of executed script
$$	the current shell's process id
$!	the last background command's process id

1.4 PROGRAMMING WITH THE BOURNE SHELL

Programming with the Bourne shell is like programming with any other language in that the Bourne shell has such statements as the assignment state, if statement, case statement, for loop, while loop, and function statement. The major difference between them is found in the syntactic rules for writing such statements. This section presents the six most important constructs of a Bourne shell script and gives examples showing how to use them effectively.

1.4.1 Variable Assignment

The syntax for variable assignment is

```
name=value
```

where value is any character string. Note that there is no space on either side of the equal sign. Here are two examples of variable assignments:

```
PATH=/usr/bin:/etc:/bin
PATH=$PATH:$HOME/bin
```

The first assignment sets the value of PATH so that the shell searches the directories /usr/bin, /etc, and /bin in that order for command. The second assignment adds the $HOME/bin directory to the end of the search path.

1.4.2 Command Substitution

Any command line can be placed within back quotation marks (`) so that the output of the command line itself can be assigned to a shell variable. This concept is known as command line substitution. The command enclosed between the back quotation marks is executed first, and then its output is assigned to the shell variable. This feature can be used to pass string data from a UNIX command or C program back to the script that invokes the command. For example:

```
OS=`uname`
```

where the uname command writes the name of the operation system you are running to the standad output. The output from the command is assigned then to the shell variable OS. If the machine you are running is an IBMRS workstation, the uname command output is AIX. A SUN workstation returns SUNOS.

1.4.3 Arithmetic Operation

The expr command provides the only arithmetic operation on integers. It evaluates a single expression and writes the result on the standard output. The most common usage of expr is to count the number of iterations inside a loop. Here is an example:

```
count=0
for  i  in filenames
do
    count=`expr  $count  + 1`
done
```

This simple script counts the number of files contained in variable filenames.

1.4.4 The Test Command

Control structures are the heart of script-writing, and the test command is the heart of each control structure. The test command is a built-in command that can be used to test the value of a specific shell variable, properties of a file or directory, properties of strings or the exit code of the last executed command. The test command also allows you to apply logic operations on the conditions under test.

Here are examples of test commands used to test a file or directory:

```
test -r file      returns true if file exists and readable
test -w file      returns true if file exists and writable
test -f file      returns true if file exists and is a regular file
test -d file      returns true if file exists and is a directory
test -s file      returns true if file exists and its size is greater than zero
```

Here are examples of test commands used to test the property of a string:

```
test -n string              returns true if string has nonzero length
test -z string              returns true if string has zero length
test string                 returns true if string is not null
test string1 = string2      returns true if string1 equals string2
test string1 != string2     returns true if string1 not equal to string2
```

Here are examples of test commands used to test numeric values:

```
test $#   -eq 0    returns true if number of arguments is zero
test $#   -ne 0    returns true if number of arguments is not zero
test $#   -gt 0    returns true if number of arguments is greater than zero
test $#   -ge 0    returns true if number of arguments is greater than or equal to
                   zero
test $#   -lt 1    returns true if number of arguments is less than one
test $#   -le 1    returns true if number of arguments is less than or equal to
                   one
```

Here is an example of the test command used to test the command exit code:

```
$SCM/admin $filename
exitcode=$?
test $exitcode -eq 1    returns true if the exit code from the command
                        $SCM/admin is 1
```

The test command also can be written by enclosing the condition in square brackets. Here is an example:

```
if   test -f filename
```

can be written as

```
if [  -f filename   ]
```

Here are examples of the test command using logical operators:

```
[  !  $command =  quit   ]
      returns true if the command string is not equal to "quit"
[   $command = cancel    -o    $command = quit   ]
      returns true if the command has a string value of "cancel" or "quit"
[   $count -ne 0    -a    $count  -gt  2   ]
      returns true if the count has a value that is not zero and is greater than
      two
```

1.4.5 The Control Structures

The Bourne shell supports these control constructs:

if-then-else	Determine between two different actions
for	Loop through a single action a fixed number of times
while	Repeat a single action while a certain condition holds true
until	Repeat a single action until a certain condition becomes true
case	Determine among many actions

1.4.5.1 If-Then-Else
The syntax for the if-then-else construct is

```
if test-condition
then
    statements
[[elif test-condition
then
    statements]
else
    statements]
fi
```

where test-condition is a test command applied to a condition.

1.4.5.2 For
The syntax for the for construct is

```
for name in list
do
    statements
done
```

where list is a list of names. These names can be spelled out explicitly or expressed implicitly through the special shell variables.

Here is an example of the for construct with names listed explicitly:

```
for workstation in ibmrs  sun  sgi  hp
do
    echo "We also work on $workstation workstation."
done
```

This example outputs the names in the list one at a time.

Here are examples of the for construct with names listed implicitly:

```
echo script $0 has $# arguments
argcount=0
for arg in $*
do
    argcount=`expr $argcount + 1`
    echo "argument  $argcount  is $arg."
done
```

The previous example first outputs the name of the script along with the number of arguments it gets. It then outputs the first, the second, the third argument, and so on.

The following two examples list all the C filenames in the current directory:

```
for file in *.c
do
    echo $file
done

for file in `ls *.c`
do
    echo $file
done
```

1.4.5.3 While
The syntax for the while construct is

```
while test-condition
do
    statements
done
```

Here is an example:

```
selection=1
while [ $selection -ne  0  ]
do
    echo "Please select one the of directory[1-4], use 0 to quit"
    read selection
done
```

In this example, the while loop continues executing until 0 is entered.

1.4.5.4 Until
The syntax for the until construct is

```
until test-condition
do
```

```
    statements
done
```

Here is an example:

```
until [  $selection  -eq  0  ]
do
   echo "Please select one the of directory[1-4], use 0 to quit"
   read selection
done
```

In this example, the loop continues executing until 0 is entered.

1.4.5.5 Case

The syntax for the case construct is

```
case $variable in
   value1)
      statements  ;;
   value2)
      statements  ;;
 ....
   *)
      statements  ;;
esac
```

where the last value, "*)", is the default value should no other value match. Normally, this is used to issue an error message.

Here is an example:

```
selection=0
while test $selection = 0
do
   echo "Please select one of the directories by entering a number[1-4]"
   echo " 1:    pipe"
   echo " 2:    timer"
   echo " 3:    socket"
   echo " 4:    lock"

   read selection
   case $selection in
   1)
      echo You are working on PIPE library.
      ;;
   2)
      echo You are working on TIMER library.
      ;;
   3)
      echo You are working on SOCKET library.
      ;;
   4)
      echo You are working on LOCK library.
      ;;
```

```
    *)
        echo Illegal selection, please try again.
        selection=0
        ;;
    esac
done
```

This script prompts the user to enter a proper number for the library name. If an inappropriate number is entered, it repeats the prompt until the proper number is entered.

1.4.6 Using Functions

The shell includes function definition and call capabilities. A function defined within a script is like another shell script, except it resides in memory. It is executed by the shell process, not a separate one. The syntax for defining a function within a script is

```
function_name ( )  {
    command_list
}
```

where command_list is a list of commands. The arguments passed to the functions are referenced through the shell positional parameters $1, $2,.. and so forth. These are different from the shell positional parameters when the script is invoked initially. Since an exit in a function terminates the shell script, the return command should be used to return a value to the original script.

The syntax for calling a function defined within a script is

```
function_name  [ arg1 arg2 ....]
```

Thus a function is called by referencing its name, followed by arguments, if needed. The returned value is stored in the shell variable $?. The following example shows how to define a function in a script, call the function, and check for the return code:

```
GetYesNo ( ) {
    prompt_message=$1
    echo $prompt_message
    ans=""
    while [  ! ans ]
    do
        read ans
        case  $ans in
            [yY])
                return 1;;
            [nN])
                return 0;;
            *)
                echo "Please answer y or n";;
        esac
    done
```

```
}
#script starts here
prompt="Do you want to continue? [y/n]"
GetYesNo  $prompt
if [ $? -eq 1 ]
then
    echo User wants to continue.
else
    echo User does not want to continue.
fi
```

1.5 SAMPLE SCRIPTS

This section presents several sample scripts that use the control constructs mentioned earlier in this chapter. The first two sample scripts work based on the UNIX grep command. The syntax for the grep command is

```
grep    pattern   filename
```

where pattern can be a fixed string or a regular expression that evaluates to a string or a number of strings and filename is the name of the file the grep command examines.

1.5.1 Displaying a User's Entry in the Password File

The following script displays a user's entry from the password file:

```
#!/bin/sh
#
#   showentry
#
USER=`whoami`
grep   $USER   /etc/passwd
```

1.5.2 Checking for a Valid Version String

The following script checks for a valid version string within a file. Here, we assume that the file to be checked must contain a string of this form

```
"  %W%     %G%     ***   "
```

which says the version string must contain three substrings: "%W%", "%G%", and "***". It can have any number of white spaces between any two adjacent substrings.

```
#!/bin/sh
#
# chkver  filename
#
if [  $#  -gt  1  ]
then
   echo  "usage: chkver  filename"
   exit 1
```

```
fi

filename=$1
grep  '%W%[ \t]*%G%[ \t]*\*\*\*'  $filename >  $HOME/tmpfile$$
if [  ! -s  $HOME/tmpfile$$  ]
then
   echo  "file  $filename does not have a valid version string"
   rm -f $HOME/tmpfile$$
   exit 1
else
   echo "file $filename has a valid version string"
fi
```

Our next three examples use the UNIX find command. The syntax for the find command is

```
find  path  selection-criteria  action
```

where path is the starting directory, so the find command examines not only this starting directory but also all its subdirectories, subdirectories of its subdirectories, and so on.

selection-criteria can be a filename, a user name, file type, last access time, and so forth. To serve our purpose, we use filename as the selection-criteria (-name filename).

action specifies the action to be taken when the selection-criteria is met. For our purpose, we want to print the full pathname of each file matching the selection criteria (-print).

Thus the find command we are going to use is

```
find  path  -name filename -print
```

1.5.3 Locating a File with a Known Name

The following script locates a file with a specific name. The syntax for invoking the script is

```
findfile  filename  path  [outfile]
```

where filename is the file to be searched and path is the directory path where search begins; outfile is an optional argument—if present, it is the output file; otherwise the output goes to the screen.

```
#!/bin/sh
#
# findfile  filename path [outfile]
#
if  [  $#  -lt 2 -o  $#  -gt  3  ]
then
   echo  "usage:   findfile  filename  path  [outfile]"
   exit 1
fi

if  [  $#  -eq  3  ]
```

```
then
   rm  -f  $3
fi

find  $2  -name  $1  -print  |  while read  filename
do
   if  [  ! -d  $filename  ]
   then
      if  [  $#  -eq  2  ]
      then
         echo $filename
      else
         echo $filename >> $3
      fi
   fi
done
```

1.5.4 Locating a Directory with a Known Directory Name

The following script locates a directory with a given directory name. The syntax
for invoking the script is

```
finddir  directory  path  [outfile]
```

where directory is the directory name to be searched and path is the directory path
where the search begins; outfile is an optional argument—if present, it is the output
file; otherwise the output goes to the screen.

```
#!/bin/sh
#
# finddir  directory path [outfile]
#
if  [  $#  -lt 2 -o  $#  -gt  3  ]
then
   echo "usage:  finddir  directory  path  [outfile]"
   exit 1
fi

if  [  $#  -eq  3  ]
then
   rm  -f  $3
fi

find  $2  -name  $1  -print  |  while read  filename
do
   if  [  -d  $filename  ]
   then
      if  [  $#  -eq  2  ]
      then
         echo $filename
      else
         echo $filename >> $3
      fi
   fi
done
```

1.5.5 Locating Files That Contain a Known String

The following script locates files that contain a known string pattern. The syntax for invoking the script is

```
findstr  string-pattern  path  [outfile]
```

where string-pattern is the string to be searched and path is the directory path where search begins; outfile is an optional argument—if present, it is the output file; otherwise the output goes to the screen.

```
#!/bin/sh
#
# findstr  string-pattern  path [outfile]
#
if  [  $#  -lt 2 -o  $#  -gt  3  ]
then
    echo "usage:  findstr  string-pattern  path  [outfile]"
    exit 1
fi

if  [  $#  -eq  3  ]
then
    rm  -f  $3
fi

find  $2  -print  |  while read  filename
do
    if  [  ! -d $filename  -a   -r $filename  ]
    then
      grep -n $1 $filename  >  tmp$$
      if [  -s  tmp$$  ]
      then
        if  [  $#  -eq  2  ]
        then
           echo $filename
        else
           echo $filename >> $3
        fi
      fi
      rm  -f  tmp$$
    fi
done
```

The following examples use the UNIX sed command. The syntax for the sed command is

```
sed  '/line-selection-rule/command'  file
```

where line-selection-rule specifies how lines are selected. If line-selection-rule is omitted, all lines are selected. If line-selection-rule contains one line number, only that line is selected. If line-selection-rule contains two line numbers, lines whose line numbers fall between these two numbers are selected.

command can be:

`p`	print the line
`d`	delete the line
`s/oldstring/newstring/`	search for the oldstring and replace with the new-string

1.5.6 Listing Source Files That Have Been Checked Out

Let us assume that we have our source files stored in the directory /usr/project/ src. We want to use sccs for the source code control. So we create a directory SCCS under the directory /usr/project/src. Every time we add a source code under the sccs control, a file with the prefix s. is created in the directory SCCS. For example, if the source code main.c is added to the sccs, a file s.main.c is created under the directory SCCS. Furthermore, whenever a file is checked out from the sccs, a file with the prefix p. is created. In the case of main.c, p.main.c is created. So by listing all the s. files, we know the source files under the sccs control, and by listing all the p. files, we know the source files that have been checked out. The following script lists all the files (without the pathname) that have been checked out:

```
#!/bin/sh
# Usage:  whatsout
#
SCCS=/usr/project/src/SCCS
pfiles=`ls  $SCCS/p.*`
for  filename in $pfiles
do
    file=`echo $filename  |  sed  's/.*SCCS\/p\.//'`
    echo $file
done
```

The following examples use the UNIX awk command. The syntax for the awk command is

```
awk  'pattern  {action}'  filename
```

The awk command examines each line from a file to determine if it matches the specific pattern. If the pattern matches, the specified action is performed on that line. If no pattern is specified, all lines are matched. For example, the command

```
awk  '{print  $1  $2 }'  p.main.c
```

prints the first two fields from the file p.main.c.

Another form of the awk command is

```
awk  -f  action-file  data-file
```

In this case, the action-file contains the actions to be taken for each line of the datafile. For example, if the action file (actfile) contains the line

```
{print  $1  $2 }
```

then this command performs the same action as the previous example:

```
awk  -f  actfile  p.main.c
```

1.5.7 List Check-Out Files with Check-Out Information

For every check-out file, a p. file is created in the SCCS directory. The p. file contains five fields: old version number, new version number, user name, check-out date, and check-out time. For example, the content of the file p.main.c may appear as

1.11   1.12   shen   05/25/96   10:21:05

The following script lists all the check-out files, along with the check-out information

File	Old-Ver	New-Ver	User	Check-Out-Date	Check-Out_Time
main.c	1.11	1.12	shen	05/25/96	10:21:05
sub.c	1.23	1.24	james	05/21/96	12:22:08

```
#!/bin/sh
# Usage:  chkoutinfo
#
SCCS=/usr/project/src/SCCS
pfiles=`ls  $SCCS/p.*`
for  filename in $pfiles
do
   file=`echo $filename  |  sed  's/.*SCCS\/p\.//'`
   echo "{print \"$file\", \"  \", \$1, \"  \", \$2,  \"  \", \$3, \"\
    \$4, \"  \", \$5}" > $HOME/tmp$$
   awk  -f  $HOME/tmp$$  $filename
done
```

1.6 SUMMARY

This chapter explained a shell and outlined the major differences between the Bourne and C shells. Because the Bourne shell is still the most popular for writing script today, we devoted most of this chapter to Bourne shell script-writing. This included how to do variable assignment, command substitution, and arithmetic operation in a script. We also showed how to use test commands within different control structures to make the script more flexible. We also showed how to use function within a script. Finally, we gave a few examples to show how powerful UNIX commands such as grep, find, sed, and awk can be used within script to perform very useful work.

MAKE

2.1 INTRODUCTION

Suppose you are working on a project that needs to read data from a data file, process the data, and display the results. You might like to divide the program into four modules, with each module performing one specific task, and have a main module coordinate the work. Let these filenames be main.c, input.c, process.c, and display.c. If you want to build an executable called "showdata," you would need to type

```
%cc -c -g main.c
%cc -c -g input.c
%cc -c -g process.c
%cc -c -g display.c
%cc -g main.o input.o process.o display.o -o showdata
```

That's a lot of typing! Furthermore, if the command needs to include user-defined include files that do not exist in the current directory and/or object libraries, these command lines become lengthier. The make command provides an easy way to do this. It can build the executable file and object library with only one command: the make command. The make command looks at a file you create, called the "makefile," and performs the necessary operations according to the instructions given in it. The default makefile is either "makefile" or "Makefile." If you choose to use a different filename for the makefile, the make command must be presented with the -f option

```
make -f mf
```

where mf is the filename of the makefile in use.

2.2 MAKEFILE FORMAT

A makefile consists of two sections: the macro definitions section, which is optional, and the target entry section. The macro definitions section contains macro definition statements and a pseudo-target entry. The macro definitions statement takes the form

```
name= string of characters
```

where string of characters can be a null string.

For example, the following macro definition defines the compilation flags to the C compiler:

```
CFLAGS= -g -c
```

Any reference to $(name) or ${name} will be substituted by the string of characters that appears to the right of the equal sign in the macro definition for name. A reference to

```
$(CFLAG)
```

is interpreted as

```
-g -c
```

A target entry takes the form

```
target: [dependents]
    [command]
    .
    .
    .
```

where target is a target name, dependents is a list of files, and command can be any UNIX command. The target name can be a filename or any artificial name. Each command line must start with a TAB. The interpretation for the target entry is that the target name depends on the list of files. If a filename is used as the target name, make checks the last modification date for the target filename against the last modification dates for the list of dependent files. If the date of any file on the dependent file list is newer than the target file, the target file is rebuilt according to the commands following the target entry's first line. Otherwise, the target file is current, and none of the commands in that target entry is executed.

A pseudo-target is a target whose name begins with a dot(.). It can be thought of as a directive to the make command. For example, .PRECIOUS is a pseudo-target name that prevents the current target's dependent files from being deleted when the make command is being terminated. For example, assume the following pseudo-target name does not exist in your makefile:

```
.PRECIOUS:    /usr/shen/libSub.a
```

Say you have issued the make command to update one object file in this object library. Suddenly, you decide to quit and press the ^c key (which the process interprets as Interrupted). The result: not only does the make process stop but the library file /usr/shen/libSub.a is removed, also. Now, you must recompile all the member objects in that object library. If, on the other hand, you include this pseudo-target in your makefile, the make process stops as you hit the ^c key and the library file /usr/shen/libSub.a remains the same.

Let us now give a simple makefile that builds the executable showdata outlined in the beginning of this chapter.

Listing 2.1 Makefile without Macros

```
showdata: main.o input.o process.o display.o
    cc -g main.o input.o process.o display.o -o showdata

main.o:  main.c
    cc -c -g main.c

input.o: input.c
    cc -c -g input.c

process.o: process.c
    cc -c -g process.c

display.o: display.c
    cc -c -g display.c
```

Listing 2.2 Makefile with Macros

```
CFLAGS= -c -g
OBJECTS= main.o input.o process.o display.o

showdata: $(OBJECTS)
    cc -g $(OBJECTS) -o showdata

main.o:  main.c
    cc -c -g main.c

input.o: input.c
    cc -c -g input.c

process.o: process.c
    cc -c -g process.c

display.o: display.c
    cc -c -g display.c
```

2.3 DYNAMIC MACROS

Whenever it reads a dependency rule, make defines several dynamic macros. This can simplify the makefile writing even further. The commonly used dynamic macros are $@, $< and $*. The $@ macro is set to the current target's target name. The $< macro is set to the name of the file that causes the action when the command is triggered by a suffix rule. The $* macro is set to the name of the file (without the suffix part) that causes the action when a suffix rule triggers the command. An example of a makefile that uses dynamic macros is shown in Listing 2.3.

2.4 THE SUFFIX RULES

On a UNIX system, all C program files have a .c suffix, all FORTRAN program files have a .f suffix, all LEX files have an .l suffix, all YACC files have a .y suffix, all object files have an .o suffix, and all object libraries have an .a suffix. Such conventions make it possible for make command to do many things automatically by acting on a set of suffix rules. By adopting this convention, the file transformations can take place only in the direction indicated by ->.

```
.y -> .c -> .o -> .a
.l -> .c -> .o -> .a
.c -> .o -> .a
.f -> .o -> .a
```

Each suffix rule takes the form

```
suffix_1[suffix_2]:
   command
   [command]

   .

   .
```

where suffix_2 is optional. When both suffixes exist, suffix_2 is the implied target file's suffix and suffix_1 is the dependent file's suffix. And command is any UNIX command to be executed when the condition is met. For example, the following suffix rule says that if you try to make prog.o and prog.c exists, the make command creates the prog.o through the command cc -g -c $<.

```
.c.o:
   cc -g -c $<
```


Listing 2.3 Makefile with Dynamic Macros and a Suffix Rule

```
#
CFLAGS = -c -g
OBJECTS = main.c input.o process.o display.o

.c.o:
   cc $(CFLAGS) $<

showdata: $(OBJECTS)
   cc -g $(OBJECTS) -o $@
```

In the case of a single suffix (with suffix_2 omitted), the rule makes an executable file from the given file. Here is an example:

Listing 2.4 Makefile Showing a Suffix Rule with a Single Suffix

```
.c:
   cc -g $< -o $@

all:   showdata
   @echo use .c rule
```

In this example, a single source file showdata.c is used to create the executable showdata.

2.4.1 Implicit Suffix Rules

The make command has a built-in set of default suffix rules, called "implicit suffix rules." When no explicit target entry is given in a makefile, the make command automatically checks these default suffix rules and uses them. You can get a complete listing of these default suffix rules by entering

```
make -p > tmpfile
```

This outputs all the default suffix rules and macros used in the rules to the file tmpfile. This output listing differs from one machine platform to the other. Listing 2.5 shows portion of the make -p command the output generates.

Listing 2.5 Default Macro Definitions and Suffix Rules

```
CCFLAGS = -o
GFLAGS =
GET = get
ASFLAGS =
AS = as
FFLAGS = -o
FC = xlf
CFLAGS = -o
CC = cc
LDFLAGS = -o
LD = ld
LFLAGS =
LEX = lex
YFLAGS =
YACC = yacc
ARFLAGS = -rv
AR = ar

.f.a:
   $(FC) -c $(FFLAGS) $<
   $(AR) $(ARFLAGS) $@ $*.o
   rm -f $*.o

.c.a:
   $(CC) -c $(CFLAGS) $<
   $(AR) $(ARFLAGS) $@ $*.o
   rm -f $*.o
```

```
.l.c:
    $(LEX) $<
    mv lex.yy.c $@

.y.c:
    $$(YACC) $(YFLAGS) $<
    mv y.tab.c $@

.l.o:
    $(LEX) $(LFLAGS) $<
    $(CC) $(CFLAGS) -c lex.yy.c
    rm lex.yy.c
    mv lex.yy.o $@

.y.o:
    $(YACC) $(YFLAGS) $<
    $(CC) $(CFLAGS) -c y.tab.c
    rm y.tab.c
    mv y.tab.c $@

.f.o:
    $(FC) $(FLAGS) -c $<

.c.o:
    $(CC) (CFLAGS) -c $<

.f:
    $(FC) $(FFLAGS) $(LDFLAGS) $< -o $@

.c:
    $(CC) $(CFLAGS) $(LDFLAGS) $< -o $@

.SUFFIXES: .o .c .c~ .f .f~ .y .y~ .l .l~ .s .s~ .h .h~
```

2.4.2 Building Your Own Suffix Rules

Although make has quite a few suffix rules built in, it is recommended that you write your own suffix rules in the makefile--even if they are exactly the same--to gain more control of what happens in the make process. The suffix rules you specify overwrite the default suffix rules. For the suffix rule to work, make sure that all suffixes you use appear on the pseudo-target .SUFFIX. You can create or add new suffix rules by adding a list of new suffixes to the makefile with the pseudo-target .SUFFIX. This pseudo-target defines the suffixes that may be used to create the suffix rules and takes the form

```
.SUFFIXES:  suffix[...]
```

The suffixes' order is significant. The one to the right can be a dependent of the one on the left. For example, the suffix list

```
.SUFFIXES:  .a .o .c .l .y
```

causes sample.c to be a dependent of sample.o, and sample.l to be a dependent of sample.c. A .SUFFIXES without a list causes the make command to ignore all suffixes. If you deal with C, LEX, and YACC source files, the following two pseudo-targets are considered appropriate in the makefile:

```
.SUFFIXES:
.SUFFIXES:  .a .o .c .l .y
```

2.5 BUILDING AN OBJECT LIBRARY

An object library is a file that contains a set of object files. Each object file is a member of this object library file. The ar command maintains each member file within the library file. (For details, refer to the *Commands Reference Manual.*)

make recognizes a target of this form:

```
libX.a(member)
```

as a reference to a library member, where libX.a is an object library, and member is any object file within this library. For example

```
libSub.a(input.o)
```

refers to an object file input.o, which is a member of the object library libSub.a.

You can create your own suffix rule to build object library by adding the .a suffix (if it is not yet in the .SUFFIXES list). For example, the suffix pairs .c.a may be used for a rule that defines how to build a library member from a C source file. The following makefile builds an object library of four members:

Listing 2.6 Makefile to Build an Object Library

```
#
.SUFFIXES:
.SUFFIXES: .a .o .c
.PRECIOUS: libSub.a

CFLAGS = -c -g
ARFLAGS = ruv

OBJECTS = libSub.a(main.o)      \
          libSub.a(input.o)     \
          libSub.a(process.o)   \
          libSub.a(display.o)

.c.a:
   cc $(CFLAGS) $<
   ar $(ARFLAGS) $@  $*.o
   rm -f $*.o

libSub.a: $(OBJECTS)
   @echo library $@ is up to date
```

2.6 INCORPORATING THE SHELL ENVIRONMENT VARIABLES

When make executes, it automatically reads the shell environment variables and adds
them to the macro definitions. When a macro is defined both in the makefile and in the
shell environment variables, the one residing in the makefile takes precedence. You
can reverse this precedence order by using the -e option in the make command.

2.7 THE MAKE COMMAND

The make command takes the form

```
make  [options] [macro definitions] [targets]
```

where macro definitions has the same format described in the makefile, except the
macro definition in this case must be enclosed by " ". For example, if you decide to
change the CFLAGS from "-g -c" as specified in the Listing 2.6 makefile to "-O -c" from
the command line, the make command is

```
make "CFLAGS = -O -c"
```

When macros are defined through the command line arguments, they receive the
highest precedence. This allows you to easily build something different using the same
makefile.

Here are descriptions of commonly used options:

Option	Description
-f filename	will use filename as the makefile
-p	prints out the complete set of macro definitions and suffix rules
-e	ignores any macro definitions that assign new values to the environment variables.(i.e. environment variables take precedence over the macro definition within the makefile)
-n	displays commands on the screen without executing them
-d	runs make command under debug mode
-r	ignores the built-in macro definitions and the suffix rules

Target is any target name in the makefile that specifies the starting target name in
the make process.

2.8 MAKEFILE EXAMPLES

This section shows a practical example of how to organize directories under a project
and the makefiles associated with it.

First, let us assume that we are working on a compiler project, so we choose
"compiler" as the project name and create a directory named "compiler" under the

path /usr2/shen. Under the compiler directory, we create four directories: src, inc, lib, and bin. All the user-defined include files are stored under the inc directory, the user-created object libraries are stored under the lib directory, and the executables are stored under the bin directory. The src directory is divided into three sub-directories: lang, sub, and main. The directory lang stores the YACC and LEX source files, the directory sub stores utility subroutine files, and the directory main stores the main program files. A main directory is required to create several executables for the project. Each executable needs a main program, so we need multiple main programs. The compiler project, for example, may require us to create two executables: one for the parser and one for the compiler. Each has its own main program, so the directory structure for the compiler project is shown in Figure 2.1.

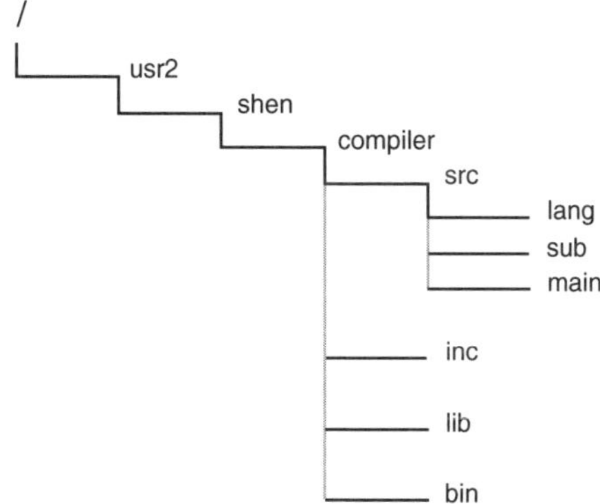

Fig. 2.1 Compiler Project Directory Structure

In each directory that contains the source files is a makefile associated with them. lang directory has one YACC source file (fgram.y) and one LEX source file (flex.l). The makefile used to create the object library libLang.a in directory /usr2/shen/compiler/lib is shown in Listing 2.7. Notice that in the makefile, we define a macro name LPATH to give us mobility. For example, if we decide to move the compiler project to the /usr1/john/compiler directory, the makefile modifies only the macro definitions for LPATH to /usr1/john/compiler. The C compiler flag CFLAGS tells the C compiler to include the user debugging codes (anything from #ifdef DEBUG to #endif), to search the directory /usr2/shen/compiler/include for include files, to compile the source in debugging mode, and to generate only object code. The d option in YFLAGS tells the YACC command to produce the y.tab.h file. The v option tells the YACC command to produce the y.output file containing the parsing table and a report on the conflicts the grammar causes. And the l option tells the YACC command to generate y.tab.c containing no numbered line directives. This allows the debugger to function properly when we trace through the YACC source file (i.e. fgram.y). The t option in LFLAGS tells the LEX command to output its lexical analyzer code to flex.c rather than yy.lex.c.

Listing 2.7 Makefile in the lang Directory

```
.SUFFIXES:
.SUFFIXES: .a .o .c .l .y

COMPILER.c=  cc
CFLAGS=         -DDEBUG -I$(INC) -g -c
CPPFLAGS=
AR=             ar
ARFLAGS=        rv
YACC=           yacc
YFLAGS=         -dvl
LEX=            lex
LFLAGS=         -t
MV=             mv
RM=             rm
SED=            sed

LPATH=       /usr2/shen/compiler

LIB=$(LPATH)/lib
INC=$(LPATH)/inc
SRC=$(LPATH)/src
BIN=$(LPATH)/bin
LANG_SRC=$(SRC)/lang
LANG_LIB= $(LIB)/libLang.a

.PRECIOUS: $(LANG_LIB)

OBJECTS=  \
   $(LANG_LIB)(fgram.o)    \
   $(LANG_LIB)(flex.o)

.c.a:
   $(COMPILE.c) $(CPPFLAGS) $(CFLAGS) $(LANG_SRC)/$<
   $(AR) $(ARFLAGS) $@ $*.o
   $(RM) $*.o

.y.a:
   $(YACC) $(YFLAGS) $(LANG_SRC)/$<
   $(MV) y.tab.h $*.h
   $(SED)  '/#line/d' y.tab.c > $*.c
   $(COMPILE.c) $(CPPFLAGS) $(CFLAGS) $*.c
   $(AR) $(ARFLAGS) $@  $*.o
   $(RM) $*.o
   $(MV) $*.c $*.c.debug

.l.a:
   $(LEX) $(LFLAGS) $(LANG_SRC)/$<  > $*.c
   $(COMPILE.c) $(CPPFLAGS) $(CFLAGS) $*.c
   $(AR) $(ARFLAGS) $@  $*.o
   $(RM) $*.o
   $(MV) $*.c $*.c.debug

$(LANG_LIB):  $(OBJECTS)
   ranlib $(LANG_LIB)
```

The makefiles for the sub and main directories are similar to the one in Listing 2.7, except they don't have the .l.a and .y.a rules. The makefile in Listing 2.8 creates the object library libSub.a, and the makefile in Listing 2.9 creates the libMain.a object library.

Listing 2.8 Makefile in the sub Directory

```
.SUFFIXES:
.SUFFIXES: .a .o .c .l .y

COMPILER.c=   cc
CFLAGS=       -DDEBUG -I$(INC) -g -c
CPPFLAGS=
AR=           ar
ARFLAGS=      rv
MV=           mv
RM=           rm

LPATH=        /usr2/shen/compiler

LIB=$(LPATH)/lib
INC=$(LPATH)/inc
SRC=$(LPATH)/src
BIN=$(LPATH)/bin
SUB_SRC=$(SRC)/sub
SUB_LIB= $(LIB)/libSub.a

.PRECIOUS: $(SUB_LIB)

OBJECTS=  \
   $(SUB_LIB)(fsub.o)    \
   $(SUB_LIB)(symbol.o)

.c.a:
   $(COMPILE.c) $(CPPFLAGS) $(CFLAGS) $(SUB_SRC)/$<
   $(AR) $(ARFLAGS) $@ $*.o
   $(RM) $*.o

$(SUB_LIB):  $(OBJECTS)
   ranlib $(SUB_LIB)
```

Listing 2.9 Makefile in the main Directory

```
.SUFFIXES:
.SUFFIXES: .a .o .c .l .y

COMPILER.c=   cc
CFLAGS=       -DDEBUG -I$(INC) -g -c
CPPFLAGS=
AR=           ar
ARFLAGS=      rv
MV=           mv
RM=           rm

LPATH=        /usr2/shen/compiler
```

```
LIB=$(LPATH)/lib
INC=$(LPATH)/inc
SRC=$(LPATH)/src
BIN=$(LPATH)/bin
MAIN_SRC=$(SRC)/main
MAIN_LIB= $(LIB)/libMain.a

.PRECIOUS: $(MAIN_LIB)

OBJECTS=   \
   $(MAIN_LIB)(fparse.o)    \
   $(MAIN_LIB)(fcomp.o)

.c.a:
   $(COMPILE.c) $(CPPFLAGS) $(CFLAGS) $(MAIN_SRC)/$<
   $(AR) $(ARFLAGS) $@ $*.o
   $(RM) $*.o

$(MAIN_LIB):  $(OBJECTS)
   ranlib $(MAIN_LIB)
```

The makefile in Listing 2.10 creates all executables for the project. In this example, two executables can be created with a make command. If only one executable is to be created, the make command must specify that target name as the argument. For example, the following make command

```
   make fparse
```

creates only the executable file fparse.

Listing 2.10 Makefile in the bin Directory

```
LPATH=       /usr2/shen/compiler
ARFLAGS=   xv
LIB=$(LPATH)/lib
BIN=$(LPATH)/bin

L= $(LIB)/lib

LIBS= \
   $(L)Lang.a  \
   $(L)Sub.a

MAIN_LIB= $(L)Main.a

all: fparse fcomp
   @echo all executables updated

fparse:
   ar $(ARFLAGS) $(MAIN_LIB) $@.o
   cc -g $@ $(LIBS)  -ll -lm  -o $(BIN)/$@

fcomp:
   ar $(ARFLAGS) $(MAIN_LIB) $@.o
   cc -g $@ $(LIBS)  -ll -lm  -o $(BIN)/$@
```

2.9 SUMMARY

This chapter explained how the make command can be used to facilitate program compilation and executable creation. The makefile format then is introduced . We also showed how dynamic macros and suffix rules can be used to simplify makefile writing further. Finally, a practical example showed how to create a directory structure, along with a makefile in each source file directory to create the object libraries, and a makefile to create the executable.

Source Code Management System

3.1 INTRODUCTION

This chapter presents a simple and yet practical source code management system (SCMS). SCMS is an interface that accepts a user's commands and makes calls to SCCS, a standard UNIX operating system package that provides source code version control. Source code version control is important when source files are updated frequently and perhaps by more than one person. SCCS allows users to retrieve a current or previous version of a file, as needed. It reduces the amount of data that must be kept on disk by recording only the differences between successive versions. As you will see, the SCMS codes are written mainly in the Bourne shell script, which in turn makes calls to SCCS commands either directly through scripts or indirectly through C program modules.

This chapter's purpose is twofold: You can use this SCMS in a production environment to manage the source codes, or you can use this to learn how to write a full-blown shell script application.

3.2 A BRIEF SCCS REVIEW

For SCCS to function properly, you need to create a sub-directory under every source code directory. Usually these sub-directories are given the name SCCS. For example, if

the source files are stored under the directory /usr/src/ipc, the directory /usr/src/ipc/
SCCS should be created.

Once the SCCS sub-directory has been created, your first step is to create an initial version of the source file and place it into the SCCS directory. This creates the so-called s. file. For example, if we have files test1.c and test2.c in the /usr/src/ipc directory initially, files s.test1.c and s.test2.c are created under the directory /usr/src/ipc/
SCCS after the creation process. These s. files contain the initial source files codes plus additional control information (usually referred to as delta information) SCCS uses to retrieve the most current version or any previous version of the source file codes.

After the s. files are created and are under the SCCS' control, you may want a read-only copy of all the source files for the listing, compilation, or a writable copy of the source file for update. When SCCS fetches a writable copy of the source, a so-called p. file is created, which locks out everyone from getting the same piece of code for update. (We use the term "copy" for getting a read-only copy of the source file and the term "checkout" for getting a writable copy.)

After a file has been checked out, you may then edit the file. Upon completion of this file editing, you then issue a command to SCCS to update the source, which is kept by SCCS. The term for updating the source back to SCCS is "checkin." When checkin a file, SCCS prompts for comment. The user is urged to type in the comment that describes the changes he or she has made. Once the file has been checked back into the SCCS, the p. file is removed and anyone is allowed to check out the file again.

SCCS allows the user to undo the checkout process; we use the term "cancel" for this purpose.

A few words about version control: When a file is initially created under SCCS' control, it is given the version number 1.0. Notice that this version number consists of two unsigned integers separated by a decimal point. The number before the decimal point is called the major version number, and the one following the decimal point is called the minor version number. Every time a file is checked out, SCCS tells you the new version number. This new version number is not in effect until the checked-out file is checked back in. Once the file is checked in, its minor version number is incremented by one. If you decide it is time to increment the major version number, you need to specify the new version number in the checkout command. In this case, you specify the new major version number (usually it is the current major version number plus one), and allow the minor version to be zero or a blank.

3.3 WHY SCMS?

Users are encouraged to use SCMS rather than SCCS command calls because

1. SCMS provides more user-friendly commands than SCCS. All commands in
    SCMS are easier to remember than SCCS' counterparts. For example, to register
    a file under the SCCS control in SCMS, you simply type

    ```
    create test1.c
    ```

While calling the SCCS command directly, you need to type

```
admin -itest1.c /usr/src/ipc/SCCS/s.test1.c
```

The effort you can save by using SCMS is obvious.

2. SCMS creates and maintains its own databases that allow SCMS to provide control information. This is done by maintaining two files under the SCCSDB directory. The first file, chklst, is a log file for every check-in and check-out activity. The second file, canlst, is a log of all the cancel commands issued.

3. SCMS provides group operations. Most of the SCMS commands allow multiple files operation in one command. For example, you can check in all the C program files through the command

```
checkin  *.c
```

4. SCMS provides a uniform interface to different operating systems.

3.4 CASE STUDY: A SOURCE CODE MANAGER

The SCMS described in this chapter provides the following commands:

☞ init: Creates two directories, SCCS and SCCSDB, under the source code directory. It sets up the proper permission for these directories. It also creates two separate files—chklst and canlst—within the SCCSDB directory.

Usage: init

Note that after the create command, the original source file is removed from that directory.

☞ create: Creates the initial version of a source file into the SCCS sub-directory.

Usage: create filename

create *.c

☞ checkout: Checks out a source code from an SCCS-controlled directory into the user's working directory for update. It creates a lock file that prevents other users from checking out the same file.

☞ checkin: Updates the source code and increases the version number. It removes the lock file that keeps everyone else from checking out the same file.

☞ copy: Makes a read-only copy into the user's working directory. More than one user can copy the same source files.

☞ cancel: Undoes the checkout command. The version number remains the same.

☞ history: Shows a certain source file's updated history.

☞ diff: Prints the differences between any two previous versions of the source file onto the standard output.

☞ whatsout: Shows a list of all files checked out, the dates they were checked out, and the names of the users who checked out these files.

☞ whatsin: Shows a list of all files under the SCCS' control.

☞ status: Shows a list of all files a specific user checked out or a specific source file's check-out status.

☞ version: Queries the current version number of a specific source file.

☞ help: Shows examples of how each SCMS command works.

☞ quit: Exits the SCMS command menu.

3.4.1 SCMS Program Structure

From a user's point of view, SCMS consists of a main menu and a sub-menu. The main menu greets the user and lists all the directories the user may choose to work with. The sub-menu lists all the commands available in the SCMS.

From the programmer's point of view, SCMS consists of several layers of scripts that may interact with C programs. The advantages of using scripts: It is easy to make changes, no compilation is needed, and it is easy to pass environment variables. In fact, all environment variables exported from the top level script are passed on to their child processes automatically. The drawback with using script is that it does not work with setuid command, which is partially why parts of the SCMS codes must be written in C code.

3.4.2 Main Script

The script file scm is SCMS' main script. It performs the following functions:

1. Checks to see if SCMS is available on that specific machine.
2. Sets the proper environment variables. For example, the environment variable TOOLBOX stores the directory name where the SCCS commands resides.
3. Echoes a greeting message.
4. Echoes available directories for selection.
5. Reads user input.
6. Sets proper environment variables DBS and SCCS, according to user input.
7. Exports environment variables.
8. Activates the submenu.

3.4.3 Submenu Script

The main script activates the submenu script. It performs the following functions:

1. Displays available commands SCMS provides.
2. Accepts and processes the user input command.
3. Activates the appropriate command script to perform the SCCS command.

3.4.4 Command Scripts

Each SCMS command has a corresponding script to perform its command. Some SCMS commands require only one script to accomplish their task, others may need more than one layer of scripts. And the bottom layer script may have to call a C code module.

3.4.5 Source Code Listings

Listings 3.1 through 3.15 are examples of script listings.

Listing 3.1 scm

```
#!/bin/sh
# Filename:      scm
# Usage:         scm
# Function:      main menu

TOP=/usr/shen/tools
SRC=/usr/shen/src
WORK=`pwd`
FIRST=YES
ERROR=NO

# defining function EchoSelectionMenu
EchoSelectionMenu ( ) {
echo   "please select the directory by the index number; enter 'q' to exit"
echo   " 1 —> FIFO        source directory"
echo   " 2 —> TIMER       source directory"
echo   " 3 —> SOCKET      source directory"
echo   " 4 —> RPC         source directory"
echo   "  "
return
}

# get the operating system name
OS=`uname -s`
if test $OS = SunOS
then
   SCM=$TOP/scm/sun
   USER=`whoami`
   TOOLBOX=/usr/sccs
elif test $OS = AIX
then
   SCM=$TOP/scm/ibmrs
   USER=`whoami`
   TOOLBOX=/usr/bin
else
   echo "SCM is not available on $OS"
fi

selection=0
while [  ! $selection  = q  ]
```

```
do
   if  [  $FIRST = YES   ]
   then
      FIRST=NO
      echo " "
      echo Welcome $USER to SCM
   fi

   EchoSelectionMenu

   read selection

   #  make sure selection not NULL
   until [  $selection ]
   do
      EchoSelectionMenu
      read command
   done

   case  $selection  in
   1)
      echo You are working on FIFO library.
      DBS=$SRC/fifo/SCCSDB
      SCCSDB=$SRC/fifo/SCCS
      echo The current directory is $WORK
      echo The SCCS directory is $SCCS
      echo The SCCSDB directory is $SCCSDB ;;

   2)
      echo You are working on TIMER library.
      DBS=$SRC/timer/SCCSDB
      SCCSDB=$SRC/timer/SCCS
      echo The current directory is $WORK
      echo The SCCS directory is $SCCS
      echo The SCCSDB directory is $SCCSDB ;;

   3)
      echo You are working on SOCKET library.
      DBS=$SRC/socket/SCCSDB
      SCCSDB=$SRC/socket/SCCS
      echo The current directory is $WORK
      echo The SCCS directory is $SCCS
      echo The SCCSDB directory is $SCCSDB ;;

   4)
      echo You are working on RPC library.
      DBS=$SRC/rpc/SCCSDB
      SCCSDB=$SRC/rpc/SCCS
      echo The current directory is $WORK
      echo The SCCS directory is $SCCS
      echo The SCCSDB directory is $SCCSDB ;;

   q | qq | quit)
      echo $USER has exited SCM.
      exit 1 ;;
   *)
```

```
        ERROR=YES
        echo That wasn\'t one of the choices. ;;
    esac

    if [ $ERROR = NO ]
    then
        echo ─────────────────────────────
        export   SCCS DBS USER SCM TOOLBOX WORK
        $SCM/scmenu
        if [ $? -eq 1 ]
        then
            exit 0
        fi
    fi

    # reset error flag
        ERROR=NO

done
```

Listing 3.2 scmenu

```
#!/bin/sh
# Usage:        scmenu
# Function:   handles menu commands
export  SCCS DBS TOOLBOX USER SCM
command=""
args=""
#define function ReadCommand
ReadCommand ( ) {
    echo ----------------------------------------------------------------
    echo
    echo Please enter command:
    read command args
}
echo Available commands are:
echo "   cancel      checkin      checkout     status      help    "
echo "   copy        create       whatsout     history     quit    "
echo "   diff        init         whatsin      version             "
# call function ReadCommand
ReadCommand
# make sure command is not NULL
until  test $command
do
    ReadCommand
done
until [ $command = quit  -o $command = q -o $command = qq ]
do
    if [ $command = cancel         -o       $command = checkout   -o  \
         $command = checkin         -o       $command = help       -o  \
         $command = copy            -o       $command = create     -o  \
         $command = whatsout        -o       $command = status     -o  \
         $command = history         -o       $command = diff       -o  \
         $command = whatsin         -o       $command = init       -o  \
```

```
        $command = version ]
    then
        $SCM/$command $args
    else
        echo Invalid command
    fi
    ReadCommand
    until  test $command
    do
        ReadCommand
    done
done
if  [  $command = qq  ]
then
    exit  1
else
    exit  0
fi
```

Listing 3.3 init

```
#!/bin/sh
# Filename:  init
# Usage:     init
# Function:  create directories SCCS and SCCSDB and
#            create files chklst and canlst under SCCSDB

if [  -f  $SCCS  ]
then
   echo file $SCCS exists, please delete it.
   exit 1
elif [  !  -d  $SCCS  ]
then
   echo create directory $SCCS
  .mkdir $SCCS
fi

if  [  -f  $DBS  ]
then
   echo file $DBS exists, please delete it.
   exit 1
elif [  !  -d  $DBS  ]
then
   echo create directory $DBS
   mkdir $DBS
   touch $DBS/chklst
   touch $DBS/canlst
fi
```

Listing 3.4 create

```
#!/bin/sh
# Filename: create
# Usage:    create filename [filename ...]
```

```
# Function: create the initial s.filename
export  DBS  SCCS TOOLBOX SCM

# check number of arguments must greater than 1
if  [  $#  -qe 1 ]
then
echo Usage: create  filename
exit 1
fi

# get the filename
for i in $*
do
   filename=$i
   if  [  ! -f  $filename  ]
   then
      echo create: file $filename does not exist
      exit 1
   fi

   $SCM/admin_sccs  $filename
   exitcode=$?
   if  [  $exitcode   -eq  1  ]
   then
      echo sccs create error
      exit 1
   fi
   echo create $filename successfully
   rm -f  $filename
done
```

Listing 3.5 checkout

```
#!/bin/sh
# checkout -- checkout one or more source module from the SCCS
#
# Usage:   checkout [options] filename [filename ...]
#      or
#          checkout [options] all.[c|h]
#
arglist=$*
WORK=`pwd`
export  SCCS DBS SCM TOOLBOX WORK

#define function
CheckOut ( )  {
   filename=$1
   options=$2
   $SCM/get_sccs  $filename  $options
   exitcode=$?
   if  [  $exitcode  -eq  1  ]
   then
      echo  checkout $filename  error
      return
   fi
```

```
# get current version number
   cd   $SCCS
   rm -f $WORK/tmp$$
   $TOOLBOX/prs  $SCCS/s.$filename  >   $WORK/tmp$$
   cd $WORK

# update log files
   $SCM/updtlog $filename co
   rm   -f   $HOME/out$$
   rm   -f   $WORK/tmp$$
   return
}

# check number of arguments must greater than 0
   if  [  $#  -eq  0  ]
   then
      echo Usage: checkout [options] filename
      exit 1
   fi

#extract options
   spaces="   "
   arg1=$1
   echo $arg1 | sed   "/-r/d"   >   $HOME/temp.$$
   if  [  -s  $HOME/temp.$$  ]
   then
      nooption=YES
      filenames=""
      count=0
      for i in $arglist
      do
         count=`expr $count + 1`
         if  [  $count -gt  0  ]
         then
            filenames=$filenames$spaces$i
         fi
      done
   else
      nooption=NO
      options=$arg1
      filenames=""
      count=0
      for i in $arglist
      do
         count=`expr $count + 1`
         if  [  $count -gt  1  ]
         then
            filenames=$filenames$spaces$i
         fi
      done
   fi
   rm -f $HOME/temp.$$

# wildcard checkout
for j in $filenames
```

```
do
   filename=$j
   if  [  $filename = all   ]
   then
      for  i  in  $SCCS/s.*
      do
         i=`echo $i | sed 's/.*SCCS\/s\.//'`
         if  [  $nooption = YES   ]
         then
            CheckOut  $i
         else
            CheckOut  $i  $options
         fi
         exitcode=$?
         if  [  $exitcode  -eq 1 ]
         then
            echo sccs command error
            exit 1
         fi
      done
      exit 0
   elif test $filename = all.c
   then
      for i in  $SCCS/s.*.c
      do
         i=`echo $i | sed 's/.*SCCS\/s\.//'`
         if  [  $nooption = YES   ]
         then
            CheckOut  $i
         else
            CheckOut  $i  $options
         fi
         exitcode=$?
         if   [  $exitcode  -eq  1 ]
         then
            echo sccs command error
            exit 1
         fi
      done
      exit 0
   elif test $filename = all.h
   then
      for i in  $SCCS/s.*.h
      do
         i=`echo $i | sed 's/.*SCCS\/s\.//'`
         if  [  $nooption = YES   ]
         then
            CheckOut  $i
         else
            CheckOut  $i  $options
         fi
         exitcode=$?
         if  [  $exitcode = 1 ]
         then
```

```
            echo sccs command error
            exit 1
        fi
    done
    exit 0
  else
#     single file checkout
    if  [  $nooption = YES  ]
    then
        CheckOut  $i
    else
        CheckOut   $i  $options
    fi
    exitcode=$?
    if test $exitcode = 1
    then
        echo sccs command error
        exit 1
    fi
  fi
done
```

Listing 3.6 checkin

```
#!/bin/sh
#  checkin -- checkin one or more source modules into the SCCS
#
#  Usage: checkin filename [filename ..]
#        or
#              checkin   *.[c|h]
#
#
USER=`whoami`
export  SCCS DBS SCM TOOLBOX  USER

#define function
CheckIn ( ) {
   filename=$1
   options=$2

# backup file
   cp  $filename  .$filename

# check for valid version string
   grep '%W%[ \t].*%G%[ \t].*\*\*\*\*'   $filename  >  $HOME/tmpfile$$
   if  [  !  -s  $HOME/tmpfile$$  ]
   then
      echo "file $filename does not have legal version string"
      echo "checkin fails"
      rm  -f  $HOME/tmpfile$$
      exit 1
   fi

# search  $SCCS/p.*  for this filename
```

```
    pfiles=`ls  $SCCS/p.*`
    for  i  in  $pfiles
    do
        file=`echo $i  |  sed  's/.*SCCS/\/p\.//'`
        if  [  $file  =  $filename  ]
        then
# check if  it is the same user
            grep  $USER  $i   >  $HOME/tmpfile$$
            if  [   !  -s  $HOME/tmpfile$$  ]
            then
                echo  checkin error:  user's name not matched
                return
            fi
            rm  -f  $HOME/tmpfile$$
        else
            echo  checkin error: $filename  has not been checked out
            return
        fi
    done

    echo checkin  $filename
    $SCM/delta_sccs  $filename
    exitcode=$?
    if  [  $exitcode  -eq  1  ]
    then
        echo sccs command error
        return
    fi

# remove backup file if it exists
    if  [  -f .$filename ]
    then
        rm   -f   .$filename
    fi

# update log file
    $SCMS/updtlog $filename ci

    return
}

# check number of arguments greater than 1
    if  [  $#   -eq   0  ]
    then
        echo Usage: checkin  filename
        exit 1
    fi

    arglist=$*
    nargs=$#

    arg1=$1
    echo $arg1  |  sed  "/-r/d"   >  $HOME/tmpfile$$
    if  [  -s  $HOME/tmpfile$$  ]
    then
        nooption=YES
```

```
      options=""
   else
      nooption=NO
      options=$arg1
   fi

   if  [  $nargs  -le  2  ]
   then
      CheckIn  $filename  $options
   else
      count=0
      for  i  in  $arglist
      do
         if  [ $nooption = YES  ]
         then
            CheckIn $i  $options
         else
            count=`expr  $count  +  1`
            if  [   $count  -gt  1  ]
            then
               CheckIn  $i  $options
            fi
         fi
      done
   fi
```

Listing 3.7 copy

```
#!/bin/sh
# copy -- get one or more readonly copies of source modules from
#         the SCCS
#
# Usage: copy [options] filename
#

# check number of arguments must greater than 1
   if  [  $#   -eq  0  ]
   then
      echo Usage: copy [options] filename
      exit 1
   fi

#extract options and filenames

   spaces="  "
   options=""
   arg1=$1
   echo $arg1 | sed "/-r/d" > temp.$$
   if  [  -s  temp.$$  ]
   then
      filenames=""
      count=0
      for i in $*
      do
```

```
            count=`expr $count + 1`
            if  [  $count   -gt   0   ]
            then
                filenames=$filenames$spaces$i
            fi
        done
    else
        options=$arg1
        filenames=""
        count=0
        for i in $*
        do
            count=`expr $count + 1`
            if  [  $count   -gt   1 ]
            then
                filenames=$filenames$spaces$i
            fi
        done
    fi
    rm -f temp.$$

# get all SCCS files
for j in $filenames
do
    filename=$j
    if  [  $filename  =  all  ]
    then
        for i in  $SCCS/s.*
        do
            echo copy $i
            $TOOLBOX/get_sccs  $options $i
            exitcode=$?
            if  [  $exitcode  -eq  1 ]
            then
                echo sccs command error
                exit 1
            fi
        done
        exit 0
    elif  [  $filename = all.c ]
    then
        for i in  $SCCS/s.*.c
        do
            echo copy $i
            $TOOLBOX/get_sccs  $options $i
            exitcode=$?
            if  [  $exitcode  -eq   1 ]
            then
                echo sccs command error
                exit 1
            fi
        done
        exit 0
    elif  [ $filename = all.h  ]
```

```
    then
        for i in  $SCCS/s.*.h
        do
            echo  copy $i
            $TOOLBOX/get_sccs  $options $i
            exitcode=$?
            if  [ $exitcode  -eq  1  ]
            then
                echo sccs command error
                exit 1
            fi
        done
        exit 0
    else
        echo copy $filename
        $TOOLBOX/get_sccs  $options $SCCS/s.$filename
        exitcode=$?
        if  [  $exitcode  -eq  1 ]
        then
            echo sccs command error
            exit 1
        fi
    fi
done
```

Listing 3.8 cancel

```
#!/bin/sh
#  cancel -- undo the checkout command previously issued to one or
#                   more source files.
#
#  Usage: cancel filename [filename ....]
#
WORK=`pwd`
export  SCCS  DBS  SCM TOOLBOX  WORK  USER

#  define function
CancelCheckOut (  )  {
   filename=$1
   if  [  !  -f  $filename  ]
   then
      echo  file  $filename does not exist
      return
   fi
# search  $SCCS/p.*  for this filename
   pfiles=`ls  $SCCS/p.*`
   for  i  in  $pfiles
   do
      file=`echo $i  |  sed  's/.*SCCS/\/p\.//'`
      if  [  $file  =  $filename  ]
      then
# check if  it is the same user
         grep  $USER $i  >  $HOME/tmpfile$$
         if  [   !  -s  $HOME/tmpfile$$  ]
```

```
            then
               echo  cancel error:  user's name not matched
               return
            fi
            rm  -f  $HOME/tmpfile$$
        else
            echo  cancel error: $filename  has not been checked out
            return
        fi
    done

    $SCM/unget_sccs  $filename
    if  [  $?  -eq  1 ]
    then
        echo  sccs command error
        return
    fi
#   remove backup file if exists
    if  [  -f   .$filename  ]
    then
        rm  -f  .$filename
    fi
    $SCM/updtlog  $filename  ca
}

# check number of arguments must greater than 1
    if  [   $#   -eq   0  ]
    then
        echo Usage: cancel  filename
        exit 1
    fi

    for i in $*
    do
       filename=$i
       CancelCheckOut  $filename
       echo cancel $filename done
    done
```

Listing 3.9 diff

```
#!/bin/sh
# diff:  print the difference between two versions
#        of a source file
#
# Usage: diff -RSID1 -RSID2 filename

if  [  $#  -ne  3  ]
then
   echo  Usage: diff -RSID1 -RSID2 filename
   exit 1
fi

arg1=$1
arg2=$2
```

```
arg3=$3
spaces=" "
echo $arg1  | sed   "/-r/d"   >    $HOME/temp.$$
if  [  -s  $HOME/temp.$$  ]
then
   echo invalid SID in argument 1
   exit 1
fi

echo $arg2  | sed   "/-r/d"   >    $HOME/temp.$$
if  [  -s  $HOME/temp.$$  ]
then
   echo invalid SID in argument 2
   exit 1
fi

filename=$SCCS/s.$arg3
args=$arg1$spaces$arg2$spaces$filename
$TOOLBOX/sccsdiff    $args
```

Listing 3.10 help

```
#!/bin/sh
#help — list the available commands and their usage examples
#
#Usage:  help
#        help command

if  [ $#   -eq  0  ]
then
   echo Available commands are:
   echo "    cancel     checkin      checkout     status     help    "
   echo "    copy       create       whatsout     history    quit    "
   echo "    diff       whatsin      version      "
   exit  0
fi

case  $1   in
cancel)
   echo "Usage: cancel filename"
   echo " ";;
init)
   echo "Usage: init"
   echo " ";;
copy)
   echo "Usage: copy [options] filename"
   echo "Examples:"
   echo "copy prog.c          ; get a readonly copy of the file prog.c"
   echo "copy prog.c prog.h" ; get two source copies
   echo "copy -r2.1 prog.c   ; get version 2.1 of the file prog.c"
   echo "copy all            ; get all the readonly copies of all"
   echo "                    ; files"
   echo " ";;
checkin)
   echo "Usage:  checkin filename ; checkin one file"
```

```
    echo "Examples:"
    echo "checkin prog.c           ; check in a single module"
    echo "checkin prog.c prog.h  ;check in two modules"
    echo "checkin  *.c             ; checkin all C program files"
    echo "checkin  *.h             ; checkin all header files"
    echo " ";;
checkout)
    echo "Usage:  checkout [options] filename"
    echo "Examples:"
    echo "checkout prog.f          ; checkout most recent copy"
    echo "checkout prog.f prog.h ;check out two source files"
    echo "checkout -r2  prog.c   ; create a new release      "
    echo "checkout -r1.3 prog.c  ; create a new branch        "
    echo "checkout all             ; checkout all files"
    echo "checkout all.c           ; checkout all C files"
    echo "checkout all.h           ; checkout all C header files"
    echo " ";;
create)
    echo "Usage:  create  filename"
    echo "Examples:"
    echo "create prog.c            ; create a s.prog.c file"
    echo "create  *.c              ; create initial copies for all C files
    echo " ";;
quit)
    echo "Usage:  quit          ; exit to first manual"
    echo "Usage:  q             ; exit to first manual"
    echo "Usage:  qq            ; exit scm"
    echo " ";;
whatsout)
    echo "Usage:  whatsout"
    echo " ";;
whatsin)
    echo "Usage:  whatsin"
    echo " ";;
help)
    echo "Usage:  help "
    echo "or       help  command_name"
    echo "Example:"
    echo "help checkout            ; inquire checkout command usage"
    echo " ";;
status)
    echo " "
    echo "Usage:"
    echo "status username "
    echo "or"
    echo "status  filename"
    echo "Example:"
    echo "status prog.c"
    echo "status shen"
    echo " ";;
diff)
    echo "Usage:  diff -rSID1  -rSID2  filename "
    echo "Example:"
    echo "diff -r1.2  -r1.3  prog.c"
```

```
    echo " ";;
history)
   echo "Usage:   history filename          ; looking  at whole history"
   echo "or       history -r1.3  filename  ; for a version"
   echo  " ";;
version)
   echo "Usage:   version filename   ; get the current version"
   echo "Example:"
   echo "version prog.c              ; inquire the current version"
   echo "                            ; of file prog.c"
*)
   echo "Error in help argument ";;
esac
```

Listing 3.11 history

```
#!/bin/sh
# history: list all or certain version history of a source file
# Usage: history [options] filename
#
if [ $#  -ne  1  -o  $#  -ne  2  ]
then
   echo  Usage: history [options] filename
   exit 1
fi

spaces="   "
arg1=$1
if [ $#    -eq   1  ]
then
   filename=$SCCS/s.$arg1
   args= $filename
else
   echo $arg1 | sed   "/-r/d"   >   $HOME/temp.$$
   if [  -s  $HOME/temp.$$  ]
   then
      echo invalid SID in argument 1
      exit 1
   fi
   arg2=$2
   filename=$SCCS/s.$arg2
   args=$arg1$spaces$filename
fi

$TOOLBOX/prs $args | more
```

Listing 3.12 status

```
#!/bin/sh
# status -- query a specific file status or a specific user
#           status regarding the checked out files.
# Usages:
#       status  -u  username
#       status  -f  filename
```

```sh
# check number of arguments must greater than 1
if   [   $#   -ne  2   ]
then
   echo "Usage:"
   echo "    status  -u username "
   echo "or"
   echo "    status  -f  filename"
   echo "Example:"
   echo "status  -f  fprog.c    ; inquire the status of prog.c"
   exit 0
fi
H=$HOME
echo '******************************************************************'
echo      File      Old-Ver      New-Ver           USER        Check-Out-Date
pfiles=`ls  $SCCS/p.*`
if  [   $1 =  "-f"  ]
then
   for j  in $pfiles
   do
      file=`echo $j  |  sed  's/.*SCCS/\/p\.//'`
      if  [   $2 =  $file  ]
      then
         echo  "{print \"$file\", \"  \",  \$1, \"        \", \$2, \" \
          \",  \$3, \"    \", \$4}"  > $H/tmp$$
         awk  -f  $H/tmp$$  $j
         echo   "  "
      fi
   done
fi
if  [   $1 =  "-u"  ]
then
   for j  in $pfiles
   do
      file=`echo $j  |  sed  's/.*SCCS/\/p\.//'`
      # check if  it is the same user
      grep  $USER  $j   > $H/ tmpfile$$
      if  [  -s  $H/tmpfile$$  ]
      then
         echo  "{print \"$file\", \"  \",  \$1, \"        \",  \$2, \" \
          \",  \$3, \"    \", \$4}"  > $H/tmp$$
         awk  -f  $H/tmp$$  $j
         echo   "  "
      fi
   done
fi
echo '******************************************************************'
rm  -f  $H/tmp$$
```

Listing 3.13 version

```sh
#!/bin/sh
#version — print the current version number of a file
#
# Usage: version filename
```

```
#
if  [  $#    -ne  1  ]
then
   echo  "Usage:  version  filename"
   exit 1
fi

spaces="    "
filename=$SCCS/s.$i
args=$filename
$TOOLBOX/prs $args > $WORK/tmp$$
$SCM/getver   $WORK/tmp$$
rm   -f $WORK/tmp$$
```

Listing 3.14 whatsin

```
#!/bin/sh
echo '*******************************************'
ls $SCCS/s.*  |  sed  's/.*SCCS\/s\.//'  |  more
echo '*******************************************'
```

Listing 3.15 whatsout

```
# !/bin/sh
# whatsout -- list the source modules that have been checked out
#
# Usage:  whatsout
#
H=$HOME
echo '***********************************************************'
echo        File      Old-Ver      New-Ver         USER         Check-Out-Date\
         Check-Out-Time
pfiles=`ls  $SCCS/p.*`
for j  in $pfiles
do
   file=`echo $j  |  sed  's/.*SCCS\/p\.//'`
   echo  "{print \"$file\", \"  \", \$1, \"      \", \$2, \"    \", \
        \$3, \"    \", \$4, \"  \",   \$5}" >  $H/tmp$$
   awk  -f $H/tmp$$  $j
   echo  "  "
done
rm  -f  $H/tmp$$
```

Listings 3-16 through 3-21 are examples of C code listings.

Listing 3.16 admin_sccs.c

```
/*
 * admin_sccs.c
 */
#include <stdio.h>
```

```c
main(argc, argv)
int argc;
char *argv[];
{

    char path[50];
    char file[80];
    char command[200];
    int mode;
    int status;
    char *strsccs;
    char *strdb;
    char *sccsdir;
    char *getenv();

    strsccs =  getenv("SCCS");
    strdb =  getenv("DBS");
    sccsdir = getenv("TOOLBOX");
    sprintf(file,"%s/s.%s\n",strsccs, argv[1]);
    sprintf(command, "%s/admin -i%s %s\n", sccsdir, argv[1], file);
    /* set the file mode to 777 */
    mode = 777;
    mode = (mode/100)*8*8 + (mode- mode/100 *100) / 10*8
       +(mode% 10);
    chmod(strsccs, mode);
    /* execute the admin command */
    status = system(command);
    /* set the file mode back to 755 */
    mode = 755;
    mode = (mode/100)*8*8 + (mode- mode/100 *100) / 10*8
       +(mode% 10);
    chmod(strsccs, mode);
    if (status == 0)
       exit(0);
    else
       exit(1);
```

Listing 3.17 delta_sccs.c

```c
/*
* delta_sccs.c
*/
#include <stdio.h>

main(argc, argv)
int argc;
char *argv[];
{

    char path[50];
    char file[80];
    char command[80];
    int mode;
    int status;
```

```c
    char *strsccs;
    char *strdb;
    char *sccsdir;
    char *getenv();

    strsccs =  getenv("SCCS");
    strdb =  getenv("DBS");
    sccsdir = getenv("TOOLBOX");
    sprintf(file,"%s/s.%s\n",strsccs, argv[1]);
    sprintf(command, "%s/delta   %s\n", sccsdir, file);
    /* set the file mode to 777 */
    mode = 777;
    mode = (mode/100)*8*8 + (mode- mode/100 *100) / 10*8
       +(mode% 10);
    chmod(strsccs, mode);
    /* execute the admin command */
    status = system(command);
    /* set the file mode back to 755 */
    mode = 755;
    mode = (mode/100)*8*8 + (mode- mode/100 *100) / 10*8
       +(mode% 10);
    chmod(strsccs, mode);
    if (status == 0)
       exit(0);
    else
       exit(1);
}
```

Listing 3.18 get_sccs.c

```c
/*
* get_sccs.c    .
*/
#include <stdio.h>

main(argc, argv)
int argc;
char *argv[];
{
    char path[50];
    char file[80];
    char command[80];
    int mode;
    int status;
    char *strsccs;
    char *strdb;
    char *sccsdir;
    char *getenv();

    strsccs =  getenv("SCCS");
    strdb =  getenv("DBS");
    sccsdir = getenv("TOOLBOX");

    sprintf(file,"%s/s.%s\n",strsccs,   argv[1]);
```

```
    if ( argv[2] == NULL)
        sprintf(command, "%s/get -e  %s\n", sccsdir, file);
    else
        sprintf(command, "%s/get -e %s %s\n", sccsdir, argv[2],   file);
    /* set the file mode to 777 */
    mode = 777;
    mode = (mode/100)*8*8 + (mode- mode/100 *100) / 10*8
        +(mode% 10);
    chmod(strsccs, mode);
    /* execute the admin command */
    status = system(command);
    /* set the file mode back to 755 */
    mode = 755;
    mode = (mode/100)*8*8 + (mode- mode/100 *100) / 10*8
        +(mode% 10);
    chmod(strsccs, mode);
    if (status == 0)
        exit(0);
    else
        exit(1);
}
```

Listing 3.19 unget_sccs.c

```
/*
* unget_sccs.c
*/
#include <stdio.h>

main(argc, argv)
int argc;
char *argv[];
{

    char path[50];
    char file[80];
    char command[80];
    int mode;
    int status;
    char *strsccs;
    char *strdb;
    char *sccsdir;
    char *getenv();

    strsccs =  getenv("SCCS");
    strdb =  getenv("DBS");
    sccsdir = getenv("TOOLBOX");

    sprintf(file,"%s/s.%s\n", strsccs, argv[1]);
    sprintf(command, "%s/unget %s\n", sccsdir, file);
    /* set the file mode to 777 */
    mode = 777;
    mode = (mode/100)*8*8 + (mode- mode/100 *100) / 10*8
        +(mode% 10);
    chmod(strsccs, mode);
```

```
   /* execute the admin command */
   status = system(command);
   /* set the file mode back to 755 */
   mode = 755;
   mode = (mode/100)*8*8 + (mode- mode/100 *100) / 10*8
      +(mode% 10);
   chmod(strsccs, mode);
   if (status == 0)
      exit(0);
   else
      exit(1);
   exit(0);
}
```

Listing 3.20 getver.c

```
/*
* getver.c
*/
#include <stdio.h>
#define MAXLINE 120

main(argc, argv)
int argc;
char *argv[];
{

   FILE *fp;
   int i,j;
   char linebuf[MAXLINE];
   char program[20];
   char version[20];

   if ((fp = fopen(argv[1], "r"))  == NULL)
   {
      printf("File open error. File name: %s\n", argv[1]);
      exit(-1);
   }
   /* extract the version string */
   while ( fgets(linebuf, MAXLINE, fp) != NULL)
   {
      if (linebuf[0] == 'D')
      {
         i = 2;  j = 0;
         while (linebuf[i] != ' ')
         {
            version[j] = linebuf[i];
            i++;    j++;
         }
         version[j] = '\0';
         printf("current version of %s is %s\n", program,    version);
         exit(0);
      }
      else if (linebuf[0] == 's' && linebuf[1] == '.')
```

```c
        {
            i = 2;   j = 0;
            while (linebuf[i] != ':')
            {
                program[j] = linebuf[i];
                i++;   j++;
            }
            program[j] = '\0';
        }
    }
}
```

Listing 3.21 updtlog.c

```c
/*
 *  updtlog - update the  checkin/checkout log files
 */
#include <stdio.h>
#include <fcntl.h>

struct flock *flock_arg;
int           flock_fd;

main(argc, argv)
int argc;
char *argv[];
{
    FILE *fp;
    FILE *fp2;
    char *date, *lognm;
    char file[40];
    char lockfile[120];
    char *getenv(), *ctime(), *getlogin();
    long time();
    long tm();
    char command[50];
    char msgs[200];
    char msg1[100], msg2[100];
    int  mode;
    int  num_tries = 0;
    char *strsccs;
    char *strdb;
    char *wkdir;
    char *ptr;

    strsccs = getenv("SCCS");
    strdb   = getenv("DBS");
    wkdir   = getenv("WORK");
    lognm   = getenv("USER");
    time(&tm);
    date = ctime(&tm);

    ptr = (char *)strchr(date, '\n');
    if ( ptr != NULL)
```

```c
   *ptr = '\0';

/* skip 3 characters which shows the day of the week */
date += 3;

sprintf(file, "%s/chklst", strdb);
/* set the permission for file chklst to 777 */
mode = 777;
mode = (mode/100)*8*8 + (mode- mode/100 *100) / 10*8
   +(mode% 10);
chmod(file, mode);
if ((fp = fopen(file, "a")) == NULL)
{
   printf("File open error: %s\n", file);
   exit(-1);
}

sprintf(lockfile, "%s/chklst", strdb);
while (lock(lockfile) != 0)
{
   printf("lock busy\n");
   sleep(1);
   num_tries++;
   if (num_tries > 5)
   {
      printf("lock error on %s\n", lockfile);
      exit(-1);
   }
}

if (strcmp(argv[2], "ci") ==  0)
{
   sprintf(msg1,"%10s   checkin  %10s at %20s from %s\n",
   lognm, argv[1], date, wkdir);
   fprintf(fp, msg1);
}
else if (strcmp(argv[2], "co") ==  0)
{
   sprintf(msg1,"%10s   checkout  %10s at %20s to %s\n",
   lognm, argv[1], date, wkdir);
   fprintf(fp, msg1);
}
else if (strcmp(argv[2], "ca") ==  0)
{
   sprintf(msg1,"%10s   cancel    %10s at %20s to %s\n",
   lognm, argv[1], date, wkdir);
   fprintf(fp, msg1);
}
else
{
   printf("Error in command argument: %s\n", argv[2]);
   exit(-1);
}
/* set the permission for file chklst back to 755 */
mode = 755;
```

```c
    mode = (mode/100)*8*8 + (mode - mode/100 *100) / 10 *8
        +(mode %s 10);
    sprintf(file, "%s/chklst", strdb);
    chmod(file, mode);
    unlock(lockfile);
    fclose(fp);
    fclose(fp2);
}

/* function for file locking */
int lock(filename)
char *filename;
{
    int rtn;

    if ((flock_fd = open(filename, O_RDWR, 0)) == NULL)
        return(2);
    if (flock_arg == NULL)
        flock_arg = (struct flock *)malloc(sizeof(struct flock));
    flock_arg->l_type = F_WRLCK;
    flock_arg->l_whence = 0;
    flock_arg->l_start = 0;
    flock_arg->l_len = 0;
    if (fcntl(flock_fd,F_SETLK,flock_arg) == -1)
    {
        close(flock_fd);
        return(3);
    }
    return(0);
}

/* function for unlocking a file */
int unlock(filename)
char *filename;
{
    if (flock_arg == NULL)
        return(2);

    flock_arg->l_type = F_UNLCK;
    flock_arg->l_whence = 0;
    flock_arg->l_start = 0;
    flock_arg->l_len = 0;
    if (fcntl(flock_fd,F_SETLK, flock_arg) == -1)
    {
        close(flock_fd);
        free(flock_arg);
        flock_arg = NULL;
        return(0);
    }
    else
        return(3);
}
```

3.5 VERSION CONTROL

Version control plays an important role in any software package release. An application package may consist of 50 program modules, and we want to know the individual version number for each. Of course, we can track this information by hand and store this information in a file. But it is much better if we embed this information into the executable file and determine the version numbers for each of the component files that comprise this executable. This is rather easy to achieve once we have all the program modules under the SCCS' control. Here is how to do it:

1. Insert the following statement into each of your C program modules following the last include statement:

   ```
   static char version[] = "%W% %G%   ***";
   ```

2. Before you compile each module, check in all the program modules that have been checked out, and use the copy command from SCMS to get the read-only copies of all source modules. When you do this, the ID keyword %W% is replaced by the special string @(#), followed by the module's filename, and the ID keyword %G% is replaced by the version number and today's date. For program module prog.c, the version string may appear as

   ```
   static char version[] = "@(#) prog.c  2.1 07/30/94   ***";
   ```

3. Compile all source files and create the executable.

The executable created in step 3 has all the version strings of all the component modules as part of the data. If we could write a program that examines this executable file and looks for all strings which start with @(#) and end with ***, we should be able to print out all the component program modules, along with their version numbers. The program verlist.c shown in Listing 3.22 does exactly that.

Listing 3.22 verlist.c

```c
#include <stdio.h>
#define BUFSIZE  8000
void copychars();
main(argc, argv)
int argc;
char *argv[];
{
   FILE   *fpin;
   int      nread;
   char   ch;
   char   buf[BUFSIZE];
   char   version[128];
   int      ,j, k;
   int      state;
   if (argc != 2)
   {
      fprintf(stderr,  "Usage: verlist  filename\n");
      exit(-1);
```

```c
       }
    if ((fpin  = fopen(argv[1], "rb")) == NULL)
    {
       fprintf(stderr, "Open file error: filename = %s\n", argv[1]);
       exit(-1);
    }
    while ( ( nread = fread(&buf[0], sizeof(char), BUFSIZE/2, fpin)) > 0)
    {
       for ( k=0;  k< nread; k++)
       {
          ch = buf[k];
          switch ( state)
          {
             case 0:
                if ( ch == '@')
                {
                   version[0] = ch;
                   state = 1;
                }
                break;
             case 1:
                if ( ch == '(')
                {
                   version[1] = ch;
                   state = 2;
                }
                else
                   state = 0;
                break;
             case 2:
                if ( ch == '#')
                {
                   version[2] = ch;
                   state = 3;
                }
                else
                   state = 0;
                break;
             case 3:
                if ( ch == ')')
                {
                   version[3] = ch;
                   state = 4;
                }
                else
                   state = 0;
                break;
             case 4:
                if ( ch == '*')
                   state = 5;
                if (j < 128)
                   version[j++]  = ch;
                else
                   state = 0;
```

```c
                break;
            case 5:
                if ( ch == '*')
                {
                    state = 6;
                    version[j++]  = ch;
                }
                else
                    state = 0;
                break;
            case 6:
                if ( ch == '*')
                {
                    state = 7;
                    version[j++]  = ch;
                }
                else
                    state = 0;
                break;
            case 7:
                if ( ch == '*')
                {
                    version[j++]  = ch;
                    version[j] = '\0';
                    fprintf(stdout, "\t%s\n", version);
                }
                state = 0;
                break;
            default:
                fprintf(stderr, "error state: %d\n", state);
                break;
        }
    }
}
fclose(fpin);
exit(0);
}
```

3.6 SUMMARY

This chapter shows how to write a source code management system (a user-friendly
interface to SCCS) using scripts that interact with C code program files. This chapter
started with a brief SCCS review and gave reasons why a user wouldn't use it directly.
We then listed 14 SCMS commands and explained each command's function. A brief
outline of the program structure for SCMS is given from the implementation point of
view. Finally, all source code listings are given at the end of the chapter. The material
presented in this chapter can be used as a case study on script-writing skills using the
Bourne shell.

LEX

4.1 INTRODUCTION

LEX is a processor (or program) that translates a LEX specification into a table-driven lexical analyzer. This table-driven lexical analyzer is given the function name yylex() for programming interface. This function is stored in the file lex.yy.c by default. This function reads characters from the input stream and detects matched patterns, which are specified in the form of regular expressions. Whenever a pattern matches, depending on how a programmer has coded the action routines, yylex() either finishes matching all the patterns before it returns to the calling program or returns a token (which is an integer value) every time a pattern is matched.

The next two sections outline the format of a LEX specification and how to construct a regular expression. Section four mentions a few LEX internal functions the LEX processor provides and programmers can access directly. Section five shows how to run the LEX processor and how to specify the control parameters to the LEX processor. Section six shows how you can use LEX to perform useful work.

4.2 THE LEX PROGRAM FORMAT

The LEX specification has the format

```
%{
    globally defined user-supplied C codes
%}
    macro definitions
%%
    patterns    actions
%%
    local C codes
```

A LEX specification is divided into three sections separated from each other by %% directives: the definitions section, the rules section, and the code section. The definitions section contains two parts: user-supplied codes and macro definitions. The user-supplied code must be enclosed between %{ and %} directives, and it may contain #include statements, external definitions, and global variable definitions. Each macro definition consists of a name, followed by one or more spaces, followed in turn by macro contents.

Here are some examples:

```
digit           [0-9]       /* decimal digit       */
letter          [A-Za-z]    /* alphabetic character */
letter_or_digit [A-Za-z0-9] /* letter or digit      */
```

Here we declare macro digit to be the set of all decimal digits, macro letter to be the set of all alphabets, and macro letter_or_digit to be the set of all alphabets and digits.

The rules section consists of a number of pattern-action pairs. Each pattern-action pair has two components: a regular expression that specifies the symbols to be matched and C code that is executed when the input matching the regular expression is found. The third section contains any number of C functions that are directly copied to the output file (lex.yy.c) when we compile a LEX specification. Anything outside the %{ and %} pairs in the definitions section is assumed to be macro definitions.

4.3 REGULAR EXPRESSION

The key to successfully writing a LEX specification relies heavily on how you create the required regular expressions to match a set of strings. This section presents a number of examples to strengthen this technique.

LEX uses regular expression to express the pattern to be matched. (A regular expression is an expression formed of a combination of letters, digits, and metacharacters.) The following characters are used as metacharacters, and each character is given a special meaning:

```
\ / . * + ? ^ $ " | ( ) { } [ ]
```


4.3.1 Rules for Constructing a Regular Expression

The following rules will help you get started:

Rule 1:   A single character that is not a metacharacter forms a regular expression.

Rule 2:   Two regular expressions concatenated form a regular expression.

Rule 3:   Two regular expressions separated by a vertical bar form a regular expression.

Rule 4:   Special meanings are given to metacharacters when they are used to form a regular expression.

Here are the regular expressions:

Regular Expression	*Meaning*
c	matches any single character c
b	matches any single character b
bc	matches any character string bc
b|c	matches characters b and c
bc|cb	matches strings bc and cb

When a metacharacter is used to form a regular expression, it has a special meaning. A *backslash* (\) is used in an escape sequence. An escape sequence is a multiple-character sequence started with backslash (\) to match a single character or a digit. Examples are:

\n	end of line character
\s	space
\t	tab
\b	back space
\ddd	number formed of three octal digits ddd

A backslash (\) is also used to take away the special meaning of a metacharacter.

\.	matches .
*	matches *
\$	matches $

A *period* (.) matches any character except newline (\n). Here are some examples:

x.z	matches any three-letter character string that starts with x and ends with z
.abc.	matches any five-letter character string with abc in the middle of the string

A *regular expression followed by a star* (*) matches that expression repeated zero or more times.

    [ ]*   matches zero or any number of spaces

A *regular expression followed by a plus* (+) matches that expression repeated one or more times.

    [ ]+   matches one or more spaces

A *regular expression followed by a question mark* (?) matches that expression repeated zero or one time.

    [ ]?   matches zero or one space

Bracket pairs ([....]) match any of characters enclosed in the brackets.

`[ \t]`	matches either one space or one tab
`[ \t]+`	matches a string that has at least one space, one tab or combinations of any number of spaces and tabs

Certain characters have a special meaning when they are inside the bracket pairs.

`-`	range of characters
`^`	negates the character class
`"`	takes away the special meaning of characters up to the next quote mark
`\`	takes away the special meaning of the next character

Here are some examples of bracketed pairs:

`[0-9]`	matches any decimal digit
`[A-Za-z]`	matches any alphabet both upper- and lowercases
`[^a-z]`	matches any character except lowercase alphabets
`[\n]`	matches a newline character
`["\\"]`	matches two backslashes

An *up arrow* (^) anchors the pattern to the beginning of a line. If the first character in a regular expression is an ^, the pattern is matched only if it is at the far left of the line.

`^[Cc]`	matches any line that starts with C or c
`^[ ][ ][ ][ ][ ]`	matches any line that starts with five spaces

A *dollar sign* ($) anchors the pattern to the end of a line. If the last character in a regular expression is a $, the expression is recognized only if it is at the far right of the line.

`[ ]+$`   matches any line that has at least one space at end of the line

`^.*$`   matches any line

Braces are used to expand a macro name. Here are two examples:

`[A-Za-z]`   letter

`[A-Za-z0-9]`   letter_or_digit

An alphanumeric symbol starting with a letter (i.e. a FORTRAN variable name) can be recognized with the following expression:

`{letter}{letter_or_digit}*`

Parentheses are used for grouping. Here is an example:

`d`   [0-9]

The following expression is used to recognize any FORTRAN floating point constant:

`[-+]?({d}+|{d}+\.{d}*|{d}*\.{d}+)([ED][-+]?{d}+)?`

A *slash* (/) is used to match a string with look-ahead symbols. A regular expression in this case consists of two parts joined together by a slash. For example, the regular expression

`MIN/[ ]*"("`

matches the character string MIN followed by any number of spaces, then followed by a left parenthesis. The token string returned is the character string MIN, which is a function name rather than a variable name.

4.3.2 Matched Text and Its Relevant Variables

LEX maintains some global variables that provide programmers with very useful information. For example, the variable yytext contains the actual text that matches a regular expression, and the variable yyleng contains the length of the matched text. The line number where the matched text is returned is stored in another variable named yylineno. The following examples use these variables often.

4.4 LEX INTERNAL FUNCTIONS

LEX provides some internal functions which are direct accessible to programmers. Furthermore, programmers can override them by providing their own versions. In doing so, they must make sure the original input-output relationship is retained. The following is a list of commonly used LEX internal functions and their definitions.

Function Name	Functions
main()	a default main() for LEX. It continues calling yylex() until a zero is returned from yylex(). It is linked automatically, if a user-defined main() is not provided. However, a user provided main() is encouraged.
int input()	reads and returns the next input character. It returns zero when it reaches the end of the file.
void unput(c)	pushes the character back into the input stream
void output(c)	outputs the character to the standard output file
int yywrap()	is automatically called by LEX at end of the input stream. It returns true if the LEX process should terminate. The default yywrap() routine always returns one.
void yymore()	is called when the programmer wants the string recognized so far to be tacked on to the next string recognized
void yyless(n)	is called to push n characters back into the input stream

4.5 THE LEX COMMAND

The LEX command translates the LEX specification into a C program named lex.yy.c by default. The following two commands translate a LEX specification in file example.l into an executable module named example:

```
lex example.l
cc lex.yy.c -o example
```

A LEX command with a -t option allows the user to redirect the C program file output to a user-specified filename. So

```
lex -t example.l > example.c
```

produces the output to the file example.c` instead of lex.yy.c.

The LEX command exits silently when it terminates normally. When the LEX specification needs more resources (such as states, transitions, or output slots), the LEX command echoes an error message, depending on the resource. For example, if it runs out of transitions, it echoes

(Error) Too many transitions

Try using %a num

which tells the user to insert a line as suggested in the macro definitions section. For example, inserting the following line into the macro definitions section allows the LEX specification as many as 5,000 transitions:

```
%a        5000
```

After you insert this line and rerun the LEX command, it prints an output similar to

```
655/1000 nodes(%e), 1240/2500 positions(%p), 67/500 (%n),
502 transitions, 75/1000 packed char classes(%k),
2002/2500 packed transitions(%a), 3658/4000 output slots(%o)
```

The ratio 655/1000 means that the LEX specification uses 655 nodes out of the 1,000 the system default provides. In general, you can use the statement

```
%x      num
```

to overwrite any of the system default values, where x is one of the following parameters and num is a decimal integer representing the new parameter size:

Parameter	Meaning
e	nodes
p	positions
n	states
k	packed character classes
a	packed transitions
o	output slots

4.6 LEX PROGRAM EXAMPLES

This section features eight listings. The first five listings demonstrate the simplicity of using the LEX specification in text manipulation. The sixth and seventh listings are lexical analyzers for a FORTRAN-like language. The only difference between the two is that Listing 4.6 calls yylex() only once, while in Listing 4.7, yylex() returns a token every time a call is made. The last example simulates the UNIX's sed command, which performs the string matching and replacing function. Although the LEX library provides a default main program, we choose to write our own because it is easier to debug. All examples, except Listing 4.7, share a common main program named lexmain.c. (File lex7main.c is the main program for Listing 4.7.) The makefiles to compile and make the executable are shown at the end of this section.

Listing 4.1 lexmain.c

```c
/*
* filename: lexmain.c
* function: driver program for LEX
*/
#include <stdio.h>

main(argc, argv)
int argc;
char *argv[];
```

```
{
   extern  FILE *yyin;
   extern  FILE *yyout;

   if ((yyin=fopen(argv[1],"r")) == NULL)
   {
      fprintf(stderr,"Unable to open input file %s\n",
         argv[1]);
      exit(-1);
   }

   if ((yyout=fopen(argv[2],"w")) == NULL)
   {
      fprintf(stderr,"Unable to open output file %s\n",   argv[2]);
      exit(-1);
   }
   yylex();
}

yywrap()
{
   return(1);
}
```

Listing 4.2 lex1.l

Listing 4.2 converts all uppercase letters into lowercase in a text file.

```
%{
/*
 *    Filename: lex1.l
 *    Function: replace upper case letters with lower case  letters
 *    Usage:    lex1  infile  outfile
 */
char  c;
char  C;
%}
%%
[A-Z]     {
             C = yytext[0];
             c = (char) ((int) C + (int) 'a' - (int) 'A');
             fprintf(yyout, "%c",c);
          }
.         fprintf(yyout, "%c", yytext[0]);
%%
```

Listing 4.3 lex2.l

Listing 4.3 adds line numbers to a text file.

```
%{
/*
 *    Filename: lex2.l
 *    Function: add line number to a text file
```

```
 *    Usage: lex2  infile  outfile
 */
%}
%%

^.*\n           fprintf(yyout,"%d\t%s", yylineno - 1, yytext);
%%
```

Listing 4.4 lex3.l

Listing 4.4 deletes blank lines from a text file.

```
%{
/*
 *   Filename: lex3.l
 *   Function: delete blank lines
 *   Usage: lex3 infile outfile
 */
%}
%%

^[ \t]*\n       ;
^.*\n           fprintf(yyout, "%s", yytext);

%%
```

Listing 4.5 lex4.l

Listing 4.5 removes the trailing blanks in every line of the text file.

```
%{
/*
 *   Filename: lex4.l
 *   Function: remove trailing blanks in every line of the  text file
 *   Usage:    lex4 infile outfile
 */
%}

%%
[ ]+$          ;
.       fprintf(yyout, "%c", yytext[0]);
%%
```

Listing 4.6 lex5.l

Listing 4.6 converts a DOS text file to a UNIX text file. The DOS text file contains \r\n at the end of each line, while the UNIX text file contains only \n at the end of each line.

```
%{
/*
 * Filename: lex5.l
 * Function: convert DOS text file to UNIX text file
```

```
 * Usage:     lex5 dosfile unixfile
 */
%}
%%
[\r][\n]   fprintf(yyout, "\n");
.          fprintf(yyout, "%c", yytext[0]);

%%
```

Listing 4.7 lex6.l

Listing 4.7 scans a FORTRAN program and outputs each token recognized along with its line number and its position within the line.

```
%{
/*
 *   Filename: lex6.l
 *   Function: This program prints out each token along with its position expressed
 *             in (line_number,  line_position) pairs from a FORTRAN program.
 *   Usage:    lex6 infile outfile
 */
#define MAXLINE   400
char      linebuf[MAXLINE];
int       linepos;
int       eof;

#undef    input
#undef    unput
#undef    output

void      PrtTok();
void      ProLit();

%}

%o        5000
%a        4000

letter              [A-Za-z_]
d                   [0-9]
letter_or_digit     [A-Za-z0-9]
other               .

%%

^[Cc].*$            ;
^[ \t]*\n           ;
".GT."              |
".LT."              |
".EQ."              |
".LE."              |
".GE."              |
".NE."              |
".OR."              |
".AND."             |
".NOT."             |
```

```
".TRUE."               |
".FALSE."              |
"+"                    |
"-"                    |
"*"                    |
"/"                    |
"**"                   |
"//"                   |
"("                    |
")"                    |
"="                    |
":"                    |
","                    |
[-+]?{d}+              |
[-+]?({d}+|{d}+\.{d}*|{d}*\.{d}+)([ED][-+]?{d}+)?  |
{letter}(letter_or_digit}*    PrtTok();
'[^']*                        ProLit();
other                         PrtTok();
%%

int readline()
{
   if (fgets(linebuf,MAXLINE, yyin) != NULL)
      return(0);
   else
      return (1);
}

int input()
{
   char  c;

   if (linebuf[linepos] == '\0')
   {
      if ((eof = readline()) != 1)
      {
         yylineno++;
         linepos = 0;
      }
   }
   if (eof)
      return(0);
   else
   {
      c = linebuf[linepos];
      linepos++;
      return(c);
   }
}

void unput(c)
char c;
{
   yytchar = c;
   linepos--;
```

```
   linebuf[linepos] = yytchar;
}

/* dummy routine for proper output alignment */
void output(c)
int c;
{
}

void PrtTok()
{
   fprintf(yyout,"    line %d col %d     %s\n",
          yylineno, linepos-yyleng+1, yytext);
}

void ProLit()
{
   char c;

   c = input();              /* skip one quote */
   c = input();
   if ( c=='\'')             /* two consecutive quotes? */
   {
      unput(c);              /* put back second quote */
      yymore();              /* tell LEX that the current matched  string will be
                               concatenated with the next matched string */
   }
   else
   {
      yyleng++;
      yytext[yyleng-1] = '\'';
      yytext[yyleng] = '\0';
      PrtTok();
   }
}
```

Listing 4.8 lex7.h

Listing 4.9 performs the same function as Listing 4.7. The difference is that yylex() returns a value every time it is called. Listing 4.8 is the header file that is used by Listing 4.9.

```
/* Filename: lex7.h
 * Function: header file
 */
#define GT      1
#define LT      2
#define EQ      3
#define LE      4
#define GE      5
#define NE      6
#define OR      7
#define AND     8
#define NOT     9
#define TRUE    10
```

```c
#define FALSE   11
#define PLUS    12
#define MINUS   13
#define TIME    14
#define DIV     15
#define POWER   16
#define LP      17
#define RP      18
#define EQUAL   19
#define ID      20
#define ICON    21
#define FCON    22
#define LI      23
#define COMMA   24
```

Listing 4.9 main.c

```c
/*
 * Filename: main.c
 * Function: main program for lex7.1
 */
#include <stdio.h>
#include "lex7.h"

main(argc, argv)
int argc;
char *argv[];
{
   extern FILE *yyin;
   extern FILE *yyout;
   extern char yytext[];
   int    tokval;

   yyin = fopen(argv[1], "r");
   if (yyin == NULL)
   {
      printf("Unable to open input file %s\n", argv[1]);
      exit(-1);
   }
   yyout = fopen(argv[2], "w");
   if (yyout == NULL)
   {
      printf("Unable to open output file %s\n", argv[2]);
      exit(-1);
   }

   while ((tokval = yylex()) != 0)
   {
      switch (tokval) {
          case GT:
          case LT:
          case EQ:
          case LE:
          case GE:
          case NE:
```

```
               printf("relational operator: %s\n", yytext);
               break;
        case OR:
        case AND:
        case NOT:
               printf("logical operator: %s\n", yytext);
               break;
        case TRUE:
        case FALSE:
               printf("logical constant: %s\n", yytext);
               break;
        case PLUS:
        case MINUS:
        case TIME:
        case DIV:
        case POWER:
               printf("arithmetic operator: %s\n", yytext);
        case LP:
        case RP:
        case COMMA:
        case EQUAL:
               printf("delimiter: %s\n", yytext);
               break;
        case ID:
               printf("identifier: %s\n", yytext);
               break;
        case ICON:
               printf("integer constant: %s\n", yytext);
               break;
        case FCON:
               printf("floating point constant: %s\n",   yytext);
               break;
        case LI:
               printf("literal constant: %s\n", yytext);
               break;
        default:
               break;
      } /* case */
   }
}

yywrap()
{
   return(1);
}
```

Listing 4.10 lex7.l

```
%{
/*
 *  Filename: lex7.l
 *  Function: The function yylex() generated from this LEX
 *  specification returns an integer value. Each value returned designates
 *            a different token found
```

```
 *  Usage:     lex7 infile outfile
 */
#include "lex7.h"
#define MAXLINE    400
char    linebuf[MAXLINE];
int     linepos;
int     eof;

#undef  input
#undef  unput
#undef  output

void    ProLit();

%}

%o      5000
%a      4000

letter              [A-Za-z_]
d                   [0-9]
letter_or_digit     [A-Za-z0-9]
other               .

%%

^[Cc].*$                                                      ;
^[ \t]*\n                                                     ;
".GT."                                            return(GT);
".LT."                                            return(LT);
".EQ."                                            return(EQ);
".LE."                                            return(LE);
".GE."                                            return(GE);
".NE."                                            return(NE);
".OR."                                            return(OR);
".AND."                                          return(AND);
".NOT."                                          return(NOT);
".TRUE."                                        return(TRUE);
".FALSE."                                      return(FALSE);
"+"                                              return(PLUS);
"-"                                             return(MINUS);
"*"                                              return(STAR);
"/"                                             return(SLASH);
"**"                                            return(POWER);
"("                                                return(LP);
")"                                                return(RP);
"="                                             return(EQUAL);
","                                             return(COMMA);
[-+]?{d}+                                        return(ICON);
[-+]?({d}+|{d}+\.{d}*|{d}*\.{d}+)([ED][-+]?{d}+)?  return(FCON);
{letter}(letter_or_digit}*                         return(ID);
'[^']*                                          {
                                                    ProLit();
                                                  return(LI);
                                                }

other                                                         ;
```

```c
%%

int readline()
{
   if (fgets(linebuf,MAXLINE, yyin) != NULL)
      return(0);
   else
      return (1);
}

int input()
{
   char   c;

   if (linebuf[linepos] == '\0')
   {
      if ((eof = readline()) != 1)
      {
         yylineno++;
         linepos = 0;
      }
   }
   if (eof)
      return(0);
   else
   {
      c = linebuf[linepos];
      linepos++;
      return(c);
   }
}

void unput(c)
char c;
{
   yytchar = c
   linepos-;
   linebuf[linepos] = yytchar;
}

/* dummy routine for proper output alignment */
void output(c)
int c;
{
}

void ProLit()
{
   char c;

   c = input();    /* skip one quote */
   c = input();
   if ( c=='\'')   /* two consecutive quotes? */
   {
      unput(c);    /* put back second quote */
```

```
      yymore();          /* tell LEX that the current matched string will be
                             concatenated with the next matched string */
   }
   else
   {
      yyleng++;
      yytext[yyleng-1] = '\'';
      yytext[yyleng] = '\0';
      PrtTok();
   }
}
```

Listing 4.11 mysed.c

Listing 4.11's C program performs a string match-and-replace function using a LEX template.

```c
/*
 * Filename: mysed.c
 * Usage:    mysed string1 string2 infile outfile
 */
#include <stdio.h>
#define MAXLINE  120

main(argc, argv)
int  argc;
char *argv[];
{
   FILE *fp;            /* file pointer for lex.template */
   FILE *fp1;           /* file pointer for tmplex.l     */
   char linebuf[MAXLINE];
   char string1[40];
   char string2[40];
   char infile[80];
   char outfile[80];
   char command[80];
   int  eof = 0;
   int  count = 0;
   int  wid = 0;
   int  status = 0;
   int  childpid = 0;

   strcpy(string1, argv[1]);
   strcpy(string2, argv[2]);
   strcpy(infile , argv[3]);
   strcpy(outfile, argv[4]);
   if ((fp = fopen("lex.template", "r") == NULL)
   {
      printf("File open error: lex.template\n");
      exit(-1);
   }
   if ((fp1 =fopen("tmplex.l", "w")) == NULL)
   {
      printf("File open error: tmplex.l\n");
```

```c
      exit(-1);
   }
   while ( !eof)
   {
      if (fgets(linebuf, MAXLINE, fp) != NULL)
      {
         if (linebuf[0]=='%' && linebuf[1]=='%')
         {
            fputs(linebuf, fp1);
            count++;
            if (count == 1)
               insertPatternAction(fp1, string1, string2);
         }
         else
            fputs(linebuf, fp1);
      }
      else
         eof = 1;
   }
   fclose(fp);
   fclose(fp1);
   sprintf(command,"make -f makefile tmplex > /dev/null");
   system(command);
   /*————————————————————
    * fork and exec the job
    *————————————————————*/
   if ((childpid=fork()) < 0)
      printf("Error forking child\n");
   else if (childpid == 0)
   { /* child process */
      execl("./tmplex", "tmplex", infile, outfile, 0);
   }
   wid = wait(&status);
}

/*————————————————————————
 * function to insert the pattern action pair into
 * lex.template file
 *————————————————————————*/
insertPatternAction(fp, string1, string2)
FILE *fp;
char *string1;
char *string2;
{
   char linebuf[MAXLINE];

   strcpy(linebuf, "\"");
   strcat(linebuf, string1);
   strcat(linebuf, "\"");
   strcat(linebuf, "           {\n");
   fputs(linebuf, fp);
   strcpy(linebuf, "                    fprintf(yyout,");
   strcat(linebuf, "\"");
   strcat(linebuf, string2);
```

```
    strcat(linebuf, "\"");
    strcat(linebuf, ");\n");
    fputs(linebuf, fp);
    strcpy(linebuf, "                        )\n");
    fputs(linebuf,fp);
}
```

The following is a listing of the lex.template file.

Listing 4.12 lex.template

```
%{
/*
 * Filename: lex.template
 */
%}
%%

.               fprintf(yyout, "%c", yytext[0]);
%%
```

Listing 4.13 Makefile

Listing 4.13 is the makefile used to generate the executable for the previous examples.

```
COMPILE.c=      cc
CFLAGS=         -c -g
LEX=            lex
RM=             rm
LINK=           cc
DEBUG=          -g
LIB=            -ll -lc

.l.o:
        @echo execute .l.o rule
        $(LEX) -t $*.l > $*.c
        $(COMPILE.c) $(CFLAGS) $*.c

.c.o:
        @echo execute .c.o
        $(COMPILE.c) $(CFLAGS) $*.c

all:    lex1 lex2 lex3 lex4 lex5 lex6 mysed
        @echo make complete

lex1:   lexmain.o lex1.o
        $(LINK) $(DEBUG) lexmain.o $@.o -o $@ $(LIB)
        $(RM) $@.c $@.o

lex2:   lexmain.o lex2.o
        $(LINK) $(DEBUG) lexmain.o $@.o -o $@ $(LIB)
        $(RM) $@.c $@.o
```

```
lex3:    lexmain.o lex3.o
         $(LINK) $(DEBUG) lexmain.o $@.o -o $@ $(LIB)
         $(RM) $@.c $@.o

lex4:    lexmain.o lex4.o
         $(LINK) $(DEBUG) lexmain.o $@.o -o $@ $(LIB)
         $(RM) $@.c $@.o

lex5:    lexmain.o lex5.o
         $(LINK) $(DEBUG) lexmain.o $@.o -o $@ $(LIB)
         $(RM) $@.c $@.o

lex6:    lexmain.o lex6.o
         $(LINK) $(DEBUG) lexmain.o $@.o -o $@ $(LIB)
         $(RM) $@.c $@.o

lex7:    lex7main.o lex7.o
         $(LINK) $(DEBUG) lex7main.o $@.o -o $@ $(LIB)
         $(RM) $@.c $@.o

tmplex:  lexmain.o tmplex.o
         $(LINK) $(DEBUG) lexmain.o $@.o -o $@ $(LIB)
         $(RM) $@.c $@.o

mysed:   mysed.o
         $(LINK) $(DEBUG) $@.o -o $@ $(LIB)
```

4.7 SUMMARY

This chapter explained how the LEX lexical analyzer works. Then we described a
LEX program format. Because regular expression plays such an important role in
writing a LEX program, we spent one section describing the rules to construct a regular expression.

When LEX program expands, it may run out of predefined storage. In this case,
the user can re-declare the size of that storage type until the error message is gone. At
the end of this chapter, we gave eight examples of LEX programs, starting from a simple application such as converting a text file from uppercase to lowercase to something
similar to the UNIX sed command.

YACC

5.1 INTRODUCTION

This chapter addresses these issues:

☞ What YACC is
☞ YACC's program format
☞ YACC's parsing operation
☞ How to tie LEX and YACC together
☞ Shift/reduce and reduce/reduce conflicts
☞ How to handle error recovery within the YACC program
☞ How to write a YACC program
☞ How to debug a YACC generated program
☞ What to do if the parser stack overflows

5.1.1 What YACC Is

Yet Another Compiler-Compiler (YACC) is a tool that translates a grammar describing a language into a parser for that language, written in Backus-Naur (BNF) form. By convention, the filename given to this grammar specification file has the suffix .y (e.g. gram.y). The grammar is presented to YACC through the command

```
yacc -d gram.y
```

This command generates two output files: y.tab.h and y.tab.c. The y.tab.h file contains #define statements for each name introduced as a %token in the gram.y file. The y.tab.c file contains the function yyparse(). The file y.tab.h must be included in the LEX specification file (the .l file) so that both yyparse() and yylex() can use the same terminal symbol representation. Since the header file y.tab.h generated from the YACC specification is included in the LEX specification file, we must make sure that the yacc command is executed before the lex command when they are compiled.

The parser YACC generates is a stack machine that consists of a large stack to hold states, a transition matrix, and a table of user-definable actions to be executed at certain points during the translation process. The result is packaged as function yyparse(), which in turn repeatedly calls yylex() to read input symbols.

5.2 YACC Program Format

A YACC program is divided into three sections: the definitions section, the rules section, and code section, which is optional. Each section is separated from one another with %% directives.

```
definitions
%%
rules
%%
codes           (optional)
```

5.2.1 The Definitions Section

The definitions section contains both declarative C code and YACC directives. The declarative C code must be surrounded by %{ and %} directives. All YACC directives must start with a percent sign, which must be in the leftmost column. The declarative C code in this section contains statements such as #include, #define, typedef, variable declarations, function prototypes, and so forth. The variables declared in this section are known globally to all functions inside or outside this program module. The YACC directives used in this section include: %union, %token, %type, %left, %right, and %nonassoc. The directive %union is used to type the value stack (See Section 5.4.1). The directive %token is used to define a token. The directive %type is used to attach %union field to a nonterminal symbol. The directive %left specifies a left-associative operator. The directive %right specifies a right-associative operator. The directive %nonassoc specifies a non-associative operator.

5.2.2 The Rules Section

The rules section contains grammar rules made of augmented productions in BNF. Each production described in BNF consists of a left-hand and a right-hand side, separated by a colon. The left-hand side consists of a single, unique nonterminal symbol. The right-hand side consists of a sequence of one or more formulations, separated from one another by a vertical bar (meaning OR). Each formulation consists of a sequence of zero or more nonterminal and terminal symbols. Only one formulation in a production may be empty. A production takes the form

```
symbol          :   formulation_1
                |   formulation_2
                .

                .
                |   formulation_n
```

For example, the production rule for argument_list can be written as

```
argument_list   :    Identifier
                |    argument_list  ','  Identifier
```

An action routine (C code) can be added to each formulation. The resulting production is called an augmented production. Here is an example:

```
argument_list    :    Identifier
                 {  /* action 1 */
                     argument_list_stmt($1->s_name);
                 }
                 |  argument_list  ','  Identifier
                 {  /* action 2 */
                     argument_list_stmt($3->s_name);
                 }
```

Note that the %prec directive can be used only in the rules section. Its function is to make an operator's precedence in a formulation the same as that of the token following the %prec directive. Listing 5.10 shows how to use the %prec directive.

5.2.3 The Code Section

The third part of the YACC input file is the code section, which is usually left empty. If code does exist, it is copied to the output file (y.tab.c). The code in this section should contain subroutines called from the actions.

5.3 YACC's Parsing Operation

YACC translates the grammar specifications into a C language program that parses the input stream according to the given specification. The parser YACC produces consists of a finite-state machine with two stacks: the state stack and the value stack. The parser reads and remembers the next input token (called the look-ahead token). The current state is always on top of the state stack. The states of the finite-state machine are given small integer numbers. Initially, the machine is in state zero, and no look-ahead token has been read. The finite-state machine has only four available actions: shift, reduce, accept, and error.

Based on the current state, the parser determines whether it needs a look-ahead token to decide the action to take. If it needs one and does not have it, it calls yylex() to obtain the next token. Using the current state and the look-ahead token if needed, the parser decides on its next action, then carries that out. As a result, the states may be pushed onto the stack or popped off the stack, and the look-ahead token may be processed or left alone. A brief description of each action follows:

5.3.1 YACC's Data Structure

YACC's data structure consists of

☞ the transition matrix

☞ the state stack

☞ the value stack

The parser function yyparse() maintains a value stack in parallel to the state stack. Whenever a symbol is accepted, the current state is pushed onto the state stack and an associated value is pushed onto the value stack. The value to be pushed during the terminal symbol's acceptance is taken from the global variable yylval yacc defines. The lexical analyzer can set it for the terminal symbol. The value to be pushed during the nonterminal symbol's reduce operation is taken from the global variable yyval yacc defines. It can be set from within the action executed during a production rule's reduce operation. The action usually needs to access the values placed on the value stack during the symbol's acceptance for the formulation that is about to be reduced. The notation $i within an action represents the value for the ith symbol in the formulation presently on the value stack. The notation $$ represents yyval, which is the value to be pushed onto the value stack during the acceptance of the nonterminal symbol. Take the following production for example:

```
expression  :  expression '-' expression
               { $$ = $1 - $3; }
```

When the formulation is reduced, the associated action { $$ = $1 - $3; } computes the appropriate difference, which is pushed onto the value stack following the reduction. The action, { $$ = $1; }, is provided by the system as default.

5.3.2 YACC's Actions

YACC performs the following actions:

☞ Shift action

This operation indicates that the look-ahead token is acceptable in the current state. The new state is pushed onto the stack and becomes the current state. The look-ahead token is pushed onto the value stack and then cleared. For example, the following action may exist in state 10:

```
Identifier    shift 5
```

This says, in state 10, if the look-ahead token is an identifier, state 5 is pushed onto the stack. Now the current state becomes state 5, which is on top of the stack, and state 10 is second from the top of the stack. In parallel to state stack, the identifier token is pushed onto the value stack.

☞ Reduce action

This operation is performed when the parser sees the right side of a grammar rule. The parser pops off as many states as symbols in the right side of the grammar rule from the state stack. The same amount of elements are popped off from the value stack, also. This assumes that the following rule is reduced:

```
expr : expr '+' expr
```

The reduce action depends on the number of symbols on the right side of the rule (which is three in this case). To reduce, the top three states are popped off the state stack. The top three elements also are popped off the value stack, and the symbol on the left side of the grammar rule is pushed onto the value stack. The parser then looks at the state uncovered on the state stack and the symbol on top of the value stack to determine the goto action, which, in effect, pushes a new state onto the state stack.

☞ Accept action

The accept action occurs when the parser has scanned the entire input stream and matched the specification. This action should take place only when the look-ahead token is the end-of-file marker and indicates that the parser has successfully completed its task.

☞ Error action

The error action signals that the parser can no longer continue parsing according to the specification. This occurs when the look-ahead symbol is illegal for a given state. When that happens, the parser generates a token symbol "error."

5.4 How to Tie the LEX and YACC Programs Together

There are two ways to tie the LEX and YACC programs together.

1. From the programming point of view, yyparse() calls yylex() and yylex() returns a token value (which is an integer) back to yyparse().
2. From the data manipulation point of view, the value stack holds the data that both yylex() and yyparse() can access.

5.4.1 Typing the Value Stack

yylval, yyval, and the value stack can be used to hold a variety of information. By default, the value stack consists of integer elements. In a compiler or parser of any language, yylval most likely holds a pointer to a symbol table entry for each terminal symbol. The value stack the parser maintains can be typed from within a YACC program.

yylval, yyval, and the value stack are defined in the parser as YYSTYPE. YYSTYPE is defined as integer, unless an explicit definition is supplied in the YACC program's definitions section. For example, the following #define statement redefines YYSTYPE as:

```
#define YYSTYPE     double
```

In general, value stack elements can be pointers to the symbol table, to character strings, and integer values for counting. So we must define the data type of value stack elements as a union of this form:

```
%union {
    struct symbol * y_sym;
    char * y_str;
    int y_num;
};
```

This is placed in the YACC specification's definitions section following the %} directive. Next, we must type those terminal symbols that are assigned a value to yylval during the lexical analysis. This is done by placing a union component, enclosed in angle brackets, between %token and the list of the terminal symbols to be typed. Here are two examples:

```
%token <y_sym> ID
%token <y_str> LI, ICON, FCON
```

Finally, we must type all nonterminal symbols for which $i or $$ are referenced. This is accomplished by making a %type definition similar to a %token definition for terminal symbols. Here is an example:

```
%type <y_sym> optional_parameter_list, parameter_list
%type <y_num> optional_argument_list, argument_list
```

Sometimes these mechanisms may not be sufficient, as in the case when a production rule may have formulations in which the action routine returns a different type of data. When such cases arise, you can type the stack on the fly by inserting the union member name, enclosed by < and >, after the first $. Here is an example:

```
symbol   :   ID
             {  $<y_sym>$ = $1; }
         |   GOTO LABEL
             {  $<y_label>$ = gen_label($2); }
```

5.5 WHAT ELSE DO WE NEED?

In order for the YACC-generated program to link properly, we need to provide two functions:

5.5.1 A User-Supplied main() Function

A YACC-generated parser does not run by itself--it needs a user-supplied main program. The main program provides the function main() which directly or indirectly calls yyparse(). If the user does not provide main(), the linker may pick up the default main() in the LEX library, and it ends calling yylex() but not yyparse().

5.5.2 An Additional User-Supplied Function

To use the YACC-generated parser, the user must provide another user-supplied function, yyerror(), which is a function yyparse() calls if an error occurs during the recognition process. yyerror() has one input argument, which is a character string that describes the cause of the error yyparse() generates. Examples of these messages yyparse() generates are "syntax error," "out of memory," and "stack overflow." yyerror() should be used to report error messages only yyparse() generates. A user-generated error message should be reported through a user-error reporting routine.

We do not recommend that you write a dummy function for yyerror() because you may lose very important error messages such as "stack overflow" or "out of memory," which are critical when debugging your program. The yyerror() function prints out a "stack overflow" message when the array representing the state stack reaches its limit. The yyerror() function provided in Listing 5.6 prints out not only the error message but also where the error occurs.

5.6 SHIFT/REDUCE AND REDUCE/REDUCE CONFLICTS

One problem with many YACC programs is that they often result in shift/reduce conflicts. When shift/reduce conflicts occur, the YACC-generated parser honors the shift operations instead of the reduce operations, which may cause unwanted results. So let us look at how these conflicts are caused, and how to eliminate them.

5.6.1 The Shift/Reduce Conflict

During the parsing process, if both of the following conditions are met in a given state, the grammar is said to have a shift/reduce conflict:

☞ The next terminal symbol is acceptable in a given state.

☞ The current state has reached a complete configuration.

When that happens, the grammar is said to be ambiguous. YACC resolves this conflict by honoring the shift operation over the reduce operation. The language designer must be sure that is the result he or she desires.

Here is an example of a grammar that causes the shift/reduce conflict:

```
statement    :   assign_statement ';'
             |   if_prefix statement
             |   if_prefix statement ELSE statement
```

When the parser finishes parsing the if_prefix statement and the next terminal symbol is ELSE, the shift/reduce conflict occurs. In that case, YACC shifts the token ELSE onto the value stack, and moves to a new state.

5.6.2 The Reduce/Reduce Conflict

A reduce/reduce conflict occurs when one formulation can be reduced to two or more nonterminal symbols. YACC resolves a reduce/reduce conflict by using the earlier grammar rule. Reduce/reduce conflicts are unacceptable in the grammar. You can avoid this result by rewriting the grammar.

5.7 SPECIFYING PRECEDENCE AND THE ASSOCIATIVITY RULE

One way to eliminate the shift/reduce conflict is by specifying the operator precedence. YACC provides ways to specify the precedence and associativity among different operators. The %left directive specifies left associative operators, the %right directive specifies right associative operators, and the %nonassoc directive specifies non-associative operators. These three directives are in the definitions section.

```
%right      '='
%left       '+'     '-'
```

specifies that + and - operators are left associative and the = operator is right associative.

The %left and %right directives not only specify the associativity of the operators but also the precedence among operators.

```
%left       '+'     '-'
%left       '*'     '/'
```

specifies that operators +, -, *, and / are all left associative, and operators * and / have higher precedence than + and - because their declarations appear later. In short, the sooner the declaration, the lower the precedence.

5.8 ERROR HANDLING

A compiler must deal with two types of errors during the compilation process. The first error type is called a "syntactic error," which means the grammar cannot generate the program presented to the compiler. The second type of error is called a "semantic error." A program can be syntactically correct and yet contain a semantic error. For example, all variables need to be declared before they are referenced in a C program. An undeclared variable is an example of a semantic error, as is a runtime error. One example of a runtime error is the divided by zero expression. A user relies heavily on YACC for syntax checking, but he or she must check the program's semantics for himself or herself. The emphasis here is on understanding how to report an error when YACC detects syntax errors and continues until the end of the program without being terminated prematurely.

5.8.1 Error Reporting

What happens when a parser encounters an error during the translation process? In the simplest case, a parser reports an error, and terminates. This can be easily accomplished by providing the function yyerror(). Whenever the parser detects an error, it calls yyerror() with an argument specifying the cause. You can add additional printouts in yyerror() to let the user know where the error occurs in the program. After reporting the error, the parser terminates.

5.8.2 Error Recovery

In most cases error reporting is not sufficient because the parser not only has to detect the error but also recover from the error and continue scanning the input until it hits the end of the input stream. This involves discarding a number of tokens from the input stream and adjusting the parser so that it can continue.

5.8.2.1 How the Parser Handles Syntax Errors YACC, fortunately, does provide a simple hook that allows the user to control this process. The error token is reserved for this purpose. The error token can be used in grammar rules. It is suggested that you place the error token where you expect errors. When an error occurs, the parser pops its stack until it enters a state where the error token is legal. It then behaves as if the error token were the current look-ahead token and performs the required action. The look-ahead token then is reset to the token that caused the error. If no special error rules have been specified, the processing halts when an error is detected.

To prevent a cascade of error messages, the parser, after detecting error, remains in an error state until three tokens have been successfully read and shifted. If an error is detected while the parser is in an error state, no message is given, and the input token is quietly deleted.

5.8.2.2 Additional Error-Handling Mechanisms YACC Provides Two other mechanisms YACC provides are yyerrok and yyclearin.

The statement yyerrok forces the parser to believe that an error has been fully recovered, and it resets the parser to its normal mode. The statement yyclearin removes the previous look-ahead token. By combining these two statements, you can find the correct place to resume when an error occurs. Here is an example:

```
statement   :   error
               {
                   resync(';');
                   yyerrok;
                   yyclearin;
               }
```

where resynch() is defined as

```
void resync(synchar)
char synchar;
{
   int  ch;
   while ((ch = input()) != 0)
   {
      if (ch == synchar)
```

```
        break;
    }
}
```

In this example, the synchronization character (';') is at the end of a statement. When a synchronization character is at the beginning of a statement, it may have to be put back to the input stream.

5.8.3 Guidelines for Placing Error Tokens

It is impossible to place the error tokens in a grammar perfectly. However, a few simple guidelines make the process easier.

☞ Try to place at least one error token close to the start rule (the highest level rule) of the grammar. This guarantees that all errors are recovered because there is a state at the bottom of the stack that can accept an error token. This may skip a large amount of tokens each time an error occurs.

☞ In the action routine following the error token, use the re-synchronizing technique described in Section 5.8.2.2.

☞ Adding more error tokens into the grammar rules often creates more shift/reduce conflicts. Adding more error tokens without further introducing shift/reduce conflicts is truly an art.

5.8.4 Semantic Error Handling

Semantic error handling can be accomplished through the call to the YYERROR macro. The YYERROR macro is defined as "goto yyerlab" in /usr/bin/yaccpar, which is a template for the YACC parser. Calling YYERROR forces the parser to go into the error state as if a syntax error has occurred. The difference between the parser-generated syntax error and this user-simulated syntax error is that yyerror() is not called in simulated syntax error. So a user must provide a message for the error cause.

5.9 How to Write a YACC Program

Writing a YACC program from scratch is a very complicated task. The following section outlines a step-by-step approach to such a task.

5.9.1 Suggested Steps in Writing a YACC Program

To write a YACC program, follow these steps:

1. Create a .y from a YACC skeleton program; write the grammar in BNF. (Listing 5.1 shows the YACC skeleton program.)

2. Create an .l file from a LEX skeleton program; write the macro definitions, pattern-matching rules, and declarative C code. (Listing 5.2 shows the LEX skeleton program.)

3. Define all the terminal symbols with %token directives, and specify the precedence rules, if necessary.

4. Write a main() function that directly or indirectly calls yyparse() and provides a yyerror() function to report the syntax error.

5. Type the value stack.

   a. The default type is an integer.

   b. For a single value type, use the following #define statement to redefine it to a new data type:

   ```
   #define YYSTYPE  double
   ```

   c. For a value stack that carries multiple data types, define the data type of the value stack elements as a union of this form

   ```
   %union {
       struct symbol * y_sym;
       char * y_str;
       int y_num;
   } :
   ```

   in a YACC program definitions section.

6. Assign values to yylval in the LEX program for those terminal symbols whose values will be referenced in the action routine.

7. Fill in the semantic part of the parser. Generally speaking, it includes expression evaluation, checking for the correct type of data, building a symbol table, and reporting any semantic errors, depending on the problem you are dealing with.

8. Define all the terminal symbols for which a value is assigned to yylval during the lexical analysis phase by placing the name of a union component, enclosed in angle brackets, between the %token and the list of terminal symbols to be typed.

   ```
   %token <y_sym> Identifier
   ```

   Define all the nonterminal symbols for which $i or $$ are referenced by making a %type definition similar to a %token definition for terminal symbols.

   ```
   %type  <y_num> optional_argument_list
   ```

   Note that this step is needed only when the value stack carries multiple data types.

9. Add the error-handling mechanisms. (Details are in Section 5.8.)

10. Prepare a makefile to generate the executable file. This includes executing YACC, LEX, and CC commands in that sequence.

Listing 5.1 YACC Skeleton Program (skel.y)

```
%{
/* begin of declarative C code */
#include <stdio.h>

%}
/* begin of YACC directives */

/*
```

```
 * terminal symbols
 */

%% /* begin of rule section */

%% /* begin of C code section */
```

Listing 5.2 LEX Skeleton Program (skel.l)

```
%{
/* begin of declarative C code */
#include "y.tab.h"

%}
/* begin of macro definition */

%% /* begin of rule section */

%% /* begin of user C code */
```

5.10 EXAMPLE 1: A BASIC CALCULATOR

In this example, we want to use YACC and LEX to implement a basic calculator with four operators (+, -, *, /) and left and right parentheses. The numbers either can be decimal or floating point numbers.

You may think that this is fairly easy--until you try it from scratch!

Let us go through this example step by step.

1. Copy the YACC skeleton file (skel.y) to file calc.y. and write the grammar rule for the calculator. The result is shown in Listing 5.3.

Listing 5.3 YACC Program for Example 1 After Step 1 (calc.y)

```
%{
/* begin of declarative C code */
#include <stdio.h>

%}

/*
 * terminal symbols
 */

%%  /* begin of rule section */

lines  :
       | lines line
       ;
line   : CR
       | expr CR

expr   : CONST
       | expr PLUS expr
       | expr MINUS expr
```

```
                | expr TIME expr
                | expr DIV  expr
                | LP expr RP
%%  /* begin of user C code */
```

2. Copy the LEX skeleton file (skel.l) to file calclex.l and write the macro definitions, pattern-matching rules, and C declarative code. The result is shown in Listing 5.4.

Listing 5.4 LEX Program for Example 1 After Step 2 (calclex.l)

```
%{
/*  begin of C declarative code */

#include  "y.tab.h"
extern    double  yylval;
int       val;

%}
/* begin of macro definitions */

digit                 [0-9]
blank                 [ \t]
other                 .

%%

"+"                   return(PLUS);
"-"                   return(MINUS);
"*"                   return(TIME);
"/"                   return(DIV);
"("                   return(LP);
")"                   return(RP);
"\n"                  return(CR);
"quit"                exit(0);
{digit}+              return(CONST);
{digit}*+\.{digit}+ |
{digit}+\.{digit}*    return(CONST);
{blank}+              ;
{other}               return(yytext[0]);

%% /* begin of user C code */
```

3. Define all the terminal symbols with a %token directive, and specify the precedence rule. The result is shown in Listing 5.5.

Listing 5.5 YACC Program for Example 1 After Step 3 (calc2.y)

```
%{
#include <stdio.h>

%}

/*
 * terminal symbols
 */

%token    CONST
```

```
%token   CR
%token   LP
%token   RP
%token   PLUS
%token   MINUS
%token   TIME
%token   DIV
%token   UMINUS

/*
 *  precedence table
 */
%left    PLUS   MINUS
%left    TIME   DIV
%left    UMINUS

%%
lines   :
        | lines line
        ;

line    : CR
        | expr CR

expr    : CONST
        | MINUS expr        %prec UMINUS
        | LP expr RP
        | expr PLUS expr
        | expr MINUS expr
        | expr TIME expr
        | expr DIV  expr
%% /* begin of user C code */
```

4. Write a main() function that directly calls yyparse() and provides a yyerror()
function. The result is shown in Listing 5.6.

Listing 5.6 Main Program for Example 1 (fparse.c)

```c
#include <stdio.h>

extern int  yydebug;
extern int  yylineno;
extern char yytext[];

main(argc, argv)
int  argc;
char *argv[];
{
#ifdef YYDEBUG
   yydebug = 1;
#endif

   yyparse();
}

/*
 *  This function must be supplied by the user
```

```
 *   for reporting errors generated by YACC parser
 */
yyerror(msg)
char *msg;
{
   fprintf(stderr, "%s " msg);
   where();
}

where()
{
   fprintf(stderr, "at line %d token=%s\n", yylineno, yytext);
}

/*
 *   This function is provided for reporting user
 *   detected errors
 */
run_error(msg)
char *msg;
{
   fprintf(stderr,"%s at line %d\n", msg, yylineno);
}
```

5. **Type the value stack.** Because the only data type in the value stack is a double data type, use

```
#define YYSTYPE  double
```

   to redefine the data type from integer to double. The result is shown in Listing 5.7.

Listing 5.7 YACC Program for Example 1 After Step 5 (calc3.y)

```
%{
/* begin of declarative C code */
#include <stdio.h>

#define YYSTYPE  double
%}

/*
 * terminal symbols
 */
%token   CONST
%token   PLUS
%token   MINUS
%token   TIME
%token   DIV
%token   LP
%token   RP
%token   CR

 /*
  *   precedence table
  */
%left    PLUS   MINUS
```

```
%left    TIME   DIV
%left    UMINUS

%%  /* begin of rule section */

lines   :
        | lines line
        ;

line    : CR
        | expr CR

expr    : CONST
        | expr PLUS expr
        | expr MINUS expr
        | expr TIME expr
        | expr DIV  expr
        | LP expr RP
%%  /* begin of user C code */
```

6. Assign values to yylval in the LEX program for those terminal symbols whose values are referenced in the action routine. In this case CONST is the only one. The result is shown in Listing 5.8.

Listing 5.8 LEX Program for Example 1 After Step 6 (calclex2.l)

```
%{
/*  begin of C declarative code */

#include  "y.tab.h"

#undef    input
#undef    unput
#undef    output
#define  MAXLINE   400

char      linebuf[MAXLINE];
int       linepos;
int       eof = 0;
int       val;

extern    double  yylval;

%}
/* begin of macro definitions */

digit                   [0-9]
blank                   [ \t]
other                   .

%%

"+"                     return(PLUS);
"-"                     return(MINUS);
"*"                     return(TIME);
"/"                     return(DIV);
"("                     return(LP);
")"                     return(RP);
```

```
"\n"                    return(CR);
"quit"                  exit(0);
{digit}+                {
                            sscanf(yytext, "%d", &val);
                            yylval = (double) val;
                            return(CONST);
                        }
{digit}*+\.{digit}+ |
{digit}+\.{digit}*      {
                            sscanf(yytext,"%lf", &yylval);
                            return(CONST);
                        }
{blank}+                ;
{other}                 return(yytext[0]);
%% /* begin of user C code */

void resync(synchar)

char synchar;
{
   int   ch;

   while ((ch = input()) != 0)
      if (ch == (int)synchar)
         break;
}

int input()
{
   char c;
   static int lineno;

   if (linebuf[linepos] == '\0')
   {
      if ((eof = readline()) != 1)
      {
         lineno++;
         yylineno = lineno;
         linepos;
      }
      else
         return(0);
   }
   c = linebuf[linepos];
   linepos++;
   return((int) c);
}

int readline()
{
   if (fgets(linebuf, MAXLINE, yyin) != NULL)
      return(0);
   else
      return(1);
}
```

```
void unput(c)
int  c;
{
   yytchar = c;
   linepos--;
   linebuf[linepos] = yytchar;
}

void output(c)
int c;
{

}
```

7. Fill in the semantic part of the parser. The result is shown in Listing 5.9.

Listing 5.9 YACC Program for Example 1 After Step 7 (calc4.y)

```
%{
/* begin of declarative C code */
#include <stdio.h>

#define YYSTYPE  double
%}

/*
 * terminal symbols
 */
%token  CONST
%token  PLUS
%token  MINUS
%token  TIME
%token  DIV
%token  LP
%token  RP
%token  CR

/*
 *  precedence table
 */
%left   PLUS   MINUS
%left   TIME   DIV
%left   UMINUS

%%  /* begin of rule section */

lines  :
       | lines line
       ;

line   : CR
       | expr CR
         {fprintf(stdout, "%.8g\n", $1);}

expr   : CONST
         {$$ = $1;}
       | expr PLUS expr
         {$$ = $1 + $3;}
```

```
          | expr MINUS expr
            {$$ = $1 - $3;}
          | expr TIME expr
            {$$ = $1 * $3;}
          | expr DIV  expr
            {$$ = $1 / $3;}
          | LP expr RP
            {$$ = $2;}
%%  /* begin of user C code */
```

8. Because the value stack in this case carries only one single data type, skip this step.

9. Add an error-handling mechanism to the grammar rules. The result is shown in Listing 5.10.

Listing 5.10 YACC Program for Example 1 After Step 9 (calc5.y)

```
%{
/* begin of declarative C code */
#include <stdio.h>

#define YYSTYPE     double

int         err = 0;

%}
/* begin of YACC directives */
/*
 * terminal symbols
 */

%token    CONST
%token    CR
%token    LP
%token    RP
%token    PLUS
%token    MINUS
%token    TIME
%token    DIV

/*
 * precedence table
 */

%left     PLUS MINUS
%left     TIME DIV
%left     UMINUS

%% /* begin of rule section */

lines   :
        | lines line
        ;

line    : CR
        | expr CR
            {
```

```
            if (!err)
                fprintf(stdout, "%.8g\n", $1);
            else
                err = 0;
            }
        | error
            {
                resync('\n');
                yyerrok;
                yyclearin;
            }
        ;

expr    : CONST
            {$$ = $1;}
        | MINUS expr        %prec UMINUS
          { $$ = -$2;}
        | LP expr RP
          {$$ = $2;}
        | expr PLUS expr
          {$$ = $1 + $3;}
        | expr MINUS expr
          {$$ = $1 - $3;}
        | expr TIME expr
          {$$ = $1 * $3;}
        | expr DIV  expr
          {  if ($3 == 0.0)
             {
                run_error("runtime error: divided by zero")
                YYERROR;
             }
             else
                $$ = $1 / $3;
          }
%%
```

10. Prepare a makefile to execute yacc, lex, and cc commands. The result is shown in
Listing 5.11.

Listing 5.11 Makefile for Example 1

```
.SUFFIXES:
.SUFFIXES:  .a .o .c .l .y

COMPILE.c=      cc
CFLAGS=         -c -g -DYYDEBUG
CPPFLAGS=
YACC=           yacc
YFLAGS=         -dvl
LEX=            lex
LFLAGS=         -t
RM=             rm
MV=             mv
CP=             cp
SED=            sed
```

```
LPATH=      /usr2/shen/sample/calculator
SRC=        $(LPATH)/src
BIN=        $(LPATH)/bin

OBJECTS=   \
   calc.o     \
   lexcalc.o \
   main.o

.y.o:
   @echo execute my .y.o rule
   $(YACC) $(YFLAGS) $(SRC)/$<
   $(SED) '/#line/d' y.tab.c > $*.c
   $(COMPILE.c) $(CPPFLAGS) $(CFLAGS) $*.c
   $(MV) $*.c $*.c.debug
   $(RM) y.tab.c

.l.o:
   @echo execute my .l.o rule
   $(LEX) $(LFLAGS) $(SRC)/$<  > $*.c
   $(COMPILE.c) $(CPPFLAGS) $(CFLAGS) $*.c
   $(MV) $*.c $*.c.debug

.c.o:
   @echo execute .c.o rule
   $(COMPILE.c) $(CPPFLAGS) $(CFLAGS) $(SRC)/$<

calc:   $(OBJECTS)
   $(COMPILE.c) -g $(OBJECTS)  -ll -lc -o $(BIN)/$@
   $(RM) *.o
```

5.11 THE Y.OUTPUT FILE

Adding the -v option to the yacc command generates an additional output file (y.output). Listing 5.12 shows the y.output file when the grammar calc.y in Listing 5.3 is submitted to the YACC through the command

```
yacc -dv calc.y
```

5.11.1 Understanding y.output

First, notice that the y.output file consists of an ascending list of states. Each state can have three parts maximum:

☞ Part one states the grammar rules.
☞ Part two shows all the legal input symbols and actions.
☞ Part three shows the goto action, which occurs after the reduce action.

In part one, all grammar rules are numbered. Part two can have, at most, four actions: accept, shift, reduce, and error. A detailed description of each action can be found in Section 5.3.2. Only the shift and reduce actions need special attention here.

For the shift action, look at state 1 in Listing 5.12. State 1 is the current state, and if the look-ahead token is CONST, it pushes state 5 to the top of the state stack, and state 5 becomes the current state.

For the reduce action, look at state 2 in listing 5.12. No matter what the look-ahead token, it applies grammar rule number two to reduce the symbol(s) on the top of the stack to the nonterminal symbol specified at the left-hand side of the rule. Immediately after this reduce action, it uses the state uncovered and the nonterminal symbol to go to a new state.

5.11.2 How to Use y.output

Listing 5.12 shows the y.output for the grammar specified in calc.y.

The best thing the y.output offers is help locating the shift/reduce and/or reduce/reduce conflicts. As you can see, states 13, 14, 15, and 16 all have shift/reduce conflict.

Listing 5.12 y.output for calc.y

```
state 0
   $accept : _lines $end
lines : _      (1)

   . reduce 1

   lines   goto 1

state 1
   $accept :  lines_$end
   lines :  lines_line
   $end   accept
   CONST   shift 5
   CR   shift 3
   vLP   shift 6
   .   error

   line   goto 2
   expr   goto 4

state 2
   lines :  lines line_     (2)
   .   reduce 2

state 3
   line :  CR_      (3)
   .   reduce 3

state 4
   line :   expr_CR
   expr :   expr_PLUS expr
   expr :   expr_MINUS expr
   expr :   expr_TIME expr
   expr :   expr_DIV expr

   CR   shift 7
```

```
    PLUS   shift 8
    MINUS   shift 9
    TIME   shift 10
    DIV   shift 11
    .  error

state 5
    expr :  CONST_     (5)

    .  reduce 5

state 6
    expr :  LP_expr RP

    CONST   shift 5
    LP   shift 6
    .  error

    expr   goto 12

state 7
    line :  expr CR_     (4)

    .  reduce 4

state 8
    expr :  expr PLUS_expr

    CONST   shift 5
    LP   shift 6
    .  error

    expr   goto 13

state 9
    expr :  expr MINUS_expr

    CONST   shift 5
    LP   shift 6
    .  error

    expr   goto 14

state 10
    expr :  expr TIME_expr

    CONST   shift 5
    LP   shift 6
    .  error

    expr   goto 15

state 11
    expr :  expr DIV_expr

    CONST   shift 5
    LP   shift 6
    .  error

    expr   goto 16
```

```
state 12
   expr :  LP expr_RP
   expr :  expr_PLUS expr
   expr :  expr_MINUS expr
   expr :  expr_TIME expr
   expr :  expr_DIV expr

   RP   shift 17
   PLUS   shift 8
   MINUS   shift 9
   TIME   shift 10
   DIV   shift 11
   .   error

13: shift/reduce conflict (shift 8, red'n 7) on PLUS
13: shift/reduce conflict (shift 9, red'n 7) on MINUS
13: shift/reduce conflict (shift 10, red'n 7) on TIME
13: shift/reduce conflict (shift 11, red'n 7) on DIV
state 13
   expr :  expr_PLUS expr
   expr :  expr PLUS expr_      (7)
   expr :  expr_MINUS expr
   expr :  expr_TIME expr
   expr :  expr_DIV expr

   PLUS   shift 8
   MINUS   shift 9
   TIME   shift 10
   DIV   shift 11
   .   reduce 7

14: shift/reduce conflict (shift 8, red'n 8) on PLUS
14: shift/reduce conflict (shift 9, red'n 8) on MINUS
14: shift/reduce conflict (shift 10, red'n 8) on TIME
14: shift/reduce conflict (shift 11, red'n 8) on DIV
state 14
   expr :  expr_PLUS expr
   expr :  expr_MINUS expr
   expr :  expr MINUS expr_     (8)
   expr :  expr_TIME expr
   expr :  expr_DIV expr

   PLUS   shift 8
   MINUS   shift 9
   TIME   shift 10
   DIV   shift 11
   .   reduce 8

15: shift/reduce conflict (shift 8, red'n 9) on PLUS
15: shift/reduce conflict (shift 9, red'n 9) on MINUS
15: shift/reduce conflict (shift 10, red'n 9) on TIME
15: shift/reduce conflict (shift 11, red'n 9) on DIV
state 15
   expr :  expr_PLUS expr
   expr :  expr_MINUS expr
   expr :  expr_TIME expr
```

```
    expr :   expr TIME expr_     (9)
    expr :   expr_DIV expr

    PLUS   shift 8
    MINUS   shift 9
    TIME   shift 10
    DIV   shift 11
    .  reduce 9

16: shift/reduce conflict (shift 8, red'n 10) on PLUS
16: shift/reduce conflict (shift 9, red'n 10) on MINUS
16: shift/reduce conflict (shift 10, red'n 10) on TIME
16: shift/reduce conflict (shift 11, red'n 10) on DIV
state 16
    expr :   expr_PLUS expr
    expr :   expr_MINUS expr
    expr :   expr_TIME expr
    expr :   expr_DIV expr
    expr :   expr DIV expr_     (10)

    PLUS   shift 8
    MINUS   shift 9
    TIME   shift 10
    DIV   shift 11
    .  reduce 10

state 17
    expr :   LP expr RP_     (6)

    .  reduce 6

10/300 terminals, 3/300 nonterminals
11/600 grammar rules, 18/1000 states
16 shift/reduce, 0 reduce/reduce conflicts reported
10/350 working sets used
memory: states,etc. 141/24000, parser 7/12000
7/600 distinct lookahead sets
6 extra closures
39 shift entries, 1 exceptions
8 goto entries
0 entries saved by goto default
Optimizer space used: input 93/24000, output 33/12000
33 table entries, 6 zero
maximum spread: 264, maximum offset: 261
```

5.12 THE YACC PATCH

Section 5.2 mentions that a YACC-generated parser may fail due to stack overflow.
One way to correct this problem is to redefine the constant YYMAXDEPTH (the size of
the stack array) to a larger value. This is not a permanent solution because chances
are you will have to increase the constant YYMAXDEPTH repeatedly. Another solution is to change the fixed array that represents the state stack to a dynamic array,

where you can realloc more space should it reach the size limit. Redefining a constant is easy, but changing the YACC parser code is quite a task.

If you look at the file y.tab.c the YACC command generates, you see that the first part of this file is a fix for all YACC programs. Actually, this piece of code is directly copied from the file /usr/lib/yaccpar. This is a skeleton parser driver for yacc command output. The end of the file /usr/bin/yaccpar, has the code

```
/*
 * code supplied by user is placed in this switch
 */
switch ( yytmp )
{
$A
}
```

The user's YACC code is placed in the switch statement to replace $A. First, copy the file /usr/lib/yaccpar to the file yacc.patch. We can modify the file yacc.patch to satisfy our needs--most importantly this file must end with the following two lines:

```
switch ( yytmp )
{
```

If we write a program (yaccpatch.c) so that it uses y.tab.c, /usr/lib/yaccpar, and yacc.patch as inputs and performs the following operations on the input files, the output file is a parser with the modifications we want:

1. Open input files /usr/bin/yaccpar, y.tab.c yacc.patch, and output file gram.c.
2. Read from yacc.patch and write to gram.c until the end of the yacc.patch file.
3. Match file /usr/bin/yaccpar and y.tab.c line for line.
4. As soon as a mismatch occurs, read from y.tab.c and write to gram.c until it encounters the end of the y.tab.c file.

The makefile portion that performs the YACC patch and the compilation is

```
.y.o:
    @echo Apply my yacc rule
    yacc -d gram.y
    yaccpatch yacc.patch gram.c
    cc -g -c gram.c
```

5.13 Debugging a YACC Program

If you ever try to debug a YACC-generated parser program using the standard debugger dbx, you may find it impossible because the debugger does not actually show the executed statements. This is caused by the #line statements inserted into the y.tab.c file during the yacc command process. You can use the vi editor to remove all the #line statements. But the simplest way is to add the -l option to the yacc command.

```
yacc -dl gram.y
```

This eliminates all the #line statements in the y.tab.c file.

We then can run debugger and set a break point at yyparse. When the debugger stops at the function yyparse()'s first executable statement, we can step through the code and examine the values of different variables.

5.14 CASE STUDY: A MINI-FORTRAN PARSER

In this example, we implement a parser for a subset of the FORTRAN language. In doing so, we restrict ourselves in certain features that a normal FORTRAN language should have. For example, our subset permits only one-dimensional array. The entire grammar for this subset of FORTRAN language is shown in Listing 5.13.

We choose a FORTRAN parser as our second example because FORTRAN differs from other languages (such as C and PASCAL) in many respects. For example, a FORTRAN label can be placed only within column one to column five. And column six is reserved to signify the continuation line. Therefore, we have to replace the LEX's input macro so that we are able to locate a token's location within a line. Again, let us follow the same procedures outlined in Section 9.1.

1. Copy the YACC skeleton file (skel.y) to file fgram.y, and write the grammar rules for the subset of FORTRAN language. This result is shown in Listing 5.13.

   Listing 5.13 YACC Program for Example 2 (fgram1.y)

```
%{
/* begin of declarative C code */

%}
/* begin of YACC directives */

/*
 * terminal symbols
 */

/*  precedence table */

%% /* begin of rule section */

program: program_units

program_units
    : program_unit
    | program_unit program_units

program_unit
    : program_definition
    | function_definition
    | subroutine_definition
    | block_definition

program_definition
    : program_heading
      declarations
```

```
        statements
        END

program_heading
    : PROGRAM ID

function_definition
    : function_heading
      declarations
      statements
      END

function_heading
    : function_declaration
      optional_parameter_list

function_declaration
    : function_type FUNCTION ID

function_type
    :
    | INTEGER
    | REAL
    | DOUBLE PRECISION
    | LOGICAL
    | CHARACTER
    | CHARACTER STAR ICON

subroutine_definition
    : subroutine_heading
      declarations
      statements
      END

subroutine_heading
    : subroutine_declaration
      optional_parameter_list

subroutine_declaration
    : SUBROUTINE ID

block_definition
    : block_heading
      declarations
      END

block_heading
    : BLOCK DATA ID
optional_parameter_list
    :
    | LP parameter_list RP

parameter_list
    : ID
    | parameter_list COMMA ID

declarations
    : declaration
```

```
              | declaration declarations

    declaration
        : type_declaration
        | data_initiation
        | parm_initiation
        | IMPLICIT NONE
        | INCLUDE LI
        | EXTERNAL var_list

    type_declaration
        : INTEGER              declarator_list
        | REAL                 declarator_list
        | LOGICAL              declarator_list
        | DOUBLE PRECISION     declarator_list
        | CHARACTER            declarator_list
        | CHARACTER STAR ICON  declarator_list

    data_initiation
        : DATA var_data_pairs

    block_declaration
        : COMMON SLASH ID SLASH var_list
    parm_initiation
        : PARAMETER LP assign_params RP

    var_data_pairs
        : var_list SLASH val_list SLASH

    assign_params
        : ID ASSIGNTO expr
        | assign_params COMMA ID ASSIGNTO expr

    var_list
        : ID
        | var_list COMMA ID
        | ID LP ICON RP

    declarator_list
        : ID
        | declarator_list COMMA ID
        | ID LP STAR RP
        | declarator_list COMMA ID LP STAR RP
        | ID LP range_expr RP
        | declarator_list COMMA ID LP range_expr RP
        | declarator_list COMMA ID LP expr RP
        | ID LP expr RP

    range_expr
        : expr COLON expr

    val_list
        : sign ICON
        | ICON
        | sign FCON
        | FCON
        | TRUE
```

```
        | FALSE
        | LI
        | ICON STAR ICON
        | ICON STAR sign ICON
        | ICON STAR FCON
        | ICON STAR sign FCON
        | ICON STAR TRUE
        | ICON STAR FALSE
        | val_list COMMA ICON
        | val_list COMMA sign ICON
        | val_list COMMA FCON
        | val_list COMMA sign FCON
        | val_list COMMA TRUE
        | val_list COMMA FALSE
        | val_list COMMA LI

statements
    : statement
    | statement statements

statement
    : simple_statement
    | compound_statement
    | LABEL simple_statement
    | LABEL compound_statement

simple_statement
    : STOP
    | RETURN
    | CONTINUE
    | GOTO ICON
    | DO ICON ID ASSIGNTO triplet
    | ID ASSIGNTO expr
    | ID LP expr RP ASSIGNTO expr
    | ID LP range_expr RP ASSIGNTO expr
    | ID LP expr RP LP range_expr RP ASSIGNTO expr
    | CALL ID LP optional_argument_list RP

triplet
    : initial_value COMMA inc final_value

initial_value
    : expr

inc
    : expr

final_value
    :
    | COMMA expr

optional_argument
    :
    | LP argument_list RP

argument_list
```

```
        : expr
        | argument_list COMMA expr

    expr_list
        : expr
        | expr_list COMMA expr

    compound_statement
        : if_prefix simple_statement
        | if_prefix then_part ENDIF
        | if_prefix then_part ELSE statements ENDIF
        | if_prefix then_part else_if_else

    if_prefix
        : IF cond
    cond
        : LP expr RP

    else_if_else
        : ELSEIF cond then_part ENDIF
        | ELSEIF cond then_part else_part ENDIF
        | ELSEIF cond then_part else_if_else

    then_part
        : THEN statements

    else_part
        : ELSE statements

    expr
        : ICON
        | FCON
        | TRUE
        | FALSE
        | LI
        | ID
        | ID LP range_expr RP
        | ID LP expr_list RP
        | ID LP expr_list RP LP range_expr RP
        | MINUS expr
        | NOT expr
        | expr POWER expr
        | expr STAR expr
        | expr SLASH expr
        | expr PLUS expr
        | expr MINUS expr
        | expr OR expr
        | expr AND expr
        | expr GT expr
        | expr LT expr
        | Stuxpr EQ expr
        | expr LE expr
        | expr GE expr
        | expr NE expr
        | expr CONCAT expr
        | LP expr RP
```

```
sign
   : PLUS
   | MINUS
```

2. Copy the LEX skeleton file (skel.l) to file flex.l, and write the macro definitions and pattern-matching rules. The result is shown in Listing 5.14.

Listing 5.14 LEX Program for Example 2 (flex2.l)

```
%{
/* begin of C declarative code */
#include    "y.tab.h"

#undef  input
#undef  unput
#undef  output

#define  MAXLINE  400

char    linebuf[MAXLINE];
int     linepos = 0;
int     eof = 0;
%}
/* begin of macro definition */

letter              [a-Za-Z_]
d                   [0-9]
letter_digit_us     [a-Za-Z0-9_]
other               .

%% /* begin of pattern matching section */

"BLOCK"             return(BLOCK);
"COMMON"            return(COMMON);
"IMPLICIT"          return(IMPLICIT);
"NONE"              return(NONE);
"INCLUDE"           return(INCLUDE);
"EXTERNAL"          return(EXTERNAL);
"PROGRAM"           return(PROGRAM);
"SUBROUTINE"        return(SUBROUTINE);
"FUNCTION"          return(FUNCTION);
"INTEGER"           return(INTEGER);
"REAL"              return(REAL);
"CHARACTER"         return(CHARACTER);
"LOGICAL"           return(LOGICAL);
"DOUBLE"            return(DOUBLE);
"PRECISION"         return(PRECISION);
"DO"                return(DO);
"IF"                return(IF);
"THEN"              return(THEN);
"ELSE"              return(ELSE);
"ELSE"[ ]*"IF"      return(ELSEIF);
"END"[ ]*"IF"       return(ENDIF);
"CONTINUE"          return(CONTINUE);
"GO"[ ]*"TO"        return(GOTO);
"CALL"              return(CALL);
```

```
"RETURN"              return(RETURN);
"PARAMETER"           return(PARAMETER);
"END"                 return(END);
"DIMENSION"           return(DIMENSION);
"DATA"                return(DATA);
"STOP"                return(STOP);
".GT."                return(GT);
".LT."                return(LT);
".EQ."                return(EQ);
".LE."                return(LE);
".GE."                return(GE);
".NE."                return(NE);
".OR."                return(OR);
".AND."               return(AND);
".NOT."               return(NOT);
".TRUE."              return(TRUE);
".FALSE."             return(FALSE);
"+"                   return(PLUS);
"-"                   return(MINUS);
"*"                   return(STAR);
"//"                  return(CONCAT);
"/"                   return(SLASH);
"**"                  return(POWER);
"("                   return(LP);
")"                   return(RP);
"="                   return(ASSIGNTO);
":"                   return(COLON);
","                   return(COMMA);
"\n"                                ; /* ignore carriage return */
^[Cc].*$                            ; /* ignore comment line */
^[ \t]*\n                           ; /* ignore blank line */
^[ ][ ][ ][ ][ ][^ ]                ; /* ignore continue character */
[ ]+                                ; /* ignore space(s) */
[\t]+                               ; /* ignore tab(s)     */
{letter}{letter_digit_us}*    return(ID);
{d}+                          return(ICON);
({d}+)([E][-+]?(d)+)   |
({d}+\.{d}*|{d}\.{d}+)([E][-+]?{d}+)?   return(FCON);
({d}+)([D][-+]?(d)+)   |
({d}+\.{d}*|{d}\.{d}+)([D][-+]?{d}+)?   return(FCON);
'[^']*'                       return(LI);
{other}               return(yytext[0]);

%% /* begin of user C code */

void resync(synchar)
char synchar;
{
   int  ch;

   while ((ch = input()) != 0)
      if (ch == (int)synchar)
         break;
}
```

```c
int input()
{
    char c;
    static int lineno;

    if (linebuf[linepos] == '\0')
    {
        if ((eof = readline()) != 1)
        {
            lineno++;
            yylineno = lineno;
            linepos;
        }
        else
            return(0);
    }
    c = linebuf[linepos];
    linepos++;
    return((int) c);
}

int readline()
{
    if (fgets(linebuf, MAXLINE, yyin) != NULL)
        return(0);
    else
        return(1);
}

void unput(c)
int  c;
{
    yytchar = c;
    linepos-;
    linebuf[linepos--] = yytchar;
}

void output(c)
int c;
{

}
```

3. Define all terminal symbols with %token directives, and specify the precedence
   rules. The result is shown in Listing 5.15.

Listing 5.15 YACC Program for Example 2 (fgram3.y)

```c
%{
/* begin of declarative C code */
#include <stdio.h>

%}
/* begin of YACC directives */

/*
```

```
    * terminal symbols
    */
%token BLOCK
%token COMMON
%token IMPLICIT
%token NONE
%token INCLUDE
%token EXTERNAL
%token PROGRAM
%token SUBROUTINE
%token FUNCTION
%token END
%token INTEGER
%token REAL
%token CHARACTER
%token LOGICAL
%token RETURN
%token CONTINUE
%token LP
%token RP
%token COMMA
%token CR
%token STAR
%token PARAMETER
%token ASSIGNTO
%token DOUBLE
%token PRECISION
%token DATA
%token CALL
%token IF
%token THEN
%token ELSE
%token ELSEIF
%token ENDIF
%token GT
%token LT
%token EQ
%token LE
%token GE
%token NE
%token PLUS
%token MINUS
%token STAR
%token SLASH
%token OR
%token AND
%token NOT
%token GOTO
%token LABEL
%token COLON
%token CONCAT
%token POWER
%token TRUE
%token FALSE
```

```
%token STOP
%token DIMENSION

/*  precedence table */
%right ASSIGNTO
%left  OR
%left  AND
%left  LE GE EQ LT NE GT
%left  COLON
%left  PLUS MINUS
%left  STAR SLASH CONCAT
%left  POWER
%left  NOT UMINUS

%% /* begin of rule section */

program: program_units

program_units
    : program_unit
    | program_unit program_units

program_unit
    : program_definition
    | function_definition
    | subroutine_definition
    | block_definition

program_definition
    : program_heading
      declarations
      statements
      END

program_heading
    : PROGRAM ID

function_definition
    : function_heading
      declarations
      statements
      END

function_heading
    : function_declaration
      optional_parameter_list

function_declaration
    : function_type FUNCTION ID

function_type
    :
    | INTEGER
    | REAL
    | DOUBLE PRECISION
    | LOGICAL
    | CHARACTER
```

```
                | CHARACTER STAR ICON

subroutine_definition
    : subroutine_heading
      declarations
      statements
      END

subroutine_heading
    : subroutine_declaration
      optional_parameter_list

subroutine_declaration
    : SUBROUTINE ID

block_definition
    : block_heading
      declarations
      END

block_heading
    : BLOCK DATA ID

optional_parameter_list
    :
    | LP parameter_list RP

parameter_list
    : ID
    | parameter_list COMMA ID

declarations
    : declaration
    | declaration declarations

declaration
    : type_declaration
    | data_initiation
    | parm_initiation
    | IMPLICIT NONE
    | INCLUDE LI
    | EXTERNAL var_list

type_declaration
    : INTEGER              declarator_list
    | REAL                 declarator_list
    | LOGICAL              declarator_list
    | DOUBLE PRECISION     declarator_list
    | CHARACTER            declarator_list
    | CHARACTER STAR ICON declarator_list

block_declaration
    : COMMON SLASH ID SLASH var_list

data_initiation
    : DATA var_data_pairs

parm_initiation
```

```
        : PARAMETER LP assign_params RP

var_data_pairs
    : var_list SLASH val_list SLASH

assign_params
    : ID ASSIGNTO expr
    | assign_params COMMA ID ASSIGNTO expr

var_list
    : ID
    | var_list COMMA ID
    | ID LP ICON RP

declarator_list
    : ID
    | declarator_list COMMA ID
    | ID LP STAR RP
    | declarator_list COMMA ID LP STAR RP
    | ID LP range_expr RP
    | declarator_list COMMA ID LP range_expr RP
    | declarator_list COMMA ID LP expr RP
    | ID LP expr RP

range_expr
    : expr COLON expr

val_list
    : sign ICON
    | ICON
    | sign FCON
    | FCON
    | TRUE
    | FALSE
    | LI
    | ICON STAR ICON
    | ICON STAR sign ICON
    | ICON STAR FCON
    | ICON STAR sign FCON
    | ICON STAR TRUE
    | ICON STAR FALSE
    | val_list COMMA ICON
    | val_list COMMA sign ICON
    | val_list COMMA FCON
    | val_list COMMA sign FCON
    | val_list COMMA TRUE
    | val_list COMMA FALSE
    | val_list COMMA LI

statements
    : statement
    | statement statements

statement
    : simple_statement
    | compound_statement
```

```
    | LABEL simple_statement
    | LABEL compound_statement

simple_statement
    : STOP
    | RETURN
    | CONTINUE
    | GOTO ICON
    | DO ICON ID ASSIGNTO triplet
    | ID ASSIGNTO expr
    | ID LP expr RP ASSIGNTO expr
    | ID LP range_expr RP ASSIGNTO expr
    | ID LP expr RP LP range_expr RP ASSIGNTO expr
    | CALL ID LP optional_argument_list RP

triplet
    : initial_value COMMA inc final_value

initial_value
    : expr

inc
    : expr

final_value
    :
    | COMMA expr

optional_argument
    :
    | LP argument_list RP

argument_list
    : expr
    | argument_list COMMA expr

expr_list
    : expr
    | expr_list COMMA expr

compound_statement
    : if_prefix simple_statement
    | if_prefix then_part ENDIF
    | if_prefix then_part ELSE statements ENDIF
    | if_prefix then_part else_if_else

if_prefix
    : IF cond

cond
    : LP expr RP

else_if_else
    : ELSEIF cond then_part ENDIF
    | ELSEIF cond then_part else_part ENDIF
    | ELSEIF cond then_part else_if_else

then_part
```

```
        : THEN statements

else_part
    : ELSE statements

expr
    : ICON
    | FCON
    | TRUE
    | FALSE
    | LI
    | ID
    | ID LP range_expr RP
    | ID LP expr_list RP
    | ID LP expr_list RP LP range_expr RP
    | MINUS expr
    | NOT expr
    | expr POWER expr
    | expr STAR expr
    | expr SLASH expr
    | expr PLUS expr
    | expr MINUS expr
    | expr OR expr
    | expr AND expr
    | expr GT expr
    | expr LT expr
    | expr EQ expr
    | expr LE expr
    | expr GE expr
    | expr NE expr
    | expr CONCAT expr
    | LP expr RP

sign
    : PLUS
    | MINUS
```

4. Write a main program that calls yyparse() and provides the yyerror() functions to report syntax errors. The result is shown in Listing 5.16.

Listing 5.16 Main Program for Example 2 (fmain4.c)

```c
#include <stdio.h>

extern int  yydebug;
extern int  yylineno;
extern int  linepos;
extern char yytext[];
extern FILE *yyin;

main(argc, argv)
int  argc;
char *argv[];
{
#ifdef YYDEBUG
    yydebug = 1;
```

```
#endif

    if ((yyin = fopen(argv[1], "r")) == NULL)
    {
       fprintf(stderr, "unable to open file %s\n", argv[1]);
       exit(-1);
    }
    yyparse();
}

/*
 *  This function must be supplied by the user
 *  for reporting errors generated by YACC parser
 */
yyerror(msg)
char *msg;
{
    fprintf(stderr, "%s " msg);
    where();
}

where()
{
    int len;
    len = strlen(yytext);
    fprintf(stderr, "at line %d:%d token=%s\n", yylineno,
            linepos-len, yytext);
}

/*
 *  This function is provided for reporting user
 *  detected errors
 */
run_error(msg)
char *msg;
{
    fprintf(stderr,"%s at line %d\n", msg, yylineno);
}
```

5. Type the value stack. A %union directive is added to the YACC program. The result is shown in Listing 5.17.

Listing 5.17 YACC Program for Example 2 (fgram5.y)

```
%{
/* begin of declarative C code */
#include <stdio.h>
#include <fcomp.h>

extern PARM_LIST *BldParmList();

%}
/* begin of YACC directives */
%union  {
    struct symbol    *y_sym;
    struct constant  *y_con;
```

```
    struct dcl_list  *y_dcl;
    struct parm_list *y_parm;
    char             *y_str;
    int               y_num;
}

/*
 * terminal symbols
 */
%token BLOCK
%token COMMON
%token IMPLICIT
%token NONE
%token INCLUDE
%token EXTERNAL
%token PROGRAM
%token SUBROUTINE
%token FUNCTION
%token END
%token INTEGER
%token REAL
%token CHARACTER
%token LOGICAL
%token RETURN
%token CONTINUE
%token LP
%token RP
%token COMMA
%token CR
%token STAR
%token PARAMETER
%token ASSIGNTO
%token DOUBLE
%token PRECISION
%token DATA
%token CALL
%token IF
%token THEN
%token ELSE
%token ELSEIF
%token ENDIF
%token GT
%token LT
%token EQ
%token LE
%token GE
%token NE
%token PLUS
%token MINUS
%token STAR
%token SLASH
%token OR
%token AND
%token NOT
```

```
%token GOTO
%token LABEL
%token COLON
%token CONCAT
%token POWER
%token FTRUE
%token FFALSE
%token STOP
%token DIMENSION

/*  precedence table */
%right ASSIGNTO
%left  OR
%left  AND
%left  LE GE EQ LT NE GT
%left  COLON
%left  PLUS MINUS
%left  STAR SLASH CONCAT
%left  POWER
%left  NOT UMINUS

%% /* begin of rule section */

program: program_units

program_units
    : program_unit
    | program_unit program_units

program_unit
    : program_definition
    | function_definition
    | subroutine_definition
    | block_definition

program_definition
    : program_heading
      declarations
      statements
      END

program_heading
    : PROGRAM ID

function_definition
    : function_heading
      declarations
      statements
      END

function_heading
    : function_declaration
      optional_parameter_list

function_declaration
    : function_type FUNCTION ID
```

```
function_type
    :
    | INTEGER
    | REAL
    | DOUBLE PRECISION
    | LOGICAL
    | CHARACTER
    | CHARACTER STAR ICON

subroutine_definition
    : subroutine_heading
      declarations
      statements
      END

subroutine_heading
    : subroutine_declaration
      optional_parameter_list

subroutine_declaration
    : SUBROUTINE ID

block_definition
    : block_heading
      declarations
      END

block_heading
    : BLOCK DATA ID

optional_parameter_list
    :
    | LP parameter_list RP

parameter_list
    : ID
    | parameter_list COMMA ID

declarations
    : declaration
    | declaration declarations

declaration
    : type_declaration
    | data_initiation
    | parm_initiation
    | IMPLICIT NONE
    | INCLUDE LI
    | EXTERNAL var_List

type_declaration
    : INTEGER               declarator_list
    | REAL                  declarator_list
    | LOGICAL               declarator_list
    | DOUBLE PRECISION      declarator_list
    | CHARACTER             declarator_list
    | CHARACTER STAR ICON declarator_list
```

```
block_declaration
   : COMMON SLASH ID SLASH var_list

data_initiation
   : DATA var_data_pairs

parm_initiation
   : PARAMETER LP assign_params RP

var_data_pairs
   : var_list SLASH val_list SLASH

assign_params
   : ID ASSIGNTO expr
   | assign_params COMMA ID ASSIGNTO expr

var_list
   : ID
   | var_list COMMA ID
   | ID LP ICON RP

declarator_list
   : ID
   | declarator_list COMMA ID
   | ID LP STAR RP
   | declarator_list COMMA ID LP STAR RP
   | ID LP range_expr RP
   | declarator_list COMMA ID LP range_expr RP
   | declarator_list COMMA ID LP expr RP
   | ID LP expr RP

range_expr
   : expr COLON expr

val_list
   : sign ICON
   | ICON
   | sign FCON
   | FCON
   | TRUE
   | FALSE
   | LI
   | ICON STAR ICON
   | ICON STAR sign ICON
   | ICON STAR FCON
   | ICON STAR sign FCON
   | ICON STAR TRUE
   | ICON STAR FALSE
   | val_list COMMA ICON
   | val_list COMMA sign ICON
   | val_list COMMA FCON
   | val_list COMMA sign FCON
   | val_list COMMA TRUE
   | val_list COMMA FALSE
   | val_list COMMA LI
```

```
statements
    : statement
    | statement statements

statement
    : simple_statement
    | compound_statement
    | LABEL simple_statement
    | LABEL compound_statement

simple_statement
    : STOP
    | RETURN
    | CONTINUE
    | GOTO ICON
    | DO ICON ID ASSIGNTO triplet
    | ID ASSIGNTO expr
    | ID LP expr RP ASSIGNTO expr
    | ID LP range_expr RP ASSIGNTO expr
    | ID LP expr RP LP range_expr RP ASSIGNTO expr
    | CALL ID LP optional_argument_list RP

triplet
    : initial_value COMMA inc final_value

initial_value
    : expr

inc
    : expr

final_value
    :
    | COMMA expr

optional_argument
    :

    | LP argument_list RP

argument_list
    : expr
    | argument_list COMMA expr

expr_list
    : expr
    | expr_list COMMA expr

compound_statement
    : if_prefix simple_statement
    | if_prefix then_part ENDIF
    | if_prefix then_part ELSE statements ENDIF
    | if_prefix then_part else_if_else

if_prefix
    : IF cond

cond
```

```
          : LP expr RP

else_if_else
      : ELSEIF cond then_part ENDIF
      | ELSEIF cond then_part else_part ENDIF
      | ELSEIF cond then_part else_if_else

then_part
      : THEN statements

else_part
      : ELSE statements

expr
      : ICON
      | FCON
      | TRUE
      | FALSE
      | LI
      | ID
      | ID LP range_expr RP
      | ID LP expr_list RP
      | ID LP expr_list RP LP range_expr RP
      | MINUS expr
      | NOT expr
      | expr POWER expr
      | expr STAR expr
      | expr SLASH expr
      | expr PLUS expr
      | expr MINUS expr
      | expr OR expr
      | expr AND expr
      | expr GT expr
      | expr LT expr
      | expr EQ expr
      | expr LE expr
      | expr GE expr
      | expr NE expr
      | expr CONCAT expr
      | LP expr RP

sign
      : PLUS
      | MINUS
```

6. Assign values to yylval in the LEX program for those terminal symbols whose values are referenced in the action routine. The result is shown in Listing 5.18.

Two functions used to store values into the stack variable yylval are grouped into the fsub.c file. The source code for fsub.c is shown in Listing 5.20. The header file fcomp.h is shown in Listing 5.21.

Listing 5.18 LEX Program for Example 2 (flex6.l)

```
%{
/* begin of C declarative code */
#include    "y.tab.h"
```

```
#include      <fcomp.h>

#undef        input
#undef        unput
#undef        output

#define       MAXLINE    400
char          linebuf[MAXLINE];
int           linepos = 0;
int           eof = 0;

PTR_SYMBOL    base_ptr     = NULL;
PTR_SYMBOL    first_symbol = NULL:
PTR_SYMBOL    last_symbol  = NULL:

/* external functions */
SYMBOL        *FindSymbol();
SYMBOL        *BldSymbol();
CONST         *BldConst();

%}
/* begin of macro definition */

letter             [a-Za-Z_]
d                  [0-9]
letter_digit_us    [a-Za-Z0-9_]
other              .

%% /* begin of pattern matching section */
"BLOCK"               return(BLOCK);
"COMMON"              return(COMMON);
"IMPLICIT"           return(IMPLICIT);
"NONE"                return(NONE);
"INCLUDE"            return(INCLUDE);
"EXTERNAL"           return(EXTERNAL);
"PROGRAM"            return(PROGRAM);
"SUBROUTINE"        return(SUBROUTINE);
"FUNCTION"           return(FUNCTION);
"INTEGER"            return(INTEGER);
"REAL"                return(REAL);
"CHARACTER"         return(CHARACTER);
"LOGICAL"            return(LOGICAL);
"DOUBLE"             return(DOUBLE);
"PRECISION"         return(PRECISION);
"DO"                  return(DO);
"IF"                  return(IF);
"THEN"               return(THEN);
"ELSE"               return(ELSE);
"ELSE"[ ]*"IF"       return(ELSEIF);
"END"[ ]*"IF"        return(ENDIF);
"CONTINUE"          return(CONTINUE);
"GO"[ ]*"TO"         return(GOTO);
"CALL"               return(CALL);
"RETURN"            return(RETURN);
"PARAMETER"       return(PARAMETER);
"END"                return(END);
```

```
"DIMENSION"          return(DIMENSION);
"DATA"                    return(DATA);
"STOP"                    return(STOP);
".GT."                      return(GT);
".LT."                      return(LT);
".EQ."                      return(EQ);
".LE."                      return(LE);
".GE."                      return(GE);
".NE."                      return(NE);
".OR."                      return(OR);
".AND."                    return(AND);
".NOT."                    return(NOT);
".TRUE."                  return(TRUE);
".FALSE."                 return(FALSE);
"+"                       return(PLUS);
"-"                       return(MINUS);
"*"                        return(STAR);
"//"                     return(CONCAT);
"/"                      return(SLASH);
"**"                     return(POWER);
"("                        return(LP);
")"                        return(RP);
"="                    return(ASSIGNTO);
":"                       return(COLON);
","                       return(COMMA);
"\n"                    ; /* ignore carriage return */
^[Cc].*$                ; /* ignore comment line */
^[ \t]*\n               ; /* ignore blank line */
^[ ][ ][ ][ ][ ][^ ]    ; /* ignore continue character */
[ ]+                    ; /* ignore space(s) */
[\t]+                   ; /* ignore tab(s)    */
{letter}{letter_digit_us}*  {
   yylval.y_sym=BldSymbol(yytext,  yylineno, NO_TYPE);
   return(ID);
}
{d}+  {
   yylval.y_con = BldConst(yytext,yylineno, INTEGER_TYPE);
   if (linepos <= 5)
      return(LABEL);
   else
      return(ICON);
}
({d}+)([E][-+]?(d)+)  |
({d}+\.{d}*|{d}\.{d}+)([E][-+]?{d}+)?   {
   yylval.y_con = BldConst(yytext,yylineno, REAL_TYPE);
   return(FCON);
}
({d}+)([D][-+]?(d)+)  |
({d}+\.{d}*|{d}\.{d}+)([D][-+]?{d}+)?   {
   yylval.y_con = BldConst(yytext,yylineno, DOUBLE_TYPE);
   return(FCON);
}
'[^']*'  {
   yylval.y_con = BldConst(yytext,yylineno, CHAR_TYPE);
```

```
        return(LI);
    }

{other}                     return(yytext[0]);

%% /* begin of user C code */

void resync(synchar)
char synchar;
{
    int   ch;

    while ((ch = input()) != 0)
        if (ch == (int)synchar)
            break;
}

int input()
{
    char c;
    static int lineno;

    if (linebuf[linepos] == '\0')
    {
        if ((eof = readline()) != 1)
        {
            lineno++;
            yylineno = lineno;
            linepos;
        }
        else
            return(0);
    }
    c = linebuf[linepos];
    linepos++;
    return((int) c);
}

int readline()
{
    if (fgets(linebuf, MAXLINE, yyin) != NULL)
        return(0);
    else
        return(1);
}

void unput(c)
int   c;
{
    yytchar = c;
    linepos-;
    linebuf[linepos--] = yytchar;
}

void output(c)
int c;
```

```
{

}
```

7. Fill in the semantic portion of the parser. The code in this section depends greatly on what you want to accomplish. In our example, we set our goal to achieve the following:

   - Build a symbol table for all identifiers and identify their types (e.g. program name, subroutine name, function name, or variable).
   - Differentiate between formal parameters and local variables.
   - Determine the variables' data type (e.g. integer, real, double precision, logical, or character).
   - List all parameters for subroutine and function definitions.
   - Determine how many arguments the CALL and function reference statements have.

The result is shown in Listing 5.19.

Listing 5.19 YACC Program for Example 2 (fgram7.y)

```
%{
/* begin of declarative C code */
#include <stdio.h>
#include <fcomp.h>

extern int        yylineno;
extern PARM_LIST *BldParmList();

%}
/* begin of YACC directives */

%union  {
    struct symbol       *y_sym;
    struct constant     *y_con;
    struct dcl_list     *y_dcl;
    struct parm_list    *y_parm;
    char                *y_str;
    int                  y_num;
}

/*
 * terminal symbols
 */
%token BLOCK
%token COMMON
%token IMPLICIT
%token NONE
%token INCLUDE
%token EXTERNAL
%token PROGRAM
%token SUBROUTINE
%token FUNCTION
%token END
%token INTEGER
```

```
        %token REAL
        %token CHARACTER
        %token LOGICAL
        %token RETURN
        %token CONTINUE
        %token LP
        %token RP
        %token COMMA
        %token CR
        %token STAR
        %token PARAMETER
        %token ASSIGNTO
        %token DOUBLE
        %token PRECISION
        %token DATA
        %token SLASH
        %token CALL
        %token IF
        %token THEN
        %token ELSE
        %token ELSEIF
        %token ENDIF
        %token GT
        %token LT
        %token EQ
        %token LE
        %token GE
        %token NE
        %token PLUS
        %token MINUS
        %token STAR
        %token OR
        %token AND
        %token DO
        %token GOTO
        %token LABEL
        %token COLON
        %token CONCAT
        %token POWER
        %token TRUE
        %token NOT
        %token FALSE
        %token STOP
        %token DIMENSION
        %token ICON
        %token FCON
        %token LI
        %token ID

        /*  precedence table */
        %right ASSIGNTO
        %left  OR
        %left  AND
        %left  LE GE EQ LT NE GT
```

```
%left   COLON
%left   PLUS MINUS
%left   STAR SLASH CONCAT
%left   POWER
%left   NOT UMINUS

%% /* begin of rule section */

program: {init();}
   program_units
   {terminate();}

program_units
   : program_unit
   | program_unit program_units

program_unit
   : program_definition
     {end_definition();}
   | function_definition
     {end_definition();}
   | subroutine_definition
     {end_definition();}
   | block_definition
     {end_definition();}

program_definition
   : program_heading
     declarations
     statements
     END

program_heading
   : PROGRAM ID
     {AddTypeToSymbol(PROG_TYPE,$2->s_name, NO_TYPE);}

function_definition
   : function_heading
     declarations
     statements
     END

function_heading
   : function_declaration
     optional_parameter_list
     {PrtParmList($2);}

function_declaration
   : function_type FUNCTION ID
     {AddTypeToSymbol(FUNC_TYPE,$3->s_name,$1);}

function_type
   : {$$ = NO_TYPE;}
   | INTEGER
     {$$ = INTEGER_TYPE;}
   | REAL
     {$$ = REAL_TYPE;}
```

```
         | DOUBLE PRECISION
           {$$ = DOUBLE_TYPE;}
         | LOGICAL
           {$$ = LOGICAL_TYPE;}
         | CHARACTER
           {$$ = CHAR_TYPE;}
         | CHARACTER STAR ICON
           {$$ = CHAR_TYPE;}

subroutine_definition
    : subroutine_heading
      declarations
      statements
      END

subroutine_heading
    : subroutine_declaration
      optional_parameter_list
      {PrtParmList($2);}

subroutine_declaration
    : SUBROUTINE ID
      {AddTypeToSymbol(SUBR_TYPE, $2->s_name,NO_TYPE);}

block_declaration
    : block_heading
      declarations
      END

block_heading
    : BLOCK DATA ID
      {AddTypeToSymbol(BLOCK_TYPE, s3->S_name,NO_TYPE);}

optional_parameter_list
    : {$$ = NULL;}
    | LP parameter_list RP
      {$$ = $2;}

parameter_list
    : ID
      {$$=BldParmList($1->s_name,NULL);
      AddTypeToSymbol(PARM_TYPE, $1->s_name, NO_TYPE);}
    | parameter_list COMMA ID
      {$$ = BldParmList($3->s_name,$1);
      AddTypeToSymbol(PARM_TYPE, $3->s_name, NO_TYPE);}

declarations
    : declarations declaration
    | declaration

declaration
    : type_declaration
    | data_initiation
    | parm_initiation
    | IMPLICIT NONE
    | INCLUDE LI
```

```
                | EXTERNAL var_list

    type_declaration
        : INTEGER declarator_list
          {AddTypesToSymbols($2, INTEGER_TYPE);}
        | REAL     declarator_list
          {AddTypesToSymbols($2, REAL_TYPE);}
        | LOGICAL  declarator_list
          {AddTypesToSymbols($2, LOGICAL_TYPE);}
        | DOUBLE PRECISION  declarator_list
          {AddTypesToSymbols($3, DOUBLE_TYPE);}
        | CHARACTER  declarator_list
          {AddTypesToSymbols($2, CHAR_TYPE);}
        | CHARACTER STAR ICON declarator_list
          {AddTypesToSymbols($4, CHAR_TYPE);}

    block_declaration
        : COMMON SLASH ID SLASH var_list
          {AddTypeToSymbol(COMMON_TYPE,$3->s_name,NO_TYPE);}

    data_initiation
        : DATA var_data_pairs

    parm_initiation
        : PARAMETER
          LP assign_params RP

    var_data_pairs
        : var_list SLASH val_list SLASH

    assign_params
        : ID ASSIGNTO expr
        | assign_params COMMA ID ASSIGNTO expr

    var_list
        : ID
        | var_list COMMA ID
        | ID LP ICON RP

    declarator_list
        : ID
          {$$ = (DCL_LIST *)BldDclList(VAR_TYPE, $1->s_name,  NULL);}
        | declarator_list COMMA ID
          {$$ = (DCL_LIST *)BldDclList(VAR_TYPE, $3->s_name,  $1);}
        | ID LP STAR RP
          {$$ = (DCL_LIST *)BldDclList(AVAR_TYPE, $1->s_name, NULL);}
        | declarator_list COMMA ID LP STAR RP
          {$$ = (DCL_LIST *)BldDclList(AVAR_TYPE, $3->s_name,  $1);}
        | ID LP range_expr RP
          {$$ = (DCL_LIST *)BldDclList(AVAR_TYPE, $1->s_name,  NULL);}
        | declarator_list COMMA ID LP range_expr RP
          {$$ = (DCL_LIST *)BldDclList(AVAR_TYPE, $3->s_name,  $1);}
        | declarator_list COMMA ID LP expr RP
          {$$ = (DCL_LIST *)BldDclList(AVAR_TYPE, $3->s_name,  $1);}
        | ID LP expr RP
          {$$ = (DCL_LIST *)BldDclList(AVAR_TYPE, $1->s_name,  NULL);}
```

```
range_expr
   : expr COLON expr

val_list
   : sign ICON
   | ICON
   | sign FCON
   | FCON
   | TRUE
   | FALSE
   | LI
   | ICON STAR ICON
   | ICON STAR sign ICON
   | ICON STAR FCON
   | ICON STAR sign FCON
   | ICON STAR TRUE
   | ICON STAR FALSE
   | val_list COMMA ICON
   | val_list COMMA sign ICON
   | val_list COMMA FCON
   | val_list COMMA sign FCON
   | val_list COMMA TRUE
   | val_list COMMA FALSE
   | val_list COMMA LI

statements
   : statement
   | statement statements

statement
   : simple_statement
   | compound_statement
   | LABEL simple_statement
   | LABEL compound_statement

simple_statement
   : STOP
     {$$=0;}
   | RETURN
     {$$=0;}
   | CONTINUE
     {$$=0;}
   | GOTO ICON
     {$$=0;}
   | DO ICON ID ASSIGNTO triplet
     {$$=0;}
   | ID ASSIGNTO expr
     {$$=0;}
   | ID LP expr RP ASSIGNTO expr
     {$$=0;}
   | ID LP range_expr RP ASSIGNTO expr
     {$$=0;}
   | ID LP expr RP LP range_expr RP ASSIGNTO expr
     {$$=0;}
   | CALL ID LP optional_argument_list RP
```

```
            {AddTypeToSymbol(SUBR_TYPE, $2->s_name,NO_TYPE);$$=0;}
    triplet
        : initial_value COMMA inc final_value

    initial_value
        : expr

    inc
        : expr

    final_value
        :
        | COMMA expr

    optional_argument
        : {$$ = 0;}
        | LP argument_list RP
          {$$ = $2;}

    argument_list
        : expr
          {$$ = 1;}
        | argument_list COMMA expr
          {$$ = $1 + 1;}

    expr_list
        : expr
          {$$=1;}
        | expr_list COMMA expr
          {$$ = $1+1;}

    compound_statement
        : if_prefix simple_statement
        | if_prefix then_part ENDIF
        | if_prefix then_part ELSE statements ENDIF
        | if_prefix then_part else_if_else

    if_prefix
        : IF cond

    cond
        : LP expr RP

    else_if_else
        : ELSEIF cond then_part ENDIF
        | ELSEIF cond then_part else_part ENDIF
        | ELSEIF cond then_part else_if_else

    then_part
        : THEN statements

    else_part
        : ELSE statements

    expr
        : ICON
        | FCON
```

```
    | TRUE
    | FALSE
    | LI
    | ID
    | ID LP range_expr RP
    | ID LP expr_list RP
      { if (!IsArray($1->s_name))
      AddTypeToSymbol(FUNC_TYPE, $1->s_name, NO_TYPE);}
    | ID LP expr_list RP LP range_expr RP
    | MINUS expr
    | NOT expr
    | expr POWER expr
    | expr STAR expr
    | expr SLASH expr
    | expr PLUS expr
    | expr MINUS expr
    | expr OR expr
    | expr AND expr
    | expr GT expr
    | expr LT expr
    | expr EQ expr
    | expr LE expr
    | expr GE expr
    | expr NE expr
    | expr CONCAT expr
    | LP expr RP

sign
    : PLUS
    | MINUS
```

Listing 5.20 Utility Functions for Example 2 (fsub.c)

```c
#include <stdio.h>
#include <fcomp.h>

extern PTR_SYMBOL base_ptr;
extern PTR_SYMBOL first_symbol;
extern PTR_SYMBOL last_symbol;
extern int        yylineno;

SYMBOL *FindSymbol();
void    PrtSymTab();

void init()
{
   yylineno = 0;
}

void terminate()
{
   PrtSymTab();
}

void end_function()
```

```c
{
   PRT_SYMBOL tptr;
   if (base_ptr == NULL)
      base_ptr = first_symbol;
   else
   {
      tptr = base_ptr;
      while (tptr->child != NULL)
         tptr = tptr->child;
      tptr->child = first_symbol;
   }
   first_symbol = NULL;
   last_symbol  = NULL;
}

SYMBOL *BldSymbol(string, line_num, symbol_type)
char *string;
int  line_num;
int  symbol_type;
{
   SYMBOL *ret_value;
   SYMBOL *tmp_ptr;

   if (first_symbol == NULL)
   {
      ret_value = (SYMBOL *) malloc(sizeof(SYMBOL));
      ret_value->s_type = symbol_type;
      ret_value->s_lineno = line_num;
      ret_value->s_name = (char *)malloc(strlen(string)+1);
      strcpy(ret_value->s_name, string);
      ret_value->next = NULL;
      ret_value->child = NULL;
      first_symbol = ret_value;
      last_symbol = first_symbol;
      return(ret_value);
   }
   else
   {
      if (ret_value = FindSymbol(string))
      {
         if (symbol_type != NO_TYPE)
            ret_value->s_type = symbol_type;
         return(ret_value);
      }
      ret_value = (SYMBOL *) malloc(sizeof(SYMBOL));
      ret_value->s_type = symbol_type;
      ret_value->s_lineno = line_num;
      ret_value->s_name = (char *)malloc(strlen(string)+1);
      strcpy(ret_value->s_name, string);
      ret_value->next = NULL;
      ret_value->child = NULL;
      last_symbol->next = ret_value;
      last_symbol = ret_value;
      return(ret_value);
```

```
   }
}

CONST *BldConst(string,line_num,const_type)
char *string;
int    line_num;
int    const_type;
{
   CONST *ret_value;
   CONST *tmp_ptr;

   ret_value = (CONST *) malloc(sizeof(CONSTANT));
   ret_value->c_type = const_type;
   ret_value->c_lineno = line_num;
   ret_value->c_str = (char *)malloc(strlen(string)+1);
   strcpy(ret_value->c_str, string);
   return(ret_value);
}

void AddTypeToSymbol(s_type, s_name, data_type)
int  s_type;
char *s_name;
int  data_type;
{
   PTR_SYMBOL tptr;
   tptr = first_symbol;
   while (tptr != NULL)
   {
      if (strcmp(s_name, tptr->s_name) == 0)
      {
         tptr->s_type = s_type;
         tptr->s_data_type = data_type;
      }
      tptr = tptr->next;
   }
}

void AddTypesToSymbols(ptr_list, data_type)
int s_type;
DCL_LIST *ptr_list;
int    data_type;
{
   DEC_LIST *tptr;

   tptr = ptr_list;
   while (tptr != NULL)
   {
      AddTypeToSymbol(tptr->s_type, tptr->s_name,    data_type);
      tptr = tptr->next;
   }
}

void PrtSymTab()
{
   PTR_SYMBOL cptr;
   PTR_SYMBOL tptr;
```

```c
        cptr = base_ptr;
        while (cptr != NULL)
        {
            printf("=========================================");
            tptr = first_symbol;
            while (tptr != NULL)
            {
                printf("%s ", tptr->s_name);
                if (tptr->s_type == PROG_TYPE)
                    printf(": program name\n");
                else if (tptr->s_type == FUNC_TYPE)
                {
                    if (tptr->s_data_type == INTEGER_TYPE)
                        printf(":is integer function\n");
                    else if (tptr->s_data_type == REAL_TYPE)
                        printf(":is real function\n");
                    else if (tptr->s_data_type == DOUBLE_TYPE)
                        printf(":is double function\n");
                    else if (tptr->s_data_type == LOGICAL_TYPE)
                        printf(":is logical function\n");
                    else if (tptr->s_data_type == CHAR_TYPE)
                        printf("is character function\n");
                    else
                        printf(": function name\n");
                }
                else if (tptr->s_name == SUBR_TYPE)
                    printf(":subroutine name\n");
                else if (tptr->s_name == BLOCK_TYPE)
                    printf(":block name\n");
                else if (tptr->s_name == COMMON_TYPE)
                    printf(":common name\n");
                else if (tptr->s_type == VAR_TYPE)
                {
                    if (tptr->s_data_type == INTEGER_TYPE)
                        printf("is integer variable\n");
                    else if (tptr->s_data_type == REAL_TYPE)
                        printf("is real variable\n");
                    else if (tptr->s_data_type == DOUBLE_TYPE)
                        printf("is double variable\n");
                    else if (tptr->s_data_type == LOGICAL_TYPE)
                        printf("is logical variable\n");
                    else if (tptr->s_data_type == CHAR_TYPE)
                        printf("is character variable\n");
                }
                else if (tptr->s_type == AVAR_TYPE)
                {
                    if (tptr->s_data_type == INTEGER_TYPE)
                        printf("is integer array variable\n");
                    else if (tptr->s_data_type == REAL_TYPE)
                        printf("is real array variable\n");
                    else if (tptr->s_data_type == DOUBLE_TYPE)
                        printf("is double array variable\n");
                    else if (tptr->s_data_type == LOGICAL_TYPE)
                        printf("is logical array variable\n");
```

```c
                  else if (tptr->s_data_type == CHAR_TYPE)
                     printf("is character array variable\n");
             }
           else if (tptr->s_name == PARM_TYPE)
              printf(": parameter\n");
           else
              printf(": no type\n");
           tptr = tptr->next;
        }
        cptr = cptr->child;
    }
}

PARM_LIST *BldParmList(s_name, ptr_list)
char *s_name;
PARM_LIST   *ptr_list;
{
    static PARM_LIST *first_ptr;
    static PARM_LIST *tptr;

    tptr = ptr_list;
    if (tptr == NULL)
    {
        first_ptr = (PARM_LIST *)malloc(sizeof(PARM_LIST));
        first_ptr->s_name = (char *)malloc(strlen(s_name)+1);
        strcpy(first_ptr->s_name, s_name);
        first_ptr->next = NULL;
        return(first_ptr);
    }
    while (tptr->next != NULL)
        tptr = tptr->next;

    tptr->next = (PARM_LIST *)malloc(sizeof(PARM_LIST));
    tptr = tptr->next;
    tptr->s_name = (char *)malloc(strlen(s_name)+1);
    strcpy(tptr->s_name, s_name);
    tptr->next = NULL;
    return(first_ptr);
}

void PrtParmList(ptr_list)
PARM_LIST *ptr_list;
{
    static PARM_LIST *tptr;

    tptr = ptr_list;
    if (tptr != NULL)
        printf(" parameters: ");
    while (tptr != NULL)
    {
        printf("%s ", tptr->s_name);
        tptr = tptr->next;
    }
    printf("\n");
}
```

```c
DCL_LIST *BldDclList(s_name, ptr_list)
char *s_name;
DCL_LIST   *ptr_list;
{
   static DCL_LIST *first_ptr;
   static DCL_LIST *tptr;

   tptr = ptr_list;
   if (tptr == NULL)
   {
      first_ptr = (DCL_LIST *)malloc(sizeof(DCL_LIST));
      first_ptr->s_name = (char *)malloc(strlen(s_name)+1);
      strcpy(first_ptr->s_name, s_name);
      first_ptr->next = NULL;
      return(first_ptr);
   }
   while (tptr->next != NULL)
      tptr = tptr->next;
   tptr->next = (DCL_LIST *)malloc(sizeof(DCL_LIST));
   tptr = tptr->next;
   tptr->s_name = (char *)malloc(strlen(s_name)+1);
   strcpy(tptr->s_name, s_name);
   tptr->next = NULL;
   return(first_ptr);
}

SYMBOL *FindSymbol(string)
char *string;
{
   SYMBOL *tptr;

   tptr = first_symbol;
   if (tptr == NULL)
      return(NULL);
   while (tptr->next != NULL)
   {
      if (strcmp(tptr->s_name, string) == 0)
         return(tptr);
      tptr = tptr->next;
   }
   if (strcmp(tptr->s_name, string) == 0)
      return(tptr);
   else
      return(NULL);
}

int IsArray(string)
char *string;
{
   PTR_SYMBOL  tptr;
   tptr = first_symbol;
   while (tptr != NULL)
   {
      if (strcmp(tptr->s_name, string) == 0)
         if (tptr->s_type == AVAR_TYPE)
```

```
            return(1);
        else
            return(0);
      tptr = tptr->next;
   }
   return(0);
}
```

Listing 5.21 Header File for Example 2 (fcomp.h)

```
/* define variable function types */
#define NO_TYPE         0
#define PROG_TYPE       1
#define FUNC_TYPE       2
#define SUBR_TYPE       3
#define VAR_TYPE        4
#define AVAR_TYPE       5
#define PARM_TYPE       6
#define BLOCK_TYPE      7
#define COMMON_TYPE     8

/* define variable data type */
#define INTEGER_TYPE   1
#define REAL_TYPE      2
#define DOUBLE_TYPE    3
#define CHAR_TYPE      4
#define LOGICAL_TYPE   5

typedef struct symbol {
   char    *s_name;
   char    *subr_name;
   int      s_type;
   int      s_data_type;
   int      s_lineno;
   int      s_linepos;
   struct symbol *child;
   struct symbol *next;
} SYMBOL, *PTR_SYMBOL;

typedef struct constant {
   char    * c_str;
   char    * subr_name;
   int      c_type;
   int      c_lineno;
   int      c_linepos;
   struct constant *next;
} CONST, *PTR_CONST;

typedef struct dcl_list {
   char *s_name;
   int   s_type;
   struct dcl_list *next;
} DCL_LIST,  *PTR_DCL_LIST;

typedef struct parm_list {
```

```
    char *s_name;
    struct parm_list *next;
} PARM_LIST, *PTR_PARM_LIST;
```

8. Define all the terminal symbols for which a value is assigned to yylval during the
lexical analysis phase with %token directives. Define all the nonterminal symbols for which $i or $$ are referenced by making a %type definition similar to the
%token definition for terminal symbols. The result is shown in Listing 5.22.

Listing 5.22 YACC Program for Example 2 (fgram8.y)

```
%{
/* begin of declarative C code */
#include <stdio.h>
#include <fcomp.h>

extern int       yylineno;
extern PARM_LIST *BldParmList();

%}
/* begin of YACC directives */

%union  {
    struct symbol     *y_sym;
    struct constant   *y_con;
    struct dcl_list   *y_dcl;
    struct parm_list  *y_parm;
    char              *y_str;
    int                y_num;
}

/*
 * terminal symbols
 */
%token BLOCK
%token COMMON
%token IMPLICIT
%token NONE
%token INCLUDE
%token EXTERNAL
%token PROGRAM
%token SUBROUTINE
%token FUNCTION
%token END
%token INTEGER
%token REAL
%token CHARACTER
%token LOGICAL
%token RETURN
%token CONTINUE
%token LP
%token RP
%token COMMA
%token CR
%token STAR
```

```
%token PARAMETER
%token ASSIGNTO
%token DOUBLE
%token PRECISION
%token DATA
%token SLASH
%token CALL
%token IF
%token THEN
%token ELSE
%token ELSEIF
%token ENDIF
%token GT
%token LT
%token EQ
%token LE
%token GE
%token NE
%token PLUS
%token MINUS
%token STAR
%token OR
%token AND
%token DO
%token GOTO
%token LABEL
%token COLON
%token CONCAT
%token POWER
%token TRUE
%token NOT
%token FALSE
%token STOP
%token DIMENSION
%token ICON
%token FCON
%token LI
%token ID

%token <y_sym> ID
%token <y_con> ICON
%token <y_con> FCON
%token <y_con> LI

%type   <y_num> function_type
%type   <y_num> expr_list
%type   <y_parm> optional_parameter_list, parameter_list
%type   <y_dcl> declarator_list
%type   <y_num> optional_argument, argument_list
%type   <y_num> simple_statement

/*  precedence table */
%right ASSIGNTO
%left  OR
%left  AND
```

```
    %left  LE GE EQ LT NE GT
    %left  COLON
    %left  PLUS MINUS
    %left  STAR SLASH CONCAT
    %left  POWER
    %left  NOT UMINUS

    %% /* begin of rule section */

    program: {init();}
       program_units
       {terminate();}

    program_units
       : program_unit
       | program_unit program_units

    program_unit
       : program_definition
         {end_definition();}
       | function_definition
         {end_definition();}
       | subroutine_definition
         {end_definition();}
       | block_definition
         {end_definition();}

    program_definition
       : program_heading
         declarations
         statements
         END

    program_heading
       : PROGRAM ID
         {AddTypeToSymbol(PROG_TYPE,$2->s_name, NO_TYPE);}

    function_definition
       : function_heading
         declarations
         statements
         END

    function_heading
       : function_declaration
         optional_parameter_list
         {PrtParmList($2);}

    function_declaration
       : function_type FUNCTION ID
         {AddTypeToSymbol(FUNC_TYPE,$3->s_name,$1);}

    function_type
       : {$$ = NO_TYPE;}
       | INTEGER
         {$$ = INTEGER_TYPE;}
       | REAL
         {$$ = REAL_TYPE;}
```

```
                    | DOUBLE PRECISION
                      {$$ = DOUBLE_TYPE;}
                    | LOGICAL
                      {$$ = LOGICAL_TYPE;}
                    | CHARACTER
                      {$$ = CHAR_TYPE;}
                    | CHARACTER STAR ICON
                      {$$ = CHAR_TYPE;}

subroutine_definition
        : subroutine_heading
          declarations
          statements
          END

subroutine_heading
        : subroutine_declaration
          optional_parameter_list
          {PrtParmList($2);}

subroutine_declaration
        : SUBROUTINE ID
          {AddTypeToSymbol(SUBR_TYPE, $2->s_name,NO_TYPE);}

block_definition
        : block_heading
          declarations
          END

block_heading
        : BLOCK DATA ID
          {AddTypeToSymbol(BLOCK_TYPE,$3->s_name, NO_TYPE);}

optional_parameter_list
        : {$$ = NULL;}
        | LP parameter_list RP
          {$$ = $2;}

parameter_list
        : ID
          {$$=BldParmList($1->s_name,NULL);
          AddTypeToSymbol(PARM_TYPE, $1->s_name, NO_TYPE);}
        | parameter_list COMMA ID
          {$$ = BldParmList($3->s_name,$1);
          AddTypeToSymbol(PARM_TYPE, $3->s_name, NO_TYPE);}

declarations
        : declarations declaration
        | declaration

declaration
        : type_declaration
        | data_initiation
        | parm_initiation
        | IMPLICIT NONE
        | INCLUDE LI
        | EXTERNAL var_list
```

```
    type_declaration
       : INTEGER declarator_list
         {AddTypesToSymbols($2, INTEGER_TYPE);}
       | REAL     declarator_list
         {AddTypesToSymbols($2, REAL_TYPE);}
       | LOGICAL  declarator_list
         {AddTypesToSymbols($2, LOGICAL_TYPE);}
       | DOUBLE PRECISION  declarator_list
         {AddTypesToSymbols($3, DOUBLE_TYPE);}
       | CHARACTER  declarator_list
         {AddTypesToSymbols($2, CHAR_TYPE);}
       | CHARACTER STAR ICON declarator_list
         {AddTypesToSymbols($4, CHAR_TYPE);}

    block_declaration
       : COMMON SLASH ID SLASH var_list
         {AddTypeToSymbol(COMMON_TYPE,$3->s_name,NO_TYPE);}

    data_initiation
       : DATA var_data_pairs

    parm_initiation
       : PARAMETER
         LP assign_params RP

    var_data_pairs
       : var_list SLASH val_list SLASH

    assign_params
       : ID ASSIGNTO expr
       | assign_params COMMA ID ASSIGNTO expr

    var_list
       : ID
       | var_list COMMA ID
       | ID LP ICON RP

    declarator_list
       : ID
         {$$ = (DCL_LIST *)BldDclList(VAR_TYPE, $1->s_name,  NULL);}
       | declarator_list COMMA ID
         {$$ = (DCL_LIST *)BldDclList(VAR_TYPE, $3->s_name,  $1);}
       | ID LP STAR RP
         {$$ = (DCL_LIST *)BldDclList(AVAR_TYPE, $1->s_name,  NULL);}
       | declarator_list COMMA ID LP STAR RP
         {$$ = (DCL_LIST *)BldDclList(AVAR_TYPE, $3->s_name,  $1);}
       | ID LP range_expr RP
         {$$ = (DCL_LIST *)BldDclList(AVAR_TYPE, $1->s_name,  NULL);}
       | declarator_list COMMA ID LP range_expr RP
         {$$ = (DCL_LIST *)BldDclList(AVAR_TYPE, $3->s_name,  $1);}
       | declarator_list COMMA ID LP expr RP
         {$$ = (DCL_LIST *)BldDclList(AVAR_TYPE, $3->s_name,  $1);}
       | ID LP expr RP
         {$$ = (DCL_LIST *)BldDclList(AVAR_TYPE, $1->s_name,  NULL);}

    range_expr
```

```
        : expr COLON expr

val_list
    : sign ICON
    | ICON
    | sign FCON
    | FCON
    | TRUE
    | FALSE
    | LI
    | ICON STAR ICON
    | ICON STAR sign ICON
    | ICON STAR FCON
    | ICON STAR sign FCON
    | ICON STAR TRUE
    | ICON STAR FALSE
    | val_list COMMA ICON
    | val_list COMMA sign ICON
    | val_list COMMA FCON
    | val_list COMMA sign FCON
    | val_list COMMA TRUE
    | val_list COMMA FALSE
    | val_list COMMA LI

statements
    : statement
    | statement statements

statement
    : simple_statement
    | compound_statement
    | LABEL simple_statement
    | LABEL compound_statement

simple_statement
    : STOP
      {$$=0;}
    | RETURN
      {$$=0;}
    | CONTINUE
      {$$=0;}
    | GOTO ICON
      {$$=0;}
    | DO ICON ID ASSIGNTO triplet
      {$$=0;}
    | ID ASSIGNTO expr
      {$$=0;}
    | ID LP expr RP ASSIGNTO expr
      {$$=0;}
    | ID LP range_expr RP ASSIGNTO expr
      {$$=0;}
    | ID LP expr RP LP range_expr RP ASSIGNTO expr
      {$$=0;}
    | CALL ID LP optional_argument_list RP
      {AddTypeToSymbol(SUBR_TYPE, $2->s_name,NO_TYPE);$$=0;}
```

```
    triplet
       : initial_value COMMA inc final_value

    initial_value
       : expr

    inc
       : expr

    final_value
       :
       | COMMA expr

    optional_argument
       : {$$ = 0;}
       | LP argument_list RP
         {$$ = $2;}

    argument_list
       : expr
         {$$ = 1;}
       | argument_list COMMA expr
         {$$ = $1 + 1;}

    expr_list
       : expr
         {$$=1;}
       | expr_list COMMA expr
         {$$ = $1+1;}

    compound_statement
       : if_prefix simple_statement
       | if_prefix then_part ENDIF
       | if_prefix then_part ELSE statements ENDIF
       | if_prefix then_part else_if_else

    if_prefix
       : IF cond

    cond
       : LP expr RP

    else_if_else
       : ELSEIF cond then_part ENDIF
       | ELSEIF cond then_part else_part ENDIF
       | ELSEIF cond then_part else_if_else

    then_part
       : THEN statements

    else_part
       : ELSE statements

    expr
       : ICON
       | FCON
       | TRUE
       | FALSE
```

```
    | LI
    | ID
    | ID LP range_expr RP
    | ID LP expr_list RP
      { if (!IsArray($1->s_name))
      AddTypeToSymbol(FUNC_TYPE, $1->s_name, NO_TYPE);}
    | ID LP expr_list RP LP range_expr RP
    | MINUS expr
    | NOT expr
    | expr POWER expr
    | expr STAR expr
    | expr SLASH expr
    | expr PLUS expr
    | expr MINUS expr
    | expr OR expr
    | expr AND expr
    | expr GT expr
    | expr LT expr
    | expr EQ expr
    | expr LE expr
    | expr GE expr
    | expr NE expr
    | expr CONCAT expr
    | LP expr RP

sign
    : PLUS
    | MINUS
```

9. Add an error-handling mechanism by adding an error token to the grammar
rules. The result is shown in Listing 5.23.

Listing 5.23 YACC Program for Example 2 (fgram9.y)

```
%{
/* begin of declarative C code */
#include <stdio.h>
#include <fcomp.h>

extern int        yylineno;
extern PARM_LIST *BldParmList();

%}
/* begin of YACC directives */

%union  {
    struct symbol    *y_sym;
    struct constant  *y_con;
    struct dcl_list  *y_dcl;
    struct parm_list *y_parm;
    char             *y_str;
    int               y_num;
}

/*
 * terminal symbols
```

```
  */
%token BLOCK
%token COMMON
%token IMPLICIT
%token NONE
%token INCLUDE
%token EXTERNAL
%token PROGRAM
%token SUBROUTINE
%token FUNCTION
%token END
%token INTEGER
%token REAL
%token CHARACTER
%token LOGICAL
%token RETURN
%token CONTINUE
%token LP
%token RP
%token COMMA
%token CR
%token STAR
%token PARAMETER
%token ASSIGNTO
%token DOUBLE
%token PRECISION
%token DATA
%token CALL
%token IF
%token THEN
%token ELSE
%token ELSEIF
%token ENDIF
%token GT
%token LT
%token EQ
%token LE
%token GE
%token NE
%token PLUS
%token MINUS
%token STAR
%token SLASH
%token OR
%token AND
%token NOT
%token GOTO
%token LABEL
%token COLON
%token CONCAT
%token POWER
%token TRUE
%token FALSE
%token STOP
```

```
%token DIMENSION
%token ICON
%token FCON
%token LI
%token ID

%token <y_sym> ID
%token <y_con> ICON
%token <y_con> FCON
%token <y_con> LI

%type   <y_num> function_type
%type   <y_num> expr_list
%type   <y_parm> optional_parameter_list, parameter_list
%type   <y_dcl> declarator_list
%type   <y_num> optional_argument, argument_list
%type   <y_num> simple_statement

/*   precedence table */
%right ASSIGNTO
%left  OR
%left  AND
%left  LE GE EQ LT NE GT
%left  COLON
%left  PLUS MINUS
%left  STAR SLASH CONCAT
%left  POWER
%left  NOT UMINUS

%% /* begin of rule section */

program: {init();}
   program_units
   {terminate();}

program_units
   : program_unit
   | program_unit program_units

program_unit
   : program_definition
     {end_definition();}
   | function_definition
     {end_definition();}
   | subroutine_definition
     {end_definition();}
   | block_definition
     {end_definition();}

program_definition
   : program_heading
     declarations
     statements
     END

program_heading
   : PROGRAM ID
```

```
              {AddTypeToSymbol(PROG_TYPE,$2->s_name, NO_TYPE);}

function_definition
    : function_heading
      declarations
      statements
      END

function_heading
    : function_declaration
      optional_parameter_list
      {PrtParmList($2);}

function_declaration
    : function_type FUNCTION ID
      {AddTypeToSymbol(FUNC_TYPE,$3->s_name,$1);}

function_type
    : {$$ = NO_TYPE;}
    | INTEGER
      {$$ = INTEGER_TYPE;}
    | REAL
      {$$ = REAL_TYPE;}
    | DOUBLE PRECISION
      {$$ = DOUBLE_TYPE;}
    | LOGICAL
      {$$ = LOGICAL_TYPE;}
    | CHARACTER
      {$$ = CHAR_TYPE;}
    | CHARACTER STAR ICON
      {$$ = CHAR_TYPE;}

subroutine_definition
    : subroutine_heading
      declarations
      statements
      END

subroutine_heading
    : subroutine_declaration
      optional_parameter_list
      {PrtParmList($2);}

subroutine_declaration
    : SUBROUTINE ID
      {AddTypeToSymbol(SUBR_TYPE, $2->s_name,NO_TYPE);}

block_definition
    : block_heading
      declarations
      END

block_heading
    : BLOCK DATA ID
      {AddTypeToSymbol(BLOCK_TYPE,$3->s_name,NO_TYPE);}

optional_parameter_list
```

```
        : {$$ = NULL;}
        | LP parameter_list RP
          {$$ = $2;}

parameter_list
        : ID
          {$$=BldParmList($1->s_name,NULL);
          AddTypeToSymbol(PARM_TYPE, $1->s_name, NO_TYPE);}
        | parameter_list COMMA ID
          {$$ = BldParmList($3->s_name,$1);
          AddTypeToSymbol(PARM_TYPE, $3->s_name, NO_TYPE);}
        | error

declarations
        : declarations declaration
        | declaration

declaration
        : type_declaration
        | data_initiation
        | parm_initiation
        | IMPLICIT NONE
        | INCLUDE LI
        | EXTERNAL var_List

type_declaration
        : INTEGER declarator_list
          {AddTypesToSymbols($2, INTEGER_TYPE);}
        | REAL     declarator_list
          {AddTypesToSymbols($2, REAL_TYPE);}
        | LOGICAL  declarator_list
          {AddTypesToSymbols($2, LOGICAL_TYPE);}
        | DOUBLE PRECISION  declarator_list
          {AddTypesToSymbols($3, DOUBLE_TYPE);}
        | CHARACTER  declarator_list
          {AddTypesToSymbols($2, CHAR_TYPE);}
        | CHARACTER STAR ICON declarator_list
          {AddTypesToSymbols($4, CHAR_TYPE);}
        | error

block_declaration
        : COMMON SLASH ID SLASH var_list
          {AddTypeToSymbol(COMMON_TYPE,$3->s_name,NO_TYPE);}

data_initiation
        : DATA var_data_pairs

parm_initiation
        : PARAMETER
          LP assign_params RP

var_data_pairs
        : var_list SLASH val_list SLASH

assign_params
        : ID ASSIGNTO expr
```

```
            | assign_params COMMA ID ASSIGNTO expr

    var_list
        : ID
        | var_list COMMA ID
        | ID LP ICON RP

    declarator_list
        : ID
          {$$ = (DCL_LIST *)BldDclList(VAR_TYPE, $1->s_name, NULL);}
        | declarator_list COMMA ID
          {$$ = (DCL_LIST *)BldDclList(VAR_TYPE, $3->s_name,  $1);}
        | ID LP STAR RP
          {$$ = (DCL_LIST *)BldDclList(AVAR_TYPE, $1->s_name,  NULL);}
        | declarator_list COMMA ID LP STAR RP
          {$$ = (DCL_LIST *)BldDclList(AVAR_TYPE, $3->s_name,  $1);}
        | ID LP range_expr RP
          {$$ = (DCL_LIST *)BldDclList(AVAR_TYPE, $1->s_name,  NULL);}
        | declarator_list COMMA ID LP range_expr RP
          {$$ = (DCL_LIST *)BldDclList(AVAR_TYPE, $3->s_name,   $1);}
        | declarator_list COMMA ID LP expr RP
          {$$ = (DCL_LIST *)BldDclList(AVAR_TYPE, $3->s_name,  $1);}
        | ID LP expr RP
          {$$ = (DCL_LIST *)BldDclList(AVAR_TYPE, $1->s_name,  NULL);}

    range_expr
        : expr COLON expr

    val_list
        : sign ICON
        | ICON
        | sign FCON
        | FCON
        | TRUE
        | FALSE
        | LI
        | ICON STAR ICON
        | ICON STAR sign ICON
        | ICON STAR FCON
        | ICON STAR sign FCON
        | ICON STAR TRUE
        | ICON STAR FALSE
        | val_list COMMA ICON
        | val_list COMMA sign ICON
        | val_list COMMA FCON
        | val_list COMMA sign FCON
        | val_list COMMA TRUE
        | val_list COMMA FALSE
        | val_list COMMA LI

    statements
        : statement
        | statement statements

    statement
        : simple_statement
```

```
        | compound_statement
        | LABEL simple_statement
        | LABEL compound_statement
        | error

   simple_statement
      : STOP
        {$$=0;}
      | RETURN
        {$$=0;}
      | CONTINUE
        {$$=0;}
      | GOTO ICON
        {$$=0;}
      | DO ICON ID ASSIGNTO triplet
        {$$=0;}
      | ID ASSIGNTO expr
        {$$=0;}
      | ID LP expr RP ASSIGNTO expr
        {$$=0;}
      | ID LP range_expr RP ASSIGNTO expr
        {$$=0;}
      | ID LP expr RP LP range_expr RP ASSIGNTO expr
        {$$=0;}
      | CALL ID LP optional_argument_list RP
        {AddTypeToSymbol(SUBR_TYPE, $2->s_name,NO_TYPE);$$=0;}

   triplet
      : initial_value COMMA inc final_value

   initial_value
      : expr

   inc
      : expr

   final_value
      :
      | COMMA expr

   optional_argument
      : {$$ = 0;}
      | LP argument_list RP
        {$$ = $2;}

   argument_list
      : expr
        {$$ = 1;}
      | argument_list COMMA expr
        {$$ = $1 + 1;}

   expr_list
      : expr
        {$$=1;}
      | expr_list COMMA expr
        {$$ = $1+1;}
```

```
compound_statement
    : if_prefix simple_statement
    | if_prefix then_part endif
    | if_prefix then_part ELSE statements endif
    | if_prefix then_part else_if_else

if_prefix
    : IF cond

cond
    : LP expr RP

else_if_else
    : ELSEIF cond then_part endif
    | ELSEIF cond then_part else_part endif
    | ELSEIF cond then_part else_if_else

endif
    : ENDIF
    | END IF

then_part
    : THEN statements

else_part
    : ELSE statements

expr
    : ICON
    | FCON
    | TRUE
    | FALSE
    | LI
    | ID
    | ID LP range_expr RP
    | ID LP expr_list RP
      { if (!IsArray($1->s_name))
            AddTypeToSymbol(FUNC_TYPE, $1->s_name, NO_TYPE);}
    | ID LP expr_list RP LP range_expr RP
    | MINUS expr
    | NOT expr
    | expr POWER expr
    | expr STAR expr
    | expr SLASH expr
    | expr PLUS expr
    | expr MINUS expr
    | expr OR expr
    | expr AND expr
    | expr GT expr
    | expr LT expr
    | expr EQ expr
    | expr LE expr
    | expr GE expr
    | expr NE expr
    | expr CONCAT expr
    | LP expr RP
```

```
sign
  : PLUS
  | MINUS

%% /* begin of user C code */

void resync(synchar)
char synchar;
{
   int ch;

   while ((ch = input()) != 0)
      if ( ch == synchar)
         break;
}
```

10. Prepare a makefile to execute yacc, lex, and cc commands. The result is shown in Listings 5.24, 5.25, and 5.26.

Listing 5.24 Makefile to Create Library libLang.a

```
.SUFFIXES:
.SUFFIXES:  .a .o .c .l .y

COMPILE.c =  cc
CFLAGS=       -DDEBUG -I(INC) -c -g
CPPFLAGS=
YACC=         yacc
YFLAGS=       -dvl
LEX=          lex
LFLAGS=       -t
RM=           rm
MV=           mv
CP=           cp
SED=          sed

LPATH=     /usr2/shen/parser
SRC=  $(LPATH)/src
INC=  $(LPATH)/inc
LIB=  $(LPATH)/lib
BIN=  $(LPATH)/bin

LANG_SRC=$(SRC)/lang
LANG_LIB=$(LIB)/libLang.a

OBJECTS=  \
   $(LANG_LIB)(fgram.o)   \
   $(LANG_LIB)(flex.o)

.PRECIOUS: $(LANG_LIB)

.y.a:
   @echo execute my .y.a rule
   $(YACC) $(YFLAGS) $(LANG_SRC)/$<
   $(SED) '/#line/d' y.tab.c > $*.c
   $(COMPILE.c) $(CPPFLAGS) $(CFLAGS) $*.c
   $(AR) $(ARFLAGS) $@ $*.o
```

```
   $(RM) $*.o y.tab.c
   $(MV) $*.c $*.c.debug

.l.a:
   @echo execute my .l.a rule
   $(LEX) $(LFLAGS) $(LANG_SRC)/$<  > $*.c
   $(COMPILE.c) $(CPPFLAGS) $(CFLAGS) $*.c
   $(RM) $*.o
   $(MV) $(LEXSRC).c $(LEXSRC).c.debug

$(LANG_LIB): $(OBJECTS)
   ranlib $(LANG_LIB)
```

Listing 5.25 Makefile to Create Library libSub.a

```
.SUFFIXES:
.SUFFIXES:  .a .o .c .l .y

COMPILE.c =  cc
CFLAGS=       -DDEBUG -I(INC) -c -g
CPPFLAGS=
RM=           rm
MV=           mv
CP=           cp
SED=          sed

LPATH=     /usr2/shen/parser
SRC=  $(LPATH)/src
INC=  $(LPATH)/inc
LIB=  $(LPATH)/lib
BIN=  $(LPATH)/bin

SUB_SRC=$(SRC)/sub
SUB_LIB=$(LIB)/libSub.a

OBJECTS=  \
   $(SUB_LIB)(fsub.o)

.PRECIOUS: $(SUB_LIB)

.c.a:
   @echo execute my .c.a rule
   $(COMPILE.c) $(CPPFLAGS) $(CFLAGS) $*.c
   $(AR) $(ARFLAGS) $@ $*.o
   $(RM) $*.o

$(SUB_LIB): $(OBJECTS)
   ranlib $(SUB_LIB)
```

Listing 5.26 Makefile to Create the Executable

```
.SUFFIXES:
.SUFFIXES:  .a .o .c .l .y

COMPILE.c =  cc
CFLAGS=       -DDEBUG -I(INC) -c -g
```

```
CPPFLAGS=
RM=             rm
MV=             mv
CP=             cp
SED=            sed

LPATH=      /usr2/shen/parser
SRC=   $(LPATH)/src
INC=   $(LPATH)/inc
LIB=   $(LPATH)/lib
BIN=   $(LPATH)/bin

MAIN_SRC=$(SRC)/main

LIBS= \
      $(LIB)/libLang.a \
      $(LIB)/libSub.a

.c.o:
      @echo my .c.o rule
      $(COMPILE.c)  $(CPPFLAGS)  $(CFLAGS)  $(MAIN_SCR)/$<

fparser: fmain.o
      cc -g  fmain.o $(LIBS)  -11  -lm  -o $(BIN)/$@
```

5.15 SUMMARY

This chapter began with a clear description of YACC. Then we outlined a YACC program format. A discussion of YACC's parsing mechanism gave a better understanding
of this YACC utility. One key issue in the chapter explained how to tie the LEX and
YACC programs together so that they can work perfectly. The shift/reduce and reduce/
reduce concepts were introduced to help the user identify the problem for a YACC program more easily. Error handling has been a major problem in writing YACC programs, and we tried to make it as simple as possible. Finally, we presented a step-by-
step procedure to write a YACC program. For readers who wish to modify the YACC
utility, a section on the YACC patch provided guidance. Two examples also were given
to demonstrate how straightforward it is to write a YACC application following this
step-by-step procedure.

The Source Code Debugger (dbx)

6.1 INTRODUCTION

Among the program development tools, dbx is one of the most useful, often used on a daily basis. dbx is an interactive debugger that operates on the source level and is line-oriented. It has two distinct running modes: post-mortem and live mode. In the post-mortem mode, the user runs an application until it crashes. After the program crashes, it creates a core file, which dbx uses to reconstruct the core image. The user issues the where dbx command to show the stack at the time the program aborted. However, this post-mortem way to debug is not recommended because it takes too long to create a core file, and it doesn't show what the program went through before it received the core dump.

To prevent an application from creating the core dump file when it aborts, you need to set the resource coredumpsize to zero in your .cshrc file, or issue a command line using

```
limit  coredumpsize  0
```

In the live debugging mode, dbx starts the application program. After the dbx loads the executable but before it starts, the user needs to set at least one breakpoint. When the program finally stops at the breakpoint, the user can examine the variables' values and look at the current stack. He or she then can step through the program and examine the relevant data values.

6.2 CREATING AN EXECUTABLE MODULE FOR DBX

For dbx to work, you must compile the programs you want to debug using the -g option, so that the object file contains the symbolic information. Take the temperature conversion program for example: You have a main program that reads the temperature in Fahrenheit and a subroutine that converts the Fahrenheit degree into Celsius. The simple makefile to create an executable module for dbx is

```
fahr_to_celsius:  main.o  sub.o
    cc  main.o sub.o  -o fahr_to_celsius

main.o:  main.c
    cc  -c -g  main.c

sub.o:     sub.o
    cc  -c -g sub.c
```

6.3 INVOKING DBX

To start the debugger, type

```
dbx options executable
```

The options differ from machine to machine. In most cases, the options are not needed. If it is necessary, use a manual page to discover the meanings for these options.

6.4 INITIAL SETUP FOR DBX (.dbxinit)

Before you run dbx, you should set up the .dbxinit in your home directory to save a lot of typing. Listing 6.1 is an example of a .dbxinit file. This .dbxinit file has two dbx commands: use and alias. The use command tells dbx where to look for the source files in the order of the directory names. In this example, dbx first searches the current directory for the source file. If it fails, it searches the /usr/shen/src/main directory for the required source file, and so on. The alias command allows the user to use short alias names instead of long command names. This example uses p as the print alias, n as the next alias, and so forth.

Listing 6.1 An Example of the .dbxinit File

```
use    .  /usr/shen/src/main   /usr/shen/src/sub     /usr/mike/src/sub
alias p  print
alias l  list
alias n  next
alias s  step
alias q  quit
alias c  cont
alias w  where
alias r  run
```

```
alias a  assign
alias rj "run -infile   /usr/shen/data/test.dat   -outfile /usr/shen/data/out.dat"
```

6.5 DBX EXPRESSIONS

dbx allows you to print expressions, which, in dbx, are combinations of variables, constants, function calls, and operators. Hexadecimal constants begin with 0x and octal constants with 0. Character constants must be enclosed in single quotes. The following operators are valid operators in forming dbx expressions:

Operator	Function
*	denotes contents of
&	denotes address of
[ ]	denotes subscript array expression
.	references a field of a structure
->	references a field from a structure pointer
(type)	type cast
sizeof	size of a variable or type

6.6 SUBCOMMANDS FOR DBX

The subcommands for dbx are standard across all platforms. After you invoke the dbx, use the help subcommand to list all the available subcommands on that machine. On a SUN workstation, use help subcommand-name to find each individual subcommand's function. On an IBMRS system, use the man dbx to discover each individual subcommand's function. You probably need only a few of the subcommands for your daily debugging work; Table 6.1 shows the often-used subcommands.

6.7 SETTING BREAKPOINTS IN DBX

There are two ways you can set a breakpoint using the stop command. The first is to set a breakpoint at the beginning of a function by using stop in function-name. For example, if you want dbx to stop at the beginning of the program, use

```
stop in main
```

The second way is to set the breakpoint at a certain line number in a certain source module. For example, if you want to stop at line 57 of module init.c, use

```
stop at "init.c":57
```

After you set all the breakpoints, double-check them using the status command.

Table 6.1 Common Subcommands for dbx

Subcommand	Function
alias	creates the aliases for dbx subcommands
assign	assigns a value to a variable
call	executes the code associated with the named function
cont	changes the program execution from step mode to continuous mode
delete	deletes breakpoint
help	prints out a synopsis of common dbx subcommands
list	lists source code
next	steps to the next line (skips function call)
print	prints symbol value
quit	quits dbx
run	starts running the program under dbx
status	shows the number of breakpoints set so far
step	steps through program at the line level (steps into function)
stop	sets breakpoint
use	sets the list of directories for a source file search
whatis	prints the declaration of a name
where	lists active procedures (i.e. top of stack)
whereis	prints the full qualifications of all symbols whose names match the specified identifier
which	prints the full qualifications of the given identifier

6.8 EXAMINING MEMORY CONTENTS

Sometimes you need to see the memory contents in certain memory locations—for example, the ASCII data. Use the command

```
address/[count] [mode]
```

This tells dbx to display the memory contents starting at the memory location expressed by address and continue until the count items are displayed on the screen. The mode specifies which format the data is displayed. Table 6.2 lists the modes that are available on most machines:

Table 6.2 Available Modes to Display Memory Content

Modes	Data Format
D	displays a word in decimal
d	displays a half-word in decimal
O	displays a word in octal
o	displays a half-word in octal
X	displays a word in hexadecimal
x	displays a half-word in hexadecimal
c	displays a byte as a character
s	displays a string of characters terminated by a null byte
f	displays a single-precision real number
F	displays a double-precision real number
E	displays an extended-precision real number

Here are some examples of displaying memory contents using these modes:

`0x00045678/20c`   displays 20 characters starting at location 0x00045678

`0x00045678/10D`   displays 10 words in decimal starting at location 0x00045678

6.9 DEBUGGING A SEPARATE PROCESS

Sometimes you need to debug a separate process that a parent process spawns off during the execution. The concurrent server using socket as the communication mechanism is one example. The server spends most of its time listening to the queue. Once the queue receives a message, the server process forks a child process to handle the incoming message. In this case, the child process is a separate process, and you cannot debug it using the normal invoking method mentioned in Section 6.3. Instead, if you know the process-id of the process currently running, use dbx's attach mechanism to attach the dbx to the process you want to debug, as Table 6.3 shows. The key is the process-id. If you know the process-id of the child process, you can attach dbx to it using its pid number. To find the child process's pid number before it terminates, you need to write an infinite loop in the code the child process must go through. While the child process is looping, you can use another window to issue a ps command and discover its pid number. Here is an example of what to write in the code the child process must go through:

```
while (debug);
```

with debug initially set to an integer value one. First, start dbx by running the parent process. After you step through the fork() statement, a child process is created. You immediately use the other window and issue a ps command, then pipe the output to a grep command to select the process' executable filename.

```
ps  ax | grep server
```

where server is the process' executable filename. You should see two lines with the same executable filenames but different pids. Let's say the child pid number is 1234. Use the following command to attach dbx to the child process (assuming that programs are running under IBMRS platform):

```
dbx -a 1234
```

Different platforms have different ways to attach dbx to a separate process. Table 6.3 shows how to attach dbx to a separate process for some of the popular platforms. After dbx has successfully attached to the child process, you must set one breakpoint at the line at the statement

```
while (debug);
```

then type the cont subcommand. dbx should stop at the breakpoint. You then use the assign subcommand to change the value of the variable "debug" to zero to break out of the loop. From that point, continue as you would normally.

Table 6.3 dbx Command Options for Attaching to a Separate Process

dbx command	Platform
dbx -a pid	IBM
dbx executable_filename pid	SUN
dbx -p pid	SGI
csd -a pid executable_filename	CONVEX

6.10 SUMMARY

This chapter's purpose is to bring the reader enough knowledge that he or she can easily set up the .dbxinit file, set breakpoints, step through the source code, print out values for variables and structures, and examine the memory contents. This chapter also discussed how to debug a separate process using dbx. Since more and more applications are taking the client/server approach, the capability to debug a separate process has become quite important.

Unix Programming

7.1 Introduction

This chapter addresses seven of the most useful UNIX programming objects: signal, FIFO, time/timer, exclusive lock, dynamic memory, socket, and RPC.

7.2 Programming with Signals

Signals are interrupts generated at a terminal (quit, interrupt, stop), by a program error (bus error, segmentation violation), or at the request of a program (kill), to inform processes of certain events occurring. Most signals terminate the receiving process.

7.2.1 How Signals Are Handled

In UNIX, when a process receives a signal, it can handle the signal in one of three ways.

☞ The process doesn't do anything specifically, and lets the operating system take care of it (i.e. handle by default).

☞ The process specifies which routine to execute when a certain interrupt signal is received (i.e. trapped by the program).

☞ The process specifies that nothing is done when a certain signal is received (i.e. ignored by the program).

7.2.2 Types of Signals

The number of signals each machine provides varies from one system to another. Use the command line kill -l to list all the signals each system provides. The output of this command for a BSD system appears as

```
HUP INT QUIT ILL TRAP ABRT EMT FPE KILL BUS SEGV SYS PIPE ALRM TERM URG STOP
TSTP CONT CHLD TTIN TTOU IO XCPU XFSZ VTALRM PROF WINCH LOST USR1 USR2
```

The actual signal numbers add the prefix SIG to each of the signals listed above. For example, the bus error signal number is SIGBUS, and the segmentation violation signal number is SIGSEGV. You can find the definitions for all signals defined in the header file /usr/include/sys/signal.h. The following list shows all the signals available in the 4.3BSD system and a brief description for each signal.

SIGHUP	hangup
SIGINT	interrupt generated by Ctrl-C on the keyboard
SIGQUIT	quit generated by Ctrl-\ on the keyboard
SIGILL	illegal instruction
SIGTRAP	trace trap
SIGABRT	abort
SIGEMT	EMT instruction
SIGFPE	floating point exception (e.g. divide by zero)
SIGKILL	kill. This signal can not be caught or ignored.
SIGBUS	bus error
SIGSEGV	segmentation violation
SIGSYS	bad argument to a system call
SIGPIPE	write on a pipe with no one to read it
SIGALRM	alarm clock
SIGTERM	software termination signal from kill
SIGURG	urgent condition on IO channel
SIGSTOP	sendable stop signal not from keyboard
SIGTSTP	stop signal generated from keyboard
SIGCONT	continue a stopped process
SIGCHLD	child process death
SIGTTIN	background read attempted from keyboard

SIGTTOU	background write attempted to terminal
SIGIO	input/output possible signal
SIGXCPU	CPU time limit exceeded
SIGXFSZ	file size limit exceeded
SIGVTALRM	virtual timer alarm
SIGPROF	profiling timer alarm
SIGWINCH	window size changed
SIGLOST	resource lost (e.g. record lock lost)
SIGUSR1	user-defined signal one
SIGUSR2	user-defined signal two

7.2.3 Sending Signals to Processes

The system call kill is used to send signals to processes. It takes two arguments: The first is the process-id of the process to receive the signal, and the second is a signal number. Here is a synopsis of this function:

```
int kill(pid, sig)
int pid;
int sig;
```

7.2.4 Handling Signals within Processes

As we mention in Section 7.2.1, a process can handle signals in three ways. If the application program does not specify how to handle each signal, the operating system takes care of it by default. If the application program specifies how to handle certain signals specifically, it either can choose to ignore these signals or trap them and do something meaningful. The system call signal allows the application program to specify which signal it wants to catch, and how it will handle it once the signal is caught. The synopsis of the signal function call is

```
int (*signal(sig, func))()
int sig;
void (*func)();
```

It simply says that signal is a function that returns a pointer to an integer. The first argument, sig, is a signal number, and the second argument is a pointer to a function.

The following program shows how certain signals can be generated either by a program or from a keyboard, and how the program can set up the signal-handling routine to process each of them.

Eight common signals are selected in this example: SIGINT, SIGQUIT, SIGFPE, SIGSEGV, SIGBUS, SIGPIPE, SIGTERM, and SIGCHLD.

The program starts by setting up the signal handler for all eight signals. It then prompts for the signal to be generated. Based on the user's input, the program goes through the case statement, and executes the appropriate code either to generate the required signal or wait for the external event to occur. Once the signal is generated, it is trapped by the signal handler, and the signal handler has control.

The signal handler examines the signal number passed to it, and uses it to print the message indicating which signal is caught. Listing 7.1 shows the results.

Listing 7.1 signal_test.c

```
/*
 * signal_test.c
 */
#include <stdio.h>
#include <signal.h>

void SigHandler();

Main(argc, argv)
int   argc;
char *argv[];
{
    int  i, n, denom, num;
    int  pid, cpid;
    int  fd[2];
    int  selection;
    int  signum;
    int  len;
    int  *iptr;
    char *cptr;
    char buf[256];
    char inbuf[256];

    /* set up signal handlers */
    signal(SIGINT,  SigHandler);
    signal(SIGQUIT, SigHandler);
    signal(SIGFPE,  SigHandler);
    signal(SIGSEGV, SigHandler);
    signal(SIGBUS,  SigHandler);
    signal(SIGPIPE, SigHandler);
    signal(SIGTERM, SigHandler);
    signal(SIGCHLD, SigHandler);

    /* prompt user for signal to be generated */
    printf("Please select the signal you want to generate.\n");
    printf("1: SIGINT\n");
    printf("2: SIGQUIT\n");
    printf("3: SIGFPE\n");
    printf("4: SIGSEGV\n");
    printf("5: SIGBUS\n");
    printf("6: SIGPIPE\n");
    printf("7: SIGTERM\n");
    printf("8: SIGCHLD\n");
```

```c
/* read user response from keyboard */
scanf("%d", &selection);

switch (selection )
{
   case 1:
      signum = SIGINT;
      break;
   case 2:
      signum = SIGQUIT;
      break;
   case 3:
      signum = SIGFPE;
      break;
   case 4:
      signum = SIGSEGV;
      break;
   case 5:
      signum = SIGBUS;
      break;
   case 6:
      signum = SIGPIPE;
      break;
   case 7:
      signum = SIGTERM;
      break;
   case  8:
      signum = SIGCHLD;
      break;
   default:
      fprintf(stdout, "Selected number is not in the range.\n");
      break;
}

switch (signum)
{
   case SIGINT:
      while (1)
      pause();
      break;
   case SIGQUIT:
      while (1)
      pause();
      break;
   case SIGFPE:
      denom = 0;
      n = 1 / denom;
      break;
   case SIGSEGV:
      buf[12345678] = 'c';
      break;
   case SIGBUS:
      num = 20;
      cptr = (char *) &num;
```

```c
                cptr++;
                iptr = (int *) cptr;
                i = *iptr;
                break;
            case SIGPIPE:
                if (pipe(fd) == -1)
                {
                    fprintf( stderr, "pipe open error\n");
                    exit(-1);
                }
                close(fd[0]);
                strcpy(buf, "Good Morning!");
                n = write(fd[1], buf, strlen(buf));
                if ( n == -1)
                {
                    fprintf(stderr, "pipe write error\n");
                    exit(-1);
                }
                else if ( n == 0)
                    fprintf(stderr, "pipe full\n");
                break;
            case SIGTERM:
                pid = getpid();
                kill(pid, SIGTERM);
                break;
            case SIGCHLD:
                if (fork() == 0)
                { /* child process */
                    exit(0);
                }
                /* parent process */
                pause();
                break;
            default:
                fprintf(stderr, "Selected number is not in the range.\n");
                break;
        }
}

void SigHandler(sig)
int sig;
{
    char  buf[80];

    signal(sig, SIG_IGN);
    switch (sig)
    {
        case SIGINT:
            signal(SIGINT, SIG_IGN);
            fprintf(stdout, "caught signal: interrupt\n");
            fprintf(stdout, "Do you want to terminate program?(y/n)");
            scanf("%s", buf);
            signal(SIGINT, SigHandler);
            if (buf[0] == 'y')
```

```
            break;
        else
            return;
    case SIGQUIT:
        fprintf(stdout, "caught signal: quit\n");
        break;
    case SIGFPE:
        fprintf(stdout, "caught signal: floating-point exception\n");
        break;
    case SIGBUS:
        fprintf(stdout, "caught signal: bus error\n");
        break;
    case SIGSEGV:
        fprintf(stdout, "caught signal: segmentation violation\n");
        break;
    case SIGPIPE:
        fprintf(stdout, "caught signal: broken pipe\n");
        break;
    case SIGTERM:
        fprintf(stdout, "caught signal: software termination\n");
        break;
    case SIGCHLD:
        fprintf(stdout, "caught signal: death of child process\n");
        break;
    default:
        break;
    }
    exit(0);
}
```

7.3 PROGRAMMING WITH FIFO

FIFO stands for first in, first out. It is similar to a one-way pipe--the first byte of data written to it is the first byte of data read from it. Unlike a pipe, however, FIFO has a name, which makes it possible for unrelated processes to communicate with each other. That is why it is also called "named pipe."

7.3.1 FIFO Programming

Programming FIFOs is similar to programming files. Processes that choose to use FIFO as the communication mechanism among them first must create the FIFOs. A FIFO is created by the mknod() system call, which is defined as

```
#include <sys/types.h>
#include <sys/stat.h>

int mknod(file, mode, dev)
char *file;
int  mode;
int  dev;
```

where file is the full-path filename (which is the FIFO's name); mode is the file access mode and needs to be logically or'ed with the S_IFIFO flag to specify that a FIFO is being created; and dev is ignored when creating a FIFO.

Once the FIFOs are created, they must be opened for reading or writing using the open() system call. Normally (i.e. when the O_NDELAY flag is not set), when a FIFO is opened for reading, the open() system call waits until another process opens it for writing. The same is true for a FIFO opened for writing. On the other hand (i.e. when the O_NDELAY flag is set), when a FIFO is opened for reading, the open() system call returns immediately regardless of whether it has been opened for writing, but an open for writing returns an error if it hasn't been opened for reading. The O_NDELAY flag can be set either when the FIFO is opened or by calling fcntl() after the FIFO has been opened. It can be cleared only by calling fcntl().

Let's assume that one process has opened a FIFO for reading and another has opened it for writing. On the reader side, a read operation can be issued in this form:

```
nread = read(rfd, buf, MAXSIZE);
```

where rfd is the file descriptor returned from the open-for-read statement, buf is the buffer for storing the FIFO's incoming data, MAXSIZE is a constant that specifies the number of bytes requested, and nread is the actual amount of data read in bytes.

There are several keys when reading a FIFO. First, each FIFO has a capacity that limits the amount of data you can write to the FIFO pipe. It is also the maximum amount of data that can be read in one read operation. A FIFO pipe's capacity is implementation dependent, and is normally a multiple of 4,096 bytes.

Secondly, if the read operation requests less data than is available in the FIFO pipe, it returns only the requested amount of data. The rest of the data remains in the pipe for subsequent reads. If the read operation requests more data than is available in the FIFO pipe, only the data available is returned.

Third, if there is no data in the FIFO pipe, but some process opens it for writing, the read waits (assuming the O_NDELAY flag is not set). If there is no data in the FIFO pipe and no process opens it for writing, a read returns zero.

On the writer's side, a write operation can be issued as

```
nwrite = write(wfd, buf, len);
```

where wfd is the file descriptor returned from the open-for-write statement, buf is the buffer where the data is to be sent to the FIFO, len is an integer variable that specifies the amount of data to be sent in bytes, and nwrite is the actual amount of data written.

If you write less than the FIFO pipe's capacity, the write operation finishes without interruption. However, if you write more data than the FIFO's capacity, that amount of data is written to the FIFO first. The writer then is blocked. When any reader reads the data in the FIFO, the writer continues writing the rest of the data to the FIFO.

If a process writes to a pipe or a FIFO, but no processes have opened it for reading, the SIGPIPE signal is generated, and the write returns -1. If the process has not set up the signal handler to handle the SIGPIPE notification, the process terminates.

Listings 7.2, 7.3, and 7.4 present code listings for a general client/server application that uses a FIFO pipe. Listing 7.2 shows a server program code, Listing 7.3 shows a client program code, and Listing 7.4 shows a common FIFO subroutine.

Listing 7.2 server_fifo.c

```c
/*
 * server_fifo.c
 */
#include <stdio.h>
#include <fcntl.h>
#include <signal.h>

#define MAXBUF   16384

extern void SigHandler();

main()
{
    int   rfd, wfd;
    char *fifo1, *fifo2;
    char mode;
    char buf[MAXBUF];
    int   n, fd;
    int   size;

    /*
     * Create the FIFOs, then open them
     */
    fifo1 = (char *)CreateFIFO("FIFO1");
    if ((rfd = open(fifo1, O_RDONLY)) < 0)
    {
        printf("open FIFO %s failed\n", fifo1);
        exit(-1);
    }
    fifo2 = (char *)CreateFIFO("FIFO2");
    if ((wfd = open(fifo2, O_WRONLY)) < 0)
    {
        printf("open FIFO %s failed\n", fifo2);
        exit(-1);
    }

    /*
     * Set up SIGPIPE signal handler
     */
    signal(SIGPIPE, SigHandler);

    while (1)
    {
        size = 0;
        while (size == 0)
        {
            if ((size = GetFIFOSize(rfd)) == 0)
                WaitMilSec(1);
        }
```

```
        /*
         * read the data from FIFO
         */
        if ((n=read(rfd, buf, MAXBUF)) <= 0)
        {
            printf("server: read error\n");
            break;
        }
        printf("server: receive %d bytes of data\n", n);
        if (write(wfd, buf, n) !=n)
        {
            printf("server: write error\n");
            break;
        }
    }
    close(rfd);
    close(wfd);
    /* Delete the FIFOs */
    if (unlink(fifo1) < 0)
        printf("server: can't unlink file %s\n", fifo1);
    if (unlink(fifo2) < 0)
        printf("server: can't unlink file %s\n", fifo2);
    exit(0);
}
```

Listing 7.3 client_fifo.c

```
/*
 * client_fifo.c
 */
#include <stdio.h>
#include <fcntl.h>
#include <signal.h>

#define MAXLINE 128
#define MAXBUF  16384

extern void SigHandler();

main()
{
    int  rfd, wfd;
    char *fifo1, *fifo2;
    char buf[MAXLINE];
    char mode;

    /*
     * Create the FIFOs, and open them
     */
    fifo1 = (char *)CreateFIFO("FIFO1");
    if ((wfd = open(fifo1, O_WRONLY)) < 0)
    {
        printf("client: open FIFO %s failed\n", fifo1);
        exit(1);
    }
```

```c
    fifo2 = (char *)CreateFIFO("FIFO2");
    if ((rfd = open(fifo2, O_RDONLY)) < 0)
    {
        printf("client: open FIFO %s failed\n", fifo2);
        exit(1);
    }

    /*
     * Set up SIGPIPE signal handler
     */
    signal(SIGPIPE, SigHandler);

    while (1)
    {
        /*
         * prompt for selecting the operation mode
         */
        printf("Please select the operation mode:\n");
        printf(" 1: Interactive mode\n");
        printf(" 2: Send mode\n");
        printf(" 3: Receive mode\n");
        printf(" 4: Echo mode\n");
        printf("  9: Quit\n");
        if (fgets(buf, MAXLINE, stdin) != NULL)
            mode = buf[0];

        switch (mode) {
            case '1': /* interactive mode */
                printf("Interactive mode selected\n");
                Interactive(rfd, wfd);
                break;
            case '2': /* send mode */
                printf("Send mode selected\n");
                SendTo(rfd, wfd);
                break;
            case '3': /* receive mode */
                printf("Receive mode selected\n");
                ReceiveFrom(rfd, wfd);
                break;
            case '4': /* echo mode */
                printf("Echo mode selected\n");
                Echo(rfd, wfd);
                break;
            case '9':
                exit(-1);
                break;
            default:
                printf("Invalid mode selection\n");
                break;
        }
    }
    close(rfd);
    close(wfd);
    exit(0);
}
```

```c
int Interactive (rfd, wfd)
int rfd;
int wfd;
{   char buf[MAXBUF];
    int n;
    int nwrite;

    printf("Please enter the data to be transferred\n");
    if (fgets(buf, MAXBUF, stdin) == NULL)
    {
        printf("client: keyboard read error\n");
        exit(1);
    }
    n = strlen(buf);
    if (buf[n-1] == '\n') n--;
    if ( n != 0)
    {
        printf("write:%s\n", buf);
        if ((nwrite = write(wfd, buf, n)) !=n)
        {
            if (nwrite == -1)
            {
                printf("FIFO write error.\n");
                printf("There are no other processes have the FIFO ");
                printf("open  for reading\n");
            }
            else
                printf("FIFO write error\n");
        }
        /*
         * Read data from FIFO and write to stdout
         */
        if ((n=read(rfd, buf, MAXBUF)) > 0)
            printf("client: data read: %s\n", buf);

        if (n < 0)
        {
            printf("client: data read error\n");
            exit(1);
        }
    }
}

int SendTo(rfd, wfd)
int rfd;
int wfd;
{
    int   n, i;
    int   len;
    int   size;
    int   nbytes;
    int   start_num;
    int   outbuf[MAXBUF];
    char linebuf[MAXLINE];
```

```c
    printf("Please enter the starting integer number.\n");
    if (fgets(linebuf, MAXLINE, stdin) != NULL)
    {
        len = strlen(linebuf);
        linebuf[len-1] = '\0';
        start_num = atoi(linebuf);
    }

    printf("Please enter number of integers to be transferred.\n");
    if (fgets(linebuf, MAXLINE, stdin) != NULL)
    {
        len = strlen(linebuf);
        linebuf[len-1] = '\0';
        size = atoi(linebuf);
    }

    nbytes = size * sizeof(int);
    for (i=start_num; i<start_num+size; i++)
        outbuf[i-start_num] = i;

    if (write(wfd, outbuf, nbytes) != nbytes)
    {
        printf("pipe write error\n");
        return(1);
    }
    return(0);
}

int ReceiveFrom(rfd, wfd)
int rfd;
int wfd;
{
    int   n;
    int   inbuf[MAXBUF];

    if ((n=read(rfd, inbuf, MAXBUF)) >0)
    {
        printf("client: %d bytes data read \n", n);
        printf("first element is %d\n", inbuf[0]);
        printf("last element is %d\n", inbuf[n/sizeof(int) -1]);
    }
    else if (n == 0)
        printf("EOF reached\n");
    else
        printf("client: data read error\n");
    return(n);
}

int Echo(rfd, wfd)
int rfd;
int wfd;
{
    SendTo(rfd, wfd);
    ReceiveFrom(rfd, wfd);
}
```

Listing 7.4 fifo_sub.c

```c
/*
 * fifo_sub.c
 */
#include <stdio.h>
#include <signal.h>
#include <sys/types.h>
#include <sys/stat.h>
#include <sys/errno.h>
#include <sys/time.h>
extern int errno;

#define PERMS    0666
#define MAXBUF   16384
#define MAXLINE 128

char * CreateFIFO(fifoname)
char *fifoname;
{
   char *fullname;

   fullname = (char *)malloc(80);
   sprintf(fullname, "/tmp/%s", fifoname);
   if ((mknod(fullname, S_IFIFO|PERMS, 0) < 0) && (errno!=EEXIST))
   {
      printf("can't create fifo %s\n", fullname);
      exit(1);
   }
   return(fullname);
}

int GetFIFOSize(fd)
int fd;
{
   struct stat sb;
   int     size;

   if (fstat(fd, &sb) == -1)
   {
      printf("fstat error\n");
      return(-1);
   }
   return(sb.st_size);
}

int WaitMilSec(msec)
int msec;
{
   struct timeval timeout;
   timeout.tv_sec = 0;
   timeout.tv_usec = 1000 * msec;

   if ((select(0,0,0,0, &timeout)) < 0)
   {
      printf("select error\n");
```

```
      sleep(1);
   }
   return(0);
}

void SigHandler(sig)
int sig;
{
   signal(sig, SIG_IGN);
   switch (sig) {
   case SIGPIPE:
      printf("caught signal: broken pipe\n");
      break;
   default:
      break;
   }
}
```

7.4 Programming with Time/Timer

In many applications, we need to know when an event takes place. So when we record the event, we also put a time stamp along with it. In other applications, we may need to measure the time spent on a critical section to justify further code optimization.

Sometimes, we want the program to check something at certain time intervals. This requires the program to suspend itself for a certain period of time. We can achieve such a goal by using a sleeping timer. (An example of the sleeping timer is the sleep() system call, which takes a single argument: the amount of time to sleep in seconds.)

Finally, we also want to safeguard ourselves against events that should have happened within a given amount of time. For example, a process may issue an RPC call to a server demon and expect the result in 10 seconds. In this case, we use the alarm() system call to schedule an alarm. If the result does not come back in time, the SIGALRM signal notifies the process.

7.4.1 Telling Time

For us to tell time, we must first get the time and express it in the right format. Two system calls in UNIX obtain the time of day: the time() and gettimeofday(). The synopses for both system calls are

```
#include <time.h>
time_t time(clock)
time_t *clock;

#include <sys/time.h>
int gettimeofday(tvalp, tzp)
struct timeval *tvalp;
struct timezone *tzp;
```

The time() system call returns the time since 00:00:00 GM, Jan 1, 1970, measured in seconds. The actual time returned is placed in the long integer the clock points to (type time_t is defined as type long). The gettimeofday() system call returns the time in terms of seconds and microseconds. The gettimeofday() call takes two arguments: a pointer to a type timeval structure, and a pointer to a type timezone structure. Both are defined in the include file <sys/time.h>.

```
struct timeval {
    long    tv_sec;              /* seconds */
    long    tv_usec;            /* and microseconds */
};

struct timezone {
    int     tz_minuteswest;  /* minutes west of Greenwich */
    int     tz_dsttime;       /* type of dst correction */
};
```

For applications that need to tell time up to the second, time() system call is sufficient. Use gettimeofday() system call when time has to be precise to a fraction of a second.

Conventionally, there are two common ways of expressing the time of the day. The first one takes the form Wed Apr 12 14:40:26 1993; the second one takes the form 12/04/93 14:40:26. The first form is more descriptive, but the second is better for comparisons.

Listing 7.5 writes to output the current time of day in the descriptive form.

Listing 7.5 ascii_time.c

```
/*
 * ascii_time.c
 */
#include <stdio.h>
#define <time.h>

main()
{
    time_t  time();
    time_t  current_time;
    char    *ctime;
    char    *date;

    time(&current_time);
    date = ctime(&current_time);
    printf("Current time of the day is %s\n", date);
}
```

This program calls ctime(), which converts the time represented in a long integer to a time represented by a 26-character descriptive form string. The ctime() call's synopsis is

```
#include <time.h>
char *ctime(clock)
time_t *clock;
```

Listing 7.6 writes to output the current time of the day in numeric form.

Listing 7.6 numeric_time.c

```c
/*
 * numeric_time.c
 */
#include <stdio.h>
#include <time.h>
main()
{
    time_t time();
    char    *ctime();
    struct tm *localtime();
    struct tm *tod;
    time_t current_time;
    char    asc_date[18];

    time(&current_time);
    tod = localtime(&current_time);
    sprintf(asc_date, "%02d/%02d/%02d %02d:%02d:%02d",
        tod->tm_mday, tod->tm_mon+1, tod->tm_year,
        tod->tm_hour, tod->tm_min, tod->tm_sec);
    printf("Current time of the day is %s\n",asc_date);
}
```

Listing 7.6 calls function localtime(), which converts the time in seconds into a tm type structure, defined in the include file time.h as

```c
struct tm {
int   tm_sec;    /* seconds   0-59            */
int   tm_min;    /* minutes   0-59            */
int   tm_hour;   /* hours     0-23            */
int   tm_mday;   /* day of the month 1-31 */
int   tm_mon;    /* month     0-11            */
int   tm_year;   /* year - 1900              */
int   tm_wday;   /* day of week 0-6          */
int   tm_yday;   /* day of year 0-365        */
int   tm_isdst;  /* 1 if daylight saving   */
};
```

7.4.2 Measuring Processing Time

Sometimes it is desirable to measure the time spent performing a certain task. For example, we may want to know which of several algorithms is the fastest. In this case, we are interested in the CPU's execution time rather than the calendar time. We can obtain the CPU's execution time through the times() system call, defined as

```c
#include <sys/types.h>
#include <sys/times.h>
struct tms *times(tm)
struct tms *tm;
```

where struct tms is defined in <sys/times.h> as follows:

```
struct tms {
    time_t   tms_utime;  /* user time                  */
    time_t   tms_stime;  /* system time                */
    time_t   tms_cutime; /* children's user time   */
    time_t   tms_cstime; /* children's system time */
};
```

All times the times() system call returns are in 1/60 seconds. The getrusage() system call is another function you can call to get the CPU usage. It returns the CPU usage time in seconds and microseconds. Because the CPU time spent executing one piece of code is generally much less than a second, the getrusage() system call replaces the times() system call. The getrusage() system call is defined as

```
#include <sys/types.h>
#include <sys/time.h>
#include <sys/resource.h>

struct rusage * getrusage(who, rusagep)
int  who;
struct rusage *rusagep;
```

where you can take only either the value RUSAGE_SELF or RUSAGE_CHILDREN, and struct rusage is defined in <sys/resource.h> as

```
struct rusage {
    struct timeval  ru_utime;  /* user time used     */
    struct timeval  ru_stime;  /* system time used   */
    long    ru_maxrss;
    long    ru_ixrss;
    long    ru_idrss;
    long    ru_isrss;
    long    ru_minflt;
    long    ru_majflt;
    long    ru_nswap;
    long    ru_inblock;
    long    ru_oublock;
    long    ru_msgsnd;
    long    ru_msgrcv;
    long    ru_nsignals;
    long    ru_nvcsw;
    long    ru_nivcsw;
};
```

If you use RUSAGE_SELF, the returned information is for the current process. Otherwise, use RUSAGE_CHILDREN to get the resource usage information for all the current process's terminated children.

Listing 7.7 compares the times spent initializing an integer array, using two different methods. The first uses a pointer to reference each integer in the array; the second uses an array index to reference each integer.

Listing 7.7 comp_time.c

```c
/*
 * comp_time.c
 */
#include <stdio.h>
#include <sys/types.h>
#include <sys/times.h>
#include <sys/time.h>
#include <sys/resource.h>

void GetTimeUsageInfo();

main(argc, argv)
int   argc;
char *argv[];
{
    struct tm *tod;
    time_t     current_time;
    int        count;
    int        rtn;
    int        size;
    int        i;
    int        *data;
    int        *ptr;
    double     clock1, ucpu1, scpu1;
    double     clock2, ucpu2, scpu2;
    double     clock3, ucpu3, scpu3;

    if (argc < 2)
    {
        printf("Usage: comp_time array_size\n");
        exit(-1);
    }
    size = atoi(argv[1]);

    data = (int *)malloc(size * sizeof(int));
    /*
     *   record begin time for method 1
     */
    GetTimeUsageInfo(&clock1, &ucpu1, &scpu1);

    ptr = data;
    for (i=0; i< size; i++)
       *ptr++ = i;
    /*
     *   record end time for method 1; it is also the begin time for method 2
     */
    GetTimeUsageInfo(&clock2, &ucpu2, &scpu2);

    for (i=0; i< size; i++)
       data[i] = i;
    /*
     *   record end time for method 2
     */
    GetTimeUsageInfo(&clock3, &ucpu3, &scpu3);
```

```
   printf("     clock time     user CPU time   System CPU time\n");
   printf(" 1:    %lf            %lf            %lf\n",
      clock2-clock1, ucpu2-ucpu1, scpu2-scpu1);
   printf(" 2:    %lf            %lf            %lf\n",
      clock3-clock2, ucpu3-ucpu2, scpu3-scpu2);
}

void GetTimeUsageInfo(clk, ucpu, scpu)
double *clk, *ucpu, *scpu;
{
   struct rusage rusage_now;
   struct timeval tnow;
   struct timezone tz;

   gettimeofday(&tnow, &tz);
   getrusage(RUSAGE_SELF, &rusage_now);
   *clk =tnow.tv_sec + tnow.tv_usec/1000000.0;
   *ucpu=rusage_now.ru_utime.tv_sec +
      rusage_now.ru_utime.tv_usec/1000000.0;
   *scpu=rusage_now.ru_stime.tv_sec +
      rusage_now.ru_stime.tv_usec/1000000.0;
   return;
}
```

7.4.3 Sleeping Timer

The sleep() system call is the most commonly used sleeping timer. It takes a single argument: the number of seconds to sleep. The program resumes after those seconds elapse. The sleep() system call's only drawback is that it provides a time resolution of seconds. You can easily implement a higher precision sleep timer with microsecond resolution by using the select() system call.

The select() system call's synopsis is

```
#include <sys/types.h>
#include <sys/time.h>
#include <sys/select.h>

int select(nfds, readfds, writefds, exceptfds, timeout)
int     nfds;
fd_set *readfds;
fd_set *writefds;
fd_set *exceptfds;
struct timeval *timeout;
```

where nfds is the number of file descriptors to check; readfds, writefds, and exceptfds point to the array of file descriptors to check to see if they are ready for reading or writing, or a certain exceptional event has occurred; and timeout points to a structure of type timeval.

The select() system call allows the user process to wait until one of the multiple events or a timeout occurs. When either happens, the user process wakes up, and the process continues. Since we are interested only in the timeout event, we can specify zero to the first argument, NULL to the second, third, and fourth arguments to the select() system call, and specify only the timeout time.

Listing 7.8 is a program that uses the select() system call to implement a sleeping timer. It verifies the result against the time() system call.

Listing 7.8 usleep.c

```c
/*
 * usleep.c
 */
#include <sys/types.h>
#include <sys/time.h>
#include <sys/select.h>

main(argc, argv)
int   argc;
char *argv[];
{
    int   atoi();
    int   i;
    struct timeval timeout;
    time_t current_time;

    if (argc != 3)
    {
        printf("Usage: usleep seconds microseconds\n");
        exit(-1);
    }

    timeout.tv_sec  = atoi(argv[1]);
    timeout.tv_usec = atoi(argv[2]);

    time(&current_time);        /* get current time in seconds */
    printf("current time in seconds: %ld\n", current_time);

    for (i=0; i<1000; i++)
        if (select(0, (fd_set *) 0, (fd_set *) 0, (fd_set *) 0, &timeout) < 0)
        {
            printf("select() call error\n");
            exit(-1);
        }

    time(&current_time);        /* get current time in seconds */
    printf("current time in seconds: %ld\n", current_time);
}
```

7.4.4 Alarm Timer

The alarm() system call is the most commonly used alarm timer. It takes a single argument: the number of seconds before the alarm sounds. When the alarm sounds, a SIGALRM signal is delivered to the process.

Listing 7.9 is a program that measures the average amount of time it takes to make a time() system call.

Listing 7.9 measure_time.c

```c
/*
 * measure_time.c
 */
#include <stdio.h>
#include <signal.h>
#include <sys/types.h>
#include <sys/time.h>

int  timeout =0;

static void SigHandler();

main(argc, argv)
int  argc;
char *argv[];
{
    long count = 0;
    time_t current_time;

    if (signal(SIGALRM, SigHandler) == BADSIG)
    {
        printf("signal error\n");
        exit(-1);
    }
    /*
     * set alarm for one second
     */
    alarm(1);
    while (! timeout)
    {    /* alarm not off yet */
        time(&current_time);
        count++;
    }
    printf("A time() call takes %lf second\n", 1.0/(float)count);
}

void SigHandler(sig)
int sig;
{
    timeout = 1;
}
```

7.5 PROGRAMMING WITH LOCKS

Two or more processes can gain exclusive access to a resource (a file, a database record, or a piece of code in main memory) through locks. Locks play an important role in writing both the kernel and application codes. The semaphore, which gains exclusive access to a critical section of code, is an example of a lock used in the kernel. A process that enters into this critical section first locks out every other process until it leaves that section. You can find many instances in the application code where one process places a lock on a database record or file while it updates it.

A common problem with the ar command is that the library is not locked when a user is updating it. Anyone can execute the ar command and thus destroy the object library.

Here are three commonly used locking mechanisms:

☞ The file-locking system calls such as lockf() and flock(): The differences between flock() and lockf() system calls are

> flock() provides file locking only (no record locking) while lockf() provides both, and

> when system call flock() is used, the lock can be seen only on the local processor, while lockf() allows other processors to see the lock. So only lockf() should be used in a networked environment.

☞ The create() system call: The create() system call fails if the file already exists, and if the calling process does not have write permission for the file. The idea is to create an ancillary file to indicate a process has a lock on another resource. However, the ancillary file that acts as the lock file might remain should the system crash. In that case, someone must manually remove the lock file--otherwise the resource is locked forever.

☞ Semaphore: This technique can be used only on the local processor.

The remaining sections discuss how to implement locks using only the lockf() system call.

7.5.1 Implementing Locks Using lockf() System Call

The synopsis for lockf() system call is

```
#include <unistd.h>

int lockf(fd, cmd, size)
int fd;
int cmd;
long size;
```

where fd is an open file descriptor (it must have the write permission for this system call to be successful); and cmd is the control value that specifies the action to take. The accepted values for cmd are defined in <unistd.h> header file as

```
#define F_ULOCK    0    /* unlock a previous locked section  */
#define F_LOCK     1    /* lock a section for exclusive use   */
#define F_TLOCK    2    /* test and lock a section            */
#define F_TEST     3    /* test to see if a section is locked */
```

Finally, size is the number of bytes to lock or unlock. If size is zero, the section that starts at the current file offsets to the end of the file is locked. Listings 7.10 and 7.11 show the results.

Listing 7.10 lock_sub.c

```c
/*
 * lock_sub.c
 */
#include <stdio.h>
#include <fcntl.h>
#include <unistd.h>

#define MAXLINE                 120
#define LOCK_SUCCEED            0
#define LOCK_EXIST              1
#define FILE_NOT_EXIST          2
#define LOCK_FAIL               3
#define UNLOCK_SUCCEED          0
#define UNLOCK_FAIL             4

int lock(filename)
char *filename;
{
   int  fd;
   int  len;
   int  nwrite;
   char buf[MAXLINE];

   /* return if file does not exist */
   fd = open(filename, O_RDWR);
   if (fd == -1)
      return(FILE_NOT_EXIST);

   lseek(fd, 0L, 0);
   if (lockf(fd, F_TEST, 0L) == 0)
   {  /* lock does not exist */
      if (lockf(fd, F_LOCK, 0L) == -1)
      {
         close(fd);
         return(LOCK_FAIL);
      }
      else
         return(LOCK_SUCCEED);
   }
   else
   {  /* lock exists */
      close(fd);
      return(LOCK_EXIST);
   }
}

int unlock(filename)
char *filename;
{
   int fd;

   /* return if file does not exist */
   fd = open(filename, O_RDWR);
   if (fd == -1)
      return(FILE_NOT_EXIST);
```

```
    lseek(fd, 0L, 0);
    if (lockf(fd, F_ULOCK, 0L) != -1)
    {
        close(fd);
        return(UNLOCK_SUCCEED);
    }
    else
        return(UNLOCK_FAIL);
}
```

Listing 7.11 test_lock.c

```c
/*
 * test_lock.c
 */
#include <stdio.h>
#include <errno.h>

#define LOCK_SUCCEED     0
#define UNLOCK_SUCCEED   0

main(argc, argv)
int  argc;
char *argv[];
{
    char filename[128];
    char hostname[80];
    char *username;
    char dotfile[128];
    char buf[256];
    char *getenv();
    int  pid;
    FILE *fp;

    if (argc < 2)
    {
        printf("Usage: test_lock  filename\n");
        exit(-1);
    }
    strcpy(filename, argv[1]);
    while (lock(filename) != LOCK_SUCCEED)
    {
        printf("lock failed\n");
        sleep(1);
    }
    gethostname(hostname, sizeof(hostname));
    username = (char *)getenv("USER");
    pid = getpid();
    sprintf(dotfile, ".%s", filename);
    if ((fp = fopen(dotfile, "w")) == NULL)
        printf("file %s open for write error\n", dotfile);
    else
    {
        sprintf(buf, "%s %s %d\n", hostname, username, pid);
        fputs(buf, fp);
```

```
        fclose(fp);
    }
    sleep(20);

    if (unlock(filename) == UNLOCK_SUCCEED)
    {
        printf("file %s unlocked\n", filename);
        unlink(dotfile);
    }
    else
        printf("unlock file %s failed\n", filename);
}
```

7.6 PROGRAMMING WITH DYNAMIC MEMORY

Dynamic memory plays a very important role in the UNIX/C programming environment. Dynamic memory is acquired through the malloc() system call. Some advantages of using dynamic memory vs. a fixed array are

☞ Memory allocations are done in execution time. The exact amount of memory can be allocated.

☞ Depending on the program control flow, some dynamic memory may not be allocated at all.

☞ Dynamic memory can be freed up once it is no longer needed.

Although the FORTRAN language does not provide this capability, a FORTRAN program can make calls to FORTRAN-callable C functions, through which the FORTRAN program effectively can use dynamic memory. These callable functions include memory allocation and deallocation routines that form the core of a dynamic memory manager, which will be presented at the end of this section.

7.6.1 Process's Memory Model

In UNIX, a process' memory organization can be depicted as Figure 7.1 shows. In this figure, a process' memory space is divided into three regions: The text region (the

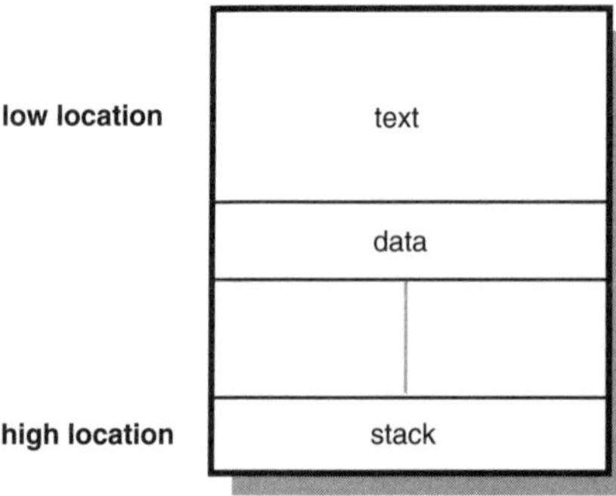

Fig. 7.1 Process's Memory Space

low memory locations) contains the code for all the functions, and space for the statically allocated global data. The data region (adjacent to the text region) contains the space for dynamic storage allocation. This region is growing from lower memory locations to higher memory locations. The stack region (the high memory locations) contains the run-time information of the functions being called. This information usually consists of the function arguments' values, the number of arguments, the return address, the return value, and the data local to that function.

7.6.2 Data Region Size and Limitations

In an operation system with virtual memory management capability, the process address space ultimately is limited by the system's total swap space, which is generally in hundreds or thousands of megabytes. Another factor also limits the data region size: the datasize limit in one of the user's resource limits, which can be found by the limit command. The limit command without any argument lists all the resource limits pertaining to a user. You also can set the datasize limit using the limit command

```
limit datasize 128000
```

which sets the data region size to 128000 kilobytes. Once the dynamically allocated memory reaches this limit, the malloc() system call fails, signifying that the process has run out of dynamic memory space.

Sometimes it is advantageous to know how much dynamic memory space is left before you call the malloc() system call. This number can be computed by subtracting the total amount of memory allocated from the datasize resource limit. The trick to finding the total allocated memory size is through the sbrk() system call and a system-defined, system-dependent variable. The sbrk() system call takes one argument that specifies the number of bytes to increment on the data region, and returns the previous upper data region boundary value. The lower data region boundary value is given by either the address of an integer variable _edata (for AIX) or etext (for SUNOS). So the amount of allocated memory in kilobytes can be computed as

```
alloc_size = ((caddr_t) sbrk(0) - (caddr_t) &extxt)/ 1024
```

or

```
alloc_size = ((caddr_t) sbrk(0) - (caddr_t) &_edata)/1024
```

depending on the system you use.

7.6.3 Writing FORTRAN-Callable C Functions

When writing a FORTRAN-callable C function, you must keep in mind a few rules. First, for a C function to be callable from a FORTRAN program, its function name must end with an underscore. Second, only lowercase letters can be used in the function name. Third, the function name may not exceed six characters (underscore not included). Fourth, FORTRAN requires all arguments to be call-by-reference. So in

calling the FORTRAN-callable C function from a C program, the parameters'
addresses are passed rather than the parameter values'.

Listing 7.12 shows how to write a FORTRAN-callable C function that returns
the amount of space (in bytes) remaining in the data region.

Listing 7.12 avail_mem.c

```c
/*
 * avail_mem.c
 */
#include <stdio.h>
#include <sys/types.h>
#include <sys/time.h>
#include <sys/resource.h>

#ifdef AIX
extern int _edata;
#endif

#ifdef SUNOS
extern int etext;
#endif

void avamem_ (nbytes, rtn_code)

int *nbytes;
int *rtn_code;
{
   struct rlimit rlp;
   long    rlimit_data;
   long    alloc_mem;

   *rtn_code = 0;
   /*
    * get the user's datasize limits
    */
   if (getrlimit(RLIMIT_DATA, &rlp) == 0)
      rlimit_data = (long)rlp.rlim_cur;      /* in bytes */
   else
   {
      printf("can't get the datasize limit\n");
      *rtn_code = -1;
      return;
   }

   /*
    * calculate the amount of allocated memory
    */
   #ifdef SUNOS
      alloc_mem=(long) ((caddr_t)sbrk(0) - (caddr_t)&etext);
   #endif

   #ifdef AIX
      alloc_mem=(long) ((caddr_t)sbrk(0) - (caddr_t)&_edata);
   #endif
```

```
/*
 *  calculate the available memory
 */
*nbytes = rlimit_data - alloc_mem;
return;
}
```

7.6.4 Case Study: A Dynamic Memory Manager

This section presents a dynamic memory manager that essentially wraps around the malloc() and free() system calls, and is capable of

☞ allocating dynamic storage for a process

☞ de-allocating storage for a process

☞ inquiring about the memory usage and memory availability

Other requirements for this dynamic memory manager include

☞ all external functions must be FORTRAN-callable

☞ can provide simple memory corruption check

☞ can collect memory usage statistics

7.6.4.1 Problem Analysis First, we can easily put two wrappers around the malloc() and free() system calls. Let these two functions be dymalloc() and dymfree(). So, whenever a C program needs dynamic memory, it calls dymalloc(), which in turn calls malloc() to actually allocate the required memory. When a process finishes with the allocated memory, it calls dymfree() instead of free() to free up the memory. dymfree() adds this free memory space to a free storage tree so that it can be reused, and therefore reduces the number of calls to malloc(). However, to do so, dymalloc() must build in the capability to search the free storage tree for free storage. If it can find free storage there, that piece is returned. Otherwise, it calls malloc() for the required memory.

The dynamic memory manager maintains an AVL-tree, a balanced tree with O(log n), even in the worst case in doing a tree search, tree insertion, and tree deletion. The amount of memory allocated is used as the key. The address field, which is the starting address of the allocated memory space, resolves duplicated keys.

Next, we must create two FORTRAN-callable functions, dymgtc_() and dymfrc_(), which are dymalloc()'s and dymfree()'s counterparts. Note that the FORTRAN-callable function name can have, at most, six characters (not including the trailing hyphen), and must end with a hyphen. Because the FORTRAN language does not allow structure, our only choice is the array data type. So, inside the FORTRAN program, you must declare an array variable.

```
INTEGER   SUMS(1)
```

Here the array size, one, is not important. Its only purpose is to tell the FOR-TRAN compiler that the variable sum is an array variable, so that it can use indexing to access part of the data. There are six arguments to the dymgtc_() function (addresses of the arguments are passed for all arguments because FORTRAN functions are call-by-reference): the function name that makes the call to dymgtc_(), the address of the first array element, the length of each element, the total number of elements, the starting index, and the return code. The first four are input arguments, and the last two are output arguments. For example, a call to dymgtc_() may look like the following in a FORTRAN program:

```
      INTEGER LEN, NUM, IDX, RCODE
      INTEGER SUMS(1)

C     assume INTEGER takes up 4 bytes and
C     100 integer storage will be allocated
         LEN = 4
         NUM = 100
      CALL  DYMGTC ('ADDINT', SUMS(1), LEN, NUM, IDX, RCODE)
```

And the following statement assigns the integer value zero into the first element of the allocated memory:

```
      SUMS(IDX) = 0
```

The major tasks within dymgtc_() include computing the amount of memory required in term of bytes, calling dymalloc() to get the required memory either from the free storage tree or from the system, and determining the value for index.

Memory corruption, so far, is the most difficult problem to debug, because memory corruption may occur in module A, and the effect appears in a totally irrelevant, module B. Usually, the author of module B is at fault—eventually, programmers discover module A is the guilty party.

Although commercial packages do a good job finding out where the memory corruption occurs, those packages usually require an enormous amount of time spent recompiling and relinking the executables. You can achieve the same results using the following mechanism:

Every time the dynamic memory manager allocates memory, it allocates 16 extra bytes. The first eight bytes are added to the front of the requested memory space, and another eight bytes are appended to the end of the same requested memory space. Two pre-determined character patterns are stored in these two eight-byte slots: One signifies the beginning of a allocated memory block; the other signifies the end of that memory block. Whenever you suspect that memory may have been corrupted, simply turn on the debugging flag. It automatically goes through each allocated memory block and examines the correctness of the patterns, both in the front and rear ends of the allocated memory block. If any one of the patterns is destroyed, memory corruption has occurred.

7.6.4.2 Data Structures   Figures 7.2 through 7.4 show the diagrams of the data structures required for this dynamic memory manager. The type definition for the table entry in Figure 7.2 is

```
      typedef struct dym_usage_table {
```

```
    char *func_name;
    int   size;
    char *start;
    char *end;
    char *prog_start;
} DYM_USAGE_STRUC;
```

The table is initially given the size NUM_USAGE_ENTRIES, which is defined as 200. Every time the table overflows, it is reallocated with 50 more entries.

Both figures 7.3 and 7.4 use the same type definition:

```
typedef struct node_struc {
    int   size;
    int   addr;
    int   bal;
    int count;
    struct node_struc *left;
    struct node_struc *right;
} NODE_STRUC, *PTR_NODE_STRUC;
```

In Figure 7.3, the size field in the node_struc structure stores the size of the memory block. The addr field stores the memory block's starting location. The bal field

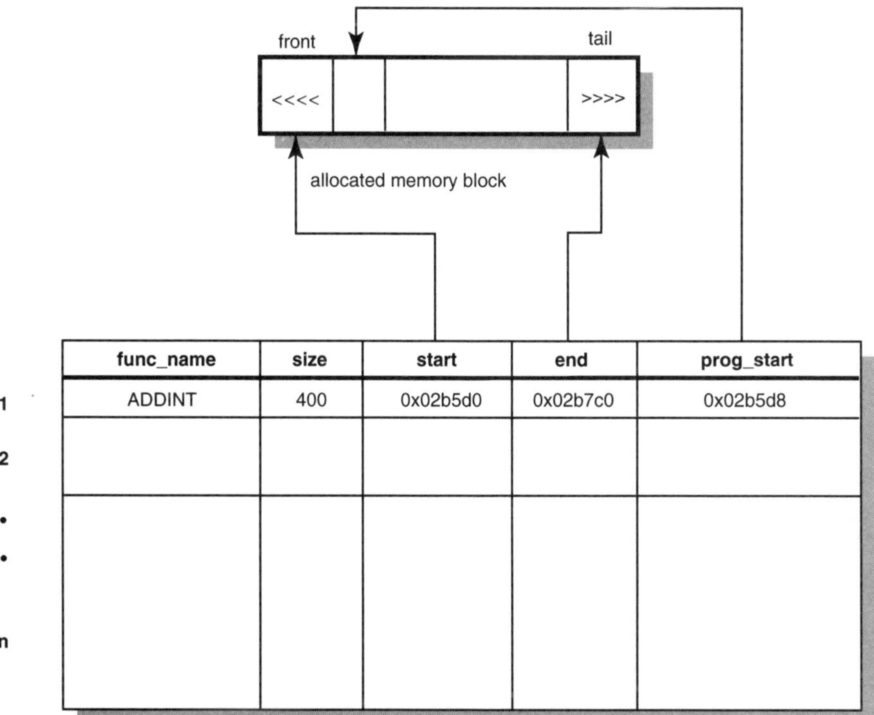

	func_name	size	start	end	prog_start
1	ADDINT	400	0x02b5d0	0x02b7c0	0x02b5d8
2					
.					
.					
n					

Fig. 7.2 Memory Usage Table

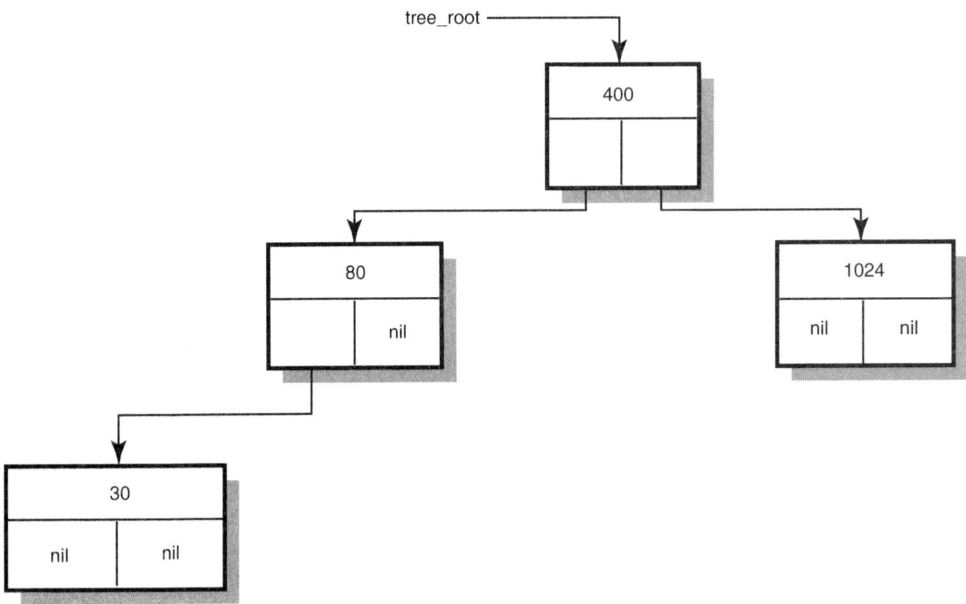

Fig. 7.3 Free Memory Tree

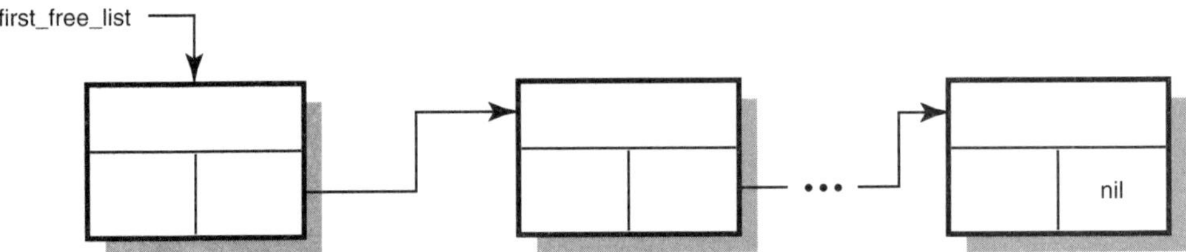

Fig. 7.4 Free Structure List

stores the difference between the height of the right and left sub-trees. The left and right fields point to the left and right sub-trees, respectively. In Figure 7.4, the only field used is the right pointer. It is interpreted as the next pointer to the next element in this free structure list. We keep this free structure list to save time allocating memory space for this structure.

The following three declarations declare the table name, the pointer to the root node of the AVL-tree, and the pointer to the first free structure list entry:

```
DYM_USAGE_TABLE *dym_use_tab;
PTR_NODE_STRUC tree_root = NULL;
PTR_NODE_STRUC first_free_list = NULL;
```

Listing 7.13 dymmgr.c

```c
/*
 *   dymmgr.c
 */
#include <stdio.h>
#include <sys/types.h>
#include <sys/resource.h>
#include <sys/time.h>

#ifdef SUNOS
extern int etext;
#endif

#ifdef AIX
extern int _edata;
#endif

#define NUM_USAGE_ENTRIES    200

typedef struct dym_usage_table {
   char *func_name;         /* calling function name      */
   int  size;               /* amount of memory in bytes  */
   char *start;             /* malloc start loc.          */
   char *end;               /* malloc up to loc.          */
   char *prog_start;        /* program start loc.         */
} DYM_USAGE_TABLE;

typedef struct node_struc {
   int  size;
   int  addr;
   int  bal;
   int count;
   struct node_struc *left;
   struct node_struc *right;
} NODE_STRUC, *PTR_NODE_STRUC;

typedef long Header;

DYM_USAGE_TABLE *dym_use_tab;
PTR_NODE_STRUC tree_root = NULL;
PTR_NODE_STRUC first_free_list = NULL;
PTR_NODE_STRUC q;

static int use_tab_size;
static int dymalloc_count = 0;
static int dymfree_count = 0;
static int dymdebug = 0;
static int new_entry_index;

void dymver_();
void dymint_();
void dymava_();

void AddToFreeTree();
void DeleteFromFreeTree();
void AddToFreeList();
```

```c
void DeleteNode();
void Balance1();
void Balance2();

PTR_NODE_STRUC GetBestFitFromFreeTree();

void dymint_(rtn_code)
int *rtn_code;
{
   static int done_init = 0;
   int   i;

   *rtn_code = 0;
   if (!done_init)
   {
      done_init = 1;
      dym_use_tab = (DYM_USAGE_TABLE *)malloc(NUM_USAGE_ENTRIES *
         sizeof(DYM_USAGE_TABLE));
      if (dym_use_tab == NULL)
      {
         printf("can't allocate space for usage table\n");
         *rtn_code = -1;
         return;
      }
      use_tab_size = NUM_USAGE_ENTRIES;

      for (i=0; i< use_tab_size; i++)
      {
         dym_use_tab[i].func_name = NULL;
         dym_use_tab[i].size = 0;
         dym_use_tab[i].start = NULL;
         dym_use_tab[i].end = NULL;
         dym_use_tab[i].prog_start = NULL;
      }
   }
   return;
}

void dymava_ (nbytes, rtn_code)
int *nbytes;
int *rtn_code;
{
   struct rlimit rlp;
   long    rlimit_data;
   long    alloc_mem;

   *rtn_code = 0;
   /*
    * get the user's datasize limits
    */
   if (getrlimit(RLIMIT_DATA, &rlp) == 0)
      rlimit_data = (long)rlp.rlim_cur;      /* in bytes */
   else
   {
      printf("can't get the datasize limit\n");
      *rtn_code = -1;
```

```c
      return;
   }

   /*
    * calculate the amount of allocated memory
    */
#ifdef SUNOS
   alloc_mem=(long) ((caddr_t)sbrk(0) - (caddr_t)&etext);
#endif

#ifdef AIX
   alloc_mem=(long) ((caddr_t)sbrk(0) - (caddr_t)&_edata);
#endif

   /*
    *  calculate the available memory
    */
    *nbytes = rlimit_data - alloc_mem;
   return;
}

char *dymalloc(nbytes, func_name)
int  nbytes;
char *func_name;
{
   int i,j;
   int rtn_code;
   int bytes_alloc;
   int best_fit_size;
   int best_fit_addr;
   int nunits;
   Header *p;
   char *front;
   char *tail;
   PTR_NODE_STRUC pnode;

   dymalloc_count++;
   if (dymdebug)
   {
      printf("dymalloc entry: %d\n", dymalloc_count);
      dymver_(&rtn_code);
      if (rtn_code != 0)
         printf("pattern destroyed\n");
   }
   if (nbytes <= 0)
   {
      printf("bytes to be allocated is less than zero\n");
      return(NULL);
   }
   /*
    *  one header for front and one for tail
    */
   nunits = (nbytes + sizeof(Header)-1)/sizeof(Header)+2;
   bytes_alloc = nunits * sizeof(Header);
   best_fit_size = 0;
```

```c
if ((pnode = GetBestFitFromFreeTree(&tree_root, bytes_alloc, &best_fit_size,
       &best_fit_addr)) == NULL)
{
   /* can't find enough space from free storage tree */
   if (( p = (Header *)malloc(bytes_alloc)) == NULL)
      return(NULL);
   else
   {
      front = (char *)p;
      tail = (char *)(p+nunits-1);
      strcpy(front, "<<<<");
      strcpy(tail, ">>>>");
   }
}
else
{
   p = (Header *)pnode->addr;
   bytes_alloc = pnode->size;
   front = (char *)p;
   tail = (char *)(p+nunits-1);
   strcpy(front, "<<<<");
   strcpy(tail, ">>>>");
}

/*
 * find an empty slot in table
 */
j = -1;
for (i=0; i<use_tab_size; i++)
{
   if (dym_use_tab[i].prog_start == NULL)
   {
      j = i;
      break;
   }
}

if ( j < 0)
{ /* table is full */
   j = use_tab_size;
   use_tab_size += 50;
   /* increase table size by 50 entries */
   dym_use_tab = (DYM_USAGE_TABLE *)realloc(dym_use_tab,
      use_tab_size*sizeof(DYM_USAGE_TABLE));
   if (dym_use_tab = NULL)
   {
      printf("realloc error\n");
      return(NULL);
   }
   for (i=use_tab_size -50; i< use_tab_size; i++)
   { /* initialize this new 50 entries */
      dym_use_tab[i].func_name = NULL;
      dym_use_tab[i].size = 0;
      dym_use_tab[i].start = NULL;
```

```c
                  dym_use_tab[i].end = NULL;
                  dym_use_tab[i].prog_start = NULL;
            }
      }
      dym_use_tab[j].func_name = (char *)malloc (strlen(func_name)  +1);
      strcpy(dym_use_tab[j].func_name, func_name);
      dym_use_tab[j].size = bytes_alloc;
      dym_use_tab[j].start = front;
      dym_use_tab[j].end = tail;
      dym_use_tab[j].prog_start = (char *)(p+1);
      new_entry_index = j;
      if (dymdebug)
      {
         dymver_(&rtn_code);
         if (rtn_code != 0)
            printf("pattern destroyed\n");
      }
      return(char *) (p+1);
}

int dymfree(p)
char *p;
{
   Header *hp;
   int    rtn_code;
   int    i,j;
   int    size;
   int    h_inc;
   PTR_NODE_STRUC pnode;

   dymfree_count++;
   if (dymdebug)
   {
      printf("dymfree entry: %d\n", dymfree_count);
      dymver_(&rtn_code);
      if (rtn_code != 0)
         printf("pattern destroyed\n");
   }

   j = -1;
   for (i=0; i<use_tab_size; i++)
   {
      if (dym_use_tab[i].prog_start == p)
      {
         hp = (Header *)dym_use_tab[i].start;
         size = dym_use_tab[i].size;
         j = i;
         break;
      }
   }
   if (j >= 0)
   {
      free(dym_use_tab[j].func_name);
      dym_use_tab[j].func_name = NULL;
      dym_use_tab[j].prog_start = NULL;
```

```
   }
   else
   {
      printf("dymfree error\n");
      return(-1);
   }
   if (first_free_list == NULL)
      pnode = (PTR_NODE_STRUC) malloc(sizeof(NODE_STRUC));
   else
   {
      pnode = first_free_list;
      first_free_list = pnode->right;
   }
   /*
    *   add this free storage to free storage tree
    */
   pnode->addr = (int)hp;
   pnode->size = size;
   pnode->left = NULL;
   pnode->right = NULL;
   AddToFreeTree(&tree_root, pnode, &h_inc);
   if (dymdebug)
   {
      printf("dymfree exit: %d\n", dymfree_count);
      dymver(&rtn_code);
      if (rtn_code != 0)
         printf("pattern destroyed\n");
   }
   return (0);
}

void dymgtc_(func_name, area, lelem, nelem, index, rtn_code)
char *func_name;
char *area;
int  *lelem;
int  *nelem;
int  *index;
int  *rtn_code;
{
   char *ptr;
   char *ptr_area;
   int    nbytes;
   long   addr;
   long   offset;
   nbytes = (*lelem) * (*nelem);
   if (*nelem <= 0 || *lelem <= 0)
   {
      *rtn_code = 2;
      return;
   }
   else
   {
      *rtn_code = 0;
      ptr_area = area;
```

```c
      offset = ptr - ptr_area;
      /* find proper array index for offset */
      if (offset < 0)
      {
         if (((-offset < 0) % (*lelem)) == 0)
            *index = offset/ (*lelem) + 1;
         else
            *index = offset/ (*lelem) + 2;
      }
      else
      {
         if (((offset) % (*lelem)) == 0)
            *index = offset/ (*lelem) + 1;
         else
            *index = offset/ (*lelem) + 2;
      }

      /* find starting address to be used by program */
      if (offset < 0)
      {
         if (((-offset) % (*lelem)) == 0)
            addr = (*index -1) * (*lelem) +
               (unsigned long) ptr_area;
         else
            addr = (*index -1) * (*lelem) +
               (unsigned long) ptr_area;
      }
      else
      {
         if (((-offset) % (*lelem)) == 0)
            addr = (*index -1) * (*lelem) +
               (unsigned long) ptr_area;
         else
            addr = (*index -1) * (*lelem) +
               (unsigned long) ptr_area;
      }
      dym_use_tab[new_entry_index].prog_start = (char*)addr;
   }
}

void dymfre_(area, lelem, nelem, index, rtn_code)
char *area;
int  *lelem;
int  *nelem;
int  *index;
int  *rtn_code;
{
   char *ptr;
   char *ptr_code;
   char *ptr_area;
   char *addr;

   if (*lelem <= 0 || *nelem <=0 )
   {
      *rtn_code = 3;
```

```c
      return;
   }
   ptr_area = area;
   if ( *index < 0)
      addr = (char *) ((*index-1)*(*lelem) +
         (unsigned long) ptr_area);
   else
      addr = (char *) ((*index-1)*(*lelem) +
         (unsigned long) ptr_area);
   *rtn_code = dymfree(addr);
}

void dymver_(rtn_code)
int *rtn_code;
{
   int   i;
   char *p;

   *rtn_code = 0;
   for (i=0; i<use_tab_size; i++)
   {
      p = dym_use_tab[i].start;
      if (p != NULL)
      {
         if (strcmp(p,  "<<<<") != 0)
         {
            *rtn_code = 1;
            return;
         }
         p = dym_use_tab[i].end;
         if (p == NULL)
         {
            *rtn_code = 2;
            return;
         }
         if (strcmp(p,  ">>>>") != 0)
         {
            *rtn_code = 1;
            return;
         }
      }
   }
   return;
}

void AddToFreeTree(root, node, h_inc)
PTR_NODE_STRUC *root;
PTR_NODE_STRUC  node;
int             *h_inc;
{
   PTR_NODE_STRUC p, p1, p2;

   if (*root == NULL)
   { /* empty tree */
      node->bal = 0;
```

```c
      node->count = 1;
      *h_inc = 1;
      *root = node;
      return;
   }

   p = *root;
   if (node->size < p->size ||
      (node->size == p->size) && (node->addr < p->addr))
   {
      AddToFreeTree(&p->left, node, h_inc);
      if (*h_inc)
      { /* left branch grows higher */
         switch (p->bal) {
         case  1: p->bal = 0;
            *h_inc = 0;
            break;
         case  0: p->bal = -1;
            break;
         case -1: /* rebalance */
            p1 = p->left;
            if (p1->bal == -1)
            { /* single LL rotation */
               p->left = p1->right;
               p1->right = p;
               p->bal = 0;
               *root = p1;
               p1->bal = 0;
            }
            else
            { /* double LR rotation */
               p2 = p1->right;
               p1->right = p2->left;
               p2->left = p1;
               p->left = p2->right;
               p2->right = p;
               if (p2->bal == -1)
                  p->bal = 1;
               else
                  p->bal = 0;
               if (p2->bal == 1)
                  p1->bal = -1;
               else
                  p1->bal = 0;
               *root = p2;
               p2->bal = 0;
            }
            *h_inc = 0;
            break;
         default:
            break;
         } /* end case */
      }
   }
```

```c
    else if (node->size > p->size ||
        (node->size == p->size) && (node->addr > p->addr))
    {
        AddToFreeTree(&p->size, node, h_inc);
        if (*h_inc)
        { /* right branch grows higher */
            switch (p->bal) {
            case -1: p->bal = 0;
                *h_inc = 0;
                break;
            case  0: p->bal = 1;
                break;
            case  1: /* rebalance */
                p1 = p->right;
                if (p1->bal == 1)
                { /* single RR rotation */
                    p->right = p1->left;
                    p1->left = p;
                    p->bal = 0;
                    *root = p1;
                    p1->bal = 0;
                }
                else
                { /* double RL rotation */
                    p2 = p1->left;
                    p1->left = p2->right;
                    p2->right = p1;
                    p->right = p2->left;
                    p2->left = p;
                    if (p2->bal == 1)
                        p->bal = -1;
                    else
                        p->bal = 0;
                    if (p2->bal == -1)
                        p1->bal = 1;
                    else
                        p1->bal = 0;
                    *root = p2;
                    p2->bal = 0;
                }
                *h_inc = 0;
                break;
            default:
                break;
            } /* end case */
        }
    }
    else
        *h_inc = 0;
}

PTR_NODE_STRUC
GetBestFitFromFreeTree(root, size, best_size, best_addr)
PTR_NODE_STRUC *root;
```

```c
int  size;
int  *best_size;
int  *best_addr;
{
   PTR_NODE_STRUC p, p1, p2, p3;
   int b1, b2;
   int h_dec;

   if (*root == NULL)
   {
      if (*best_size == 0)
         return (NULL);
      else
      {
         DeleteFromFreeTree(&tree_root, *best_size,   *best_addr, &h_dec);
         return(first_free_list);
      }
   }

   p = *root;
   if (size < p->size)
   {
      *best_size = p->size;
      *best_addr = p->addr;
      GetBestFitFromFreeTree(&p->left, size, best_size,  best_addr);
   }
   else if (size > p->size)
      GetBestFitFromFreeTree(&p->right, size, best_size, best_addr);
   else
   {
      *best_size = p->size;
      *best_addr = p->addr;
      DeleteFromFreeTree(&tree_root, *best_size, *best_addr,  &h_dec);
      return(first_free_list);
   }
}

void DeleteFromFreeTree(root, size, addr, h_dec)
PTR_NODE_STRUC *root;
int  size;
int  addr;
int  *h_dec;
{
   PTR_NODE_STRUC p, p1, p2, p3;
   int  b1, b2;

   if (*root = NULL)
   {
      printf("Can't be deleted from tree, key not matched\n");
      *h_dec = 0;
      return;
   }
   p = *root;
   if (size < p->size)
   {
```

```c
         DeleteFromFreetree(&p->left, size, addr, h_dec);
      if (*h_dec)
         Balance1(root, h_dec);
   }
   else if (size > p->size)
   {
      DeleteFromFreetree(&p->right, size, addr, h_dec);
      if (*h_dec)
         Balance2(root, h_dec);
   }
   else
   {
      if (addr < p->addr)
      {
         DeleteFromFreeTree(&p->left, size, addr, h_dec);
         if (*h_dec)
            Balance1(root, h_dec);
      }
      else if (addr > p->addr)
      {
         DeleteFromFreeTree(&p->right, size, addr, h_dec);
         if (*h_dec)
            Balance2(root, h_dec);
      }
      else
      {
         q = p;
         if (q->right == NULL)
         {
            *root = q->left;
            *h_dec = 1;
            AddToFreeList(q);
         }
         else if (q->left == NULL)
         {
            *root = q->right;
            *h_dec = 1;
            AddToFreeList(q);
         }
         else
         {
            DeleteNode(&q->left, h_dec);
            if (*h_dec)
               Balance1(root, h_dec);
         }
      }
   }
}

void AddToFreeList(p)
PTR_NODE_STRUC p;
{
   p->right = first_free_list;
   first_free_list = p;
```

```c
}

void Balance1(root, h_dec)
PTR_NODE_STRUC *root;
int   *h_dec;
{
   int b1, b2;
   PTR_NODE_STRUC p, p1, p2;

   p = *root;
   switch (p->bal) {
   case -1: p->bal = 0;
      break;
   case  0: p->bal = 1;
      *h_dec = 0;
      break;
   case  1: p1 = p->right;
      b1 = p1->bal;
      if (b1 >= 0)
      { /* single RR rotation */
         p->right = p1->left;
         p1->left = p;
         if (b1 == 0)
         {
            p->bal = 1;
            p1->bal = -1;
            *h_dec = 0;
         }
         else
         {
            p->bal = 0;
            p1->bal= 0;
         }
         *root = p1;
      }
      else
      {
         /* double RL rotation */
         p2 = p1->left;
         b2 = p2->bal;
         p1->left = p2->right;
         p2->right = p1;
         p->right = p2->left;
         p2->left = p;
         if (b2 == 1)
            p->bal = -1;
         else
            p->bal = 0;
         if (b2 == -1)
            p1->bal = 1;
         else
            p1->bal = 0;
         *root = p2;
         p2->bal = 0;
```

```c
      }
      break;
   default:
      break;
   }
}

void Balance2(root, h_dec)
PTR_NODE_STRUC *root;
int   *h_dec;
{
   int b1, b2;
   PTR_NODE_STRUC p, p1, p2;

   p = *root;
   switch (p->bal) {
   case  1: p->bal = 0;
      break;
   case  0: p->bal = -1;
      *h_dec = 0;
      break;
   case -1: p1 = p->left;
      b1 = p1->bal;
      if (b1 <= 0)
      { /* single LL rotation */
         p->left = p1->right;
         p1->right = p;
         if (b1 == 0)
         {
            p->bal = -1;
            p1->bal = 1;
            *h_dec = 0;
         }
         else
         {
            p->bal = 0;
            p1->bal= 0;
         }
         *root = p1;
      }
      else
      {
         /* double LR rotation */
         p2 = p1->right;
         b2 = p2->bal;
         p1->right = p2->left;
         p2->left = p1;
         p->left = p2->right;
         p2->right = p;
         if (b2 == -1)
            p->bal = 1;
         else
            p->bal = 0;
         if (b2 == 1)
```

```
            p1->bal = -1;
        else
            p1->bal = 0;
        *root = p2;
        p2->bal = 0;
    }
    break;
    default:
        break;
    }
}

void DeleteNode(root, h_dec)
PTR_NODE_STRUC *root;
int *h_dec;
{
    PTR_NODE_STRUC p, p1, p2;
    int b1, b2;
    int tmp_size, tmp_addr;

    p = *root;
    if ( p->right != NULL)
    {
        DeleteNode(&p->right, h_dec);
        if (*h_dec)
            balance2(root, h_dec);
    }
    else
    {
        tmp_size = q->size;
        tmp_addr = q->addr;
        q->size = p->size;
        q->addr = p->addr;
        *root = p->left;
        p->size = tmp_size;
        p->addr = tmp_addr;
        AddToFreeList(p);
        *h_dec = 1;
    }
}
```

7.7 Programming with Sockets

Sockets are the base for the network programming in 4.3 BSD. They are a generalized UNIX file-access mechanism that provides a communication endpoint.

An application program requests that the operating system open a socket when it needs to communicate through the network. The operating system in turn returns an integer that allows the application program to reference the socket. This returned integer is referred to as a socket descriptor, and it is used like the file descriptor. The main difference is that the operating system binds a file descriptor to a specific file when the application opens a file. When a socket is opened, however, it is not bound to a specific destination address. The application program can choose to supply the destination address each time it uses the socket, or it can bind the destination address to the socket and avoid specifying the destination address every time it transfers the data. The first case is called a user datagram protocol (UDP), and the latter is called a transmission control protocol (TCP).

Depending on the services the transport layer provides, there are three commonly used socket types: SOCK_STREAM, SOCK_DGRAM, and SOCK_RAW. SOCK_STREAM is a stream socket that uses the connection-oriented services the TCP protocol provides at the transport layer. SOCK_DGRAM is a datagram socket that uses connectionless services the UDP protocol provides at the transport layer. SOCK_RAW is a raw socket that does not use any services from the transport layer; instead, it directly interfaces with the IP protocol at the network layer.

7.7.1 Domains and Socket Addresses

Sockets created by different programs use host names and port numbers to refer to one another. These host names must be translated into network addresses for use. There are several ways to specify these network addresses. Each address format is called a domain; the UNIX domain (AF_UNIX) and the Internet domain (AF_INET) are two well-known domains. We restrict our discussion to the Internet domain (the UNIX implementation of DARPA Internet protocols). The combination of the network addresses and the port numbers is referred to as a socket address.

7.7.2 Internet Addresses

Each host on the Internet is assigned a unique 32-bit Internet address used in all communication with the host. Conceptually, each Internet address is a (netid, hostid) pair. The netid identifies the network, and the hostid identifies the host on that network. This 32-bit Internet address normally is represented by the dotted decimal notation. For example, the following 32-bit Internet address

```
10000000 00001010 00000010 00011110
```

is written as

```
128.10.2.30
```

7.7.3 TCP Ports

For a process in host A to communicate with a process in host B, two levels of addressing are needed. On the higher level, each host on network must have a unique global network address. This allows the data to be delivered to the proper host. On the lower level, each process within a host must have an address unique within the host. This allows the data to be delivered ultimately to the proper process. These latter addresses are known as port numbers. TCP services are identified with port numbers. Table 7.1 shows a few well-known ports.

Table 7.1 Some Well-Known Ports

Port Number	Protocol	Services
7	tcp	echo
13	tcp	daytime
21	tcp	ftp
37	tcp	time
43	tcp	whois
79	tcp	finger
513	tcp	login
513	udp	who

7.7.4 Socket Descriptors

A 5-tuple is associated with the socket descriptor. It is represented as

```
{protocol, loc_addr, loc_process, rem_addr, rem_process}
```

where protocol is either TCP or UDP; loc_addr is the local host's Internet address; loc_process is the local port number; rem_addr is the remote host's Internet address; and rem_process is the remote port number.

7.7.5 Data Structures

Two socket address structure representations are required in the networking system calls. One is protocol specific, and the other is common to all protocols. The user employs the protocol-specific socket address structure, and the kernel uses the other socket structure. Both are defined as

```
/* socket address, Internet style, used by programmer */

#include <netinet/in.h>

struct sockaddr_in  {
short           sin_family;     /* AF_INET */
u_short         sin_port;       /* 16 bit port number */
struct in_addr  sin_addr;       /* 32 bit netid/hostid */
char            sin_zero[8];    /* not used */
};
```

where struct in_addr is defined further as

```
/* Internet address, network byte ordered */
struct in_addr {
u_long  s_addr;         /* 32 bit netid/hostid */
};

/* socket address, common style, used by kernel */
```

```
#include <sys/socket.h>

struct sockaddr {
u_short   sa_family;      /* address family */
char      sa_data[14];    /* up to 14 bytes of protocol-specific address */
}
```

Struct hostent is another useful data structure used in the network programming. This is the structure the function call gethostbyname() returns. Through the call to function gethostbyname(), you can obtain all the Internet address information about any host. Struct hostent's structure is

```
/* structure returned by network data base library */
#include <netdb.h>

struct hostent {
char   *h_name;          /* host name */
char   **h_aliases;      /* alias list */
int    h_addrtype;       /* host address type */
int    h_length;         /* length of address */
char   **h_addr_list;    /* list of addresses */
};
#define h_addr h_addr_list[0]; /* 1st address in list */
```

7.7.6 Socket-Related System Calls and Library Functions

The following chart explains all the socket-related system calls used in this book.

system call: socket()

function: creates an endpoint for communication, and returns a socket descriptor representing the endpoint

synopsis:

```
#include <sys/types.h>
#include <sys/socket.h>

int socket (domain, type, protocol)
int domain;
int type;
int protocol;
```

where domain is the address domain (AF_INET is used for Internet protocols); type is the type of socket created (for the stream socket, SOCK_STREAM); and protocol specifies the network protocol used. If TCP is used, it is set to IPPROTO_TCP, which is the constant zero.

system call: bind()

function: associates a socket descriptor to a local socket address

synopsis:

```
#include <sys/types.h>
#include <sys/socket.h>

int bind(sockfd, sock_addr, len)
```

```
int sockfd;
struct sockaddr *sock_addr;
int len;
```

where sockfd is the socket descriptor, sock_addr points to a structure that contains the socket address, and len is the size of the structure in bytes.

system call: connect()

function: establishes a connection between two sockets

synopsis:

```
#include <sys/types.h>
#include <sys/socket.h>

int connect(sockfd, serv_addr, len)
int sockfd;
struct sockaddr *serv_addr;
int len;
```

where sockfd is the socket descriptor; serv_addr points to the socket address; and len is the size of the structure in bytes.

system call: listen()

function: creates a connection request queue, and indicates that it is ready to receive incoming connections

synopsis:

```
#include <sys/types.h>
#include <sys/socket.h>

int listen (sockfd, queue_len)
int sockfd;
int queue_len;
```

where sockfd is the socket descriptor, and queue_len is the maximum queue length for pending connection requests.

system call: accept()

function: takes the first connection request on queue and creates another socket with the same properties as sockfd

synopsis:

```
#include <sys/types.h>
#include <sys/socket.h>

int accept(sockfd, cli_addr, len)
int sockfd;
struct sockaddr *cli_addr;
int len;
```

where sockfd is the socket descriptor, cli_addr points to the socket address, and len is the size of the structure in bytes.

system call: read()

function: reads in data through the socket descriptor and stores it in a buffer

synopsis:

```
#include <sys/types.h>
#include <sys/socket.h>

int read(sockfd, buf, len)
int sockfd;
char *buf;
int len
```

where sockfd is the socket descriptor, buf points to the buffer where the data is stored, and len is the amount of data to be read in bytes.

system call: write()
function: writes out data through the socket descriptor
synopsis:

```
#include <sys/types.h>
#include <sys/socket.h>

int write(sockfd, buf, len)
int sockfd;
char *buf;
int len
```

where sockfd is the socket descriptor, buf points to the buffer holding the data to be sent, and len is the amount of data to be sent in bytes.

system call: close()
function: closes the socket associated with the socket descriptor
synopsis:

```
#include <sys/types.h>
#include <sys/socket.h>

int close(sockfd)
int sockfd;
```

where sockfd is the socket descriptor.

system call: select()
function: monitors activity on a set of sockets to determine if (1)any sock-
                    ets are ready for reading or writing or (2) a time-out expires
synopsis:

```
#include <sys/time.h>
#include <sys/types.h>
#include <sys/select.h>

int select(nfds, readfds, writefds, exceptfds, timeout)
int nfds;
fd_set readfds;
fd_set writefds;
fd_set exceptfds;
struct timeval *timeout;
```

where nfds is the number of socket descriptors to check; readfds points to a bit mask of descriptors to check for reading; writefds points to a bit mask of descriptors to check for writing; exceptfds points to a bit mask of descriptors to check for exceptional conditions; and timeout specifies the time to wait before the select() call completes.

7.7.7 Socket Programming Using the TCP Protocol

Client/server applications must have a server process for each application. A server process can communicate with a number of client processes. The client process initiates the requests, or dialogues, and the server process responds. For the client process to initiate communication, it must know the server process's hostname from which it can get the server's Internet address through the function call gethostbyname().

Before the communication starts, both the server and client processes must open a socket of their own. At the time the socket is opened, it knows only which protocol will be used (TCP or UDP). The server then binds its socket descriptor to its local Internet address and port number, and waits for the client processes to make the connection. Once the connection is made, the server's socket descriptor has all the information in its 5-tuple filled in (including the remote Internet address and port number), and the data exchange begins.

7.7.7.1 Server Programming   Here are the instructions that provide a step outline of a general server program:

1. Open a socket.

   This is done with the socket() system call. It creates a socket to use for the communication, and returns a socket descriptor for the program to use. The input arguments must specify the protocol for the address family (AF_UNIX or AF_INET) and the socket type (SOCK_STREAM or SOCK_DGRAM).

2. Associate the socket descriptor with the local IP address and port number.

   This is done with the bind() system call. The input arguments must provide the socket descriptor, the address of a structure that specifies the local IP address, and the service port number.

3. Specify a queue length for server.

   This is done with the listen() system call. It sets the socket in the listen mode, and also sets the queue length for the incoming connection requests.

4. Wait for the connection from the clients.

   This is done with the accept() system call. It waits until the connection request arrives, and removes the connection from the queue.

5. After the connection is made, if the server process is an iterative server, it goes to a loop that processes requests and sends the results back to the client. If the server process is a concurrent server, it forks a new process to handle the client requests. The read() system call is used to read requests from clients, and the write() system call is used to return the results.

6. Go back to step 4.

7.7.7.2 Client Programming   Here are the instructions that provide a step outline of a general client program:

1. Open a socket.

    It performs the same function as on server side.

2. Connect to the server.

    This is done with the connect() system call. It allows the client process to specify the remote endpoint address for a previously created socket. For sockets that use the TCP protocol, the result of the connect() system call is an established connection between the local client and the remote server.

3. Send a service request to the server, and wait for responses.

    The write() system call is used to send a request to the server, and the read() system call is used to receive the results from the server.

4. Upon receiving the results, if there still are requests to be sent, return to step three; else go to step five.

5. Close socket.

    This is done with the close() system call. It terminates communication gracefully and removes the socket.

7.7.8 Case Study: A Client/Server Application Based on Sockets

This section presents an example of a client/server application that uses sockets as the communication mechanism. This application features a server that can communicate with a number of clients. The server can behave either as an iterative or a concurrent server, depending on what the client chooses. If one client chooses to run the server in the iterative mode, communication between the server and other clients is blocked until that client finishes its session with the server.

This server provides three basic functions: echo, query, and broadcast. With echo, whatever you key in on the client side is transferred to the server and echoed back to the client. For a query function, start the command with the keyword "query," followed by the UNIX command you want to issue to the server. This is useful when the client's application load module is very big because it eliminates the need to fork a process through the system() system call. For the broadcast function, start the command with the keyword "broadcast," followed by the name and value of the attribute you want to broadcast. The server broadcasts this attribute's name and value pair to the client it has chosen to listen.

For the client to receive the broadcast message, it must register to the server the kind of event it wants to listen to. This is done with the listen command, which starts with the keyword "listen," followed by the event name.

Listings 7.14, 7.15, and 7.16 present code listings for client/server applications. Listing 7.14 shows a common socket subroutine, Listing 7.15 shows a server program code, and Listing 7.16 shows a client program code.

Listing 7.14 socket_sub.c

```c
/*
 * socket_sub.c
 */
#include <stdio.h>
#include <sys/time.h>
#include <sys/types.h>
#include <sys/socket.h>
#include <netinet/in.h>
#include <arpa/inet.h>
#include <netdb.h>

#define SRV_TCP_PORT    7000
#define MAXFD           9999

struct sockaddr_in srv_addr;
struct sockaddr_in cli_addr;

int     cli_len;
char    hostname[64];

struct hostent * GetHostAddressInfo()
{
    struct hostent *hp;

    gethostname(hostname, sizeof(hostname));
    if ((hp = gethostbyname(hostname)) == NULL)
        return(NULL);
    else
        return(hp);
}

/*
 * open a socket
 */
int OpenSocket()
{
    int sockfd;

    sockfd = socket(AF_INET, SOCK_STREAM, 0);
    return(sockfd);
}

/*
 * server binds its local address to socket
 */
int BindToLocalAddress(sockfd, hp)
int sockfd;
struct hostent *hp;
{
    bzero((char*)&srv_addr, sizeof(srv_addr));
    srv_addr.sin_family = AF_INET;
    bcopy(hp->h_addr, &srv_addr.sin_addr, hp->h_length);
    srv_addr.sin_port = htons(SRV_TCP_PORT);
    return(bind(sockfd, (struct sockaddr*)&srv_addr,  sizeof(srv_addr)));
}
```

```c
void SetQueueLength(sockfd, len)
int sockfd;
{
    listen(sockfd, len);
}

int WaitForClientConnection(sockfd)
int sockfd;
{
    int newsockfd;
    fd_set ready;
    struct timeval to;

    FD_ZERO(&ready);
    FD_SET(sockfd, &ready);
    to.tv_sec = 0;
    to.tv_usec = 0;
    if (select(sockfd+1, &ready, (fd_set *) 0,
        (fd_set *) 0, &to) < 0)
    {
        perror("select");
        return(-1);
    }
    if (!FD_ISSET(sockfd, &ready))
        return(MAXFD);
    cli_len = sizeof(cli_addr);
    newsockfd = accept(sockfd, (struct sockaddr *)&cli_addr,  &cli_len);
    return(newsockfd);
}

int ConnectToServer(sockfd, name)
int  sockfd;
char *name;
{
    struct hostent *hp;
    if ((hp = gethostbyname(name)) == NULL)
        return (-1);

    /*
     * Fill in the structure "srv_addr" with the address of the server
     */
    bzero((char *)&srv_addr, sizeof(srv_addr));
    srv_addr.sin_family = AF_INET;
    bcopy(hp->h_addr, &srv_addr.sin_addr, hp->h_length);
    srv_addr.sin_port = htons(SRV_TCP_PORT);
    /*
     * connect to server
     */
    if (connect(sockfd, (struct sockaddr *)&srv_addr,
            sizeof(srv_addr)) < 0)
        return(-1);
    else
        return(0);
}
```

```c
/*
 * read n bytes from a socket descriptor
 */
int readn(fd, ptr, maxlen)
int fd;
char *ptr;
int maxlen;
{
    int n, rc;
    char c;

    rc = read(fd, ptr, maxlen);
    *(ptr+rc) = '\0';
    return(rc);
}

/*
 * write n bytes to a socket descriptor
 */
int writen(fd, ptr, nbytes)
int   fd;
char *ptr;
int   nbytes;
{
    int nleft, nwritten;
    nleft = nbytes;
    while (nleft > 0)
    {
        nwritten = write(fd, ptr, nleft);
        if (nwritten <= 0) return(nwritten);   /* error */
        nleft = nleft - nwritten;
        ptr = ptr + nwritten;
    }
    return(nbytes - nleft);
}
void ErrOut(msg)
char *msg;
{
    fprintf(stderr, "%s\n", msg);
}
```

Listing 7.15 server_socket.c

```c
/*
 *   server_socket.c
 */
#include   <stdio.h>
#include   <signal.h>
#include   <sys/types.h>
#include   <sys/socket.h>
#include   <sys/select.h>
#include   <sys/time.h>

#define   MAXLINE      512
#define   MAXFD        9999
```

```
#define   True           1
/*
 * define communication modes
 */
#define  UNDEFINED      0
#define  CONCURRENT     1
#define  ITERATIVE      2

/*
 * define event types
 */
#define   NO_EVENT       0
#define   SCALE_CHANGE  1
#define   COLOR_CHANGE  2

typedef struct client_info {
   int   srv_sockfd;
   char cli_hostname[64];
   int   cli_pid;
   int   event_type;
   struct client_info *next;
} Client_Info;

Client_Info *first_client = NULL;

int   newsockfd;
int   sockfd;
/*
 * Internal functions
 */

void BuildClientList();
void RemoveFromClientList();
void IntHandler();
void GetComMode();
struct hostent *GetHostAddressInfo();

main(argc, argv)
int argc;
char *argv[ ];
{
   int   i;
   int   cli_mode;
   int   cli_pid;
   int   cli_event;
   char cli_hostname[64];
   struct hostent *hp;
   Client_Info *tmptr;

   signal(SIGPIPE, IntHandler);
   if ((hp = GetHostAddressInfo()) == NULL)
   {
      ErrOut("Can't get the host address information");
      exit(1);
   }
   /*
```

```
 * Open a TCP socket
 */
if ((sockfd=OpenSocket()) <0)
{
   ErrOut("server: can't open a socket");
   exit(1);
}
/*
 * Bind our local address to the socket descriptor
 */
i = 0;
while (BindToLocalAddress(sockfd, hp))
{
   ErrOut("server: can't bind local address");
   sleep(5);
   if (i++ > 20)
      exit(1);
}

SetQueueLength(sockfd, 5);

while (True)
{
   /*
    * Wait for connection from a client process
    */
   newsockfd = WaitForClientConnection(sockfd);
   if (newsockfd < 0)
      ErrOut("server: accept connection error");
   else if (newsockfd == MAXFD)
   {
      tmptr = first_client;
      while (tmptr != NULL)
      {
         ProcessRequest(tmptr->srv_sockfd);
         tmptr = tmptr->next;
      }
   }
   else
   {
      GetComMode(newsockfd, &cli_mode,cli_hostname, &cli_pid);
      if (cli_mode == CONCURRENT)
      {
         /* concurrent mode */
         BuildClientList(&first_client, newsockfd,
            cli_hostname, cli_pid, NO_EVENT);
         ForkProcess(sockfd, newsockfd);
      }
      else if (cli_mode == ITERATIVE)
      { /* iterative mode */
         BuildClientList(&first_client, newsockfd,
            cli_hostname, cli_pid, NO_EVENT);
         ProcessRequest(newsockfd);
      }
```

```c
      }
    }
}

/*
 * broadcast message to appropriate clients according to
 * the events they want to listen
 */
void BroadcastMessage(message, event_type)
char *message;
int    event_type;
{
   int n, rtn;
   char  outline[MAXLINE];
   Client_Info *tmptr, *ptr;

   if (first_client == NULL)
   {
      printf("Event list is empty\n");
      return;
   }

   tmptr = first_client;
   while (tmptr != NULL)
   {
      if (event_type == tmptr->event_type)
      {
         sprintf(outline, "%s\n", message);
         n = strlen(outline);
         rtn = writen(tmptr->srv_sockfd, outline, n);
         if (rtn != n)
         {
            ErrOut("BroadcastMessage: writen error\n");
            RemoveFromClientList(&first_client,
               tmptr->srv_sockfd);
         }
      }
      tmptr = tmptr->next;
   }
}

void IntHandler()
{
   signal(SIGPIPE, IntHandler);
   ErrOut("IntHandler: pipe broken");
}

void BuildClientList(first_client,sockfd,hostname,pid,event_type)
Client_Info **first_client;
int   sockfd;
char hostname[];
int   pid;
int event_type;
{
   Client_Info *tmptr, *ptr;
```

```c
    if (*first_client == NULL)
    {
        tmptr=(Client_Info *)malloc(sizeof(Client_Info));
        tmptr->srv_sockfd = sockfd;
        strcpy(tmptr->cli_hostname, hostname);
        tmptr->cli_pid = pid;
        tmptr->event_type = event_type;
        tmptr->next = NULL;
        *first_client = tmptr;
        return;
    }

    ptr = *first_client;
    while (ptr->next != NULL)
    {
        if (ptr->srv_sockfd == sockfd)
            return;
        ptr = ptr->next;
    }
    tmptr = (Client_Info *)malloc(sizeof(Client_Info));
    tmptr->srv_sockfd = sockfd;
    strcpy(tmptr->cli_hostname, hostname);
    tmptr->cli_pid = pid;
    tmptr->event_type = event_type;
    tmptr->next = NULL;
    ptr->next = tmptr;
    return;
}

void RemoveFromClientList(first_client, sockfd)
Client_Info **first_client;
int sockfd;
{
    Client_Info *tmptr, *ptr;

    tmptr = *first_client;
    if (tmptr->srv_sockfd == sockfd)
    {
        close(sockfd);
        *first_client = tmptr->next;
        free(tmptr);
        return;
    }
    tmptr = *first_client;
    while (tmptr != NULL)
    {
        if (tmptr->srv_sockfd == sockfd)
        {
            close(sockfd);
            ptr->next = tmptr->next;
            free(tmptr);
            return;
        }
        ptr = tmptr;
        tmptr = tmptr->next;
```

```c
   }
}

int ForkProcess(sockfd, newsockfd)
int sockfd;
int newsockfd;
{
   int childpid;

   if ((childpid = fork()) < 0)
      Errout("server: fork error");
   else if (childpid == 0)
   { /* child process */
      close(sockfd);       /* close original socket */
      ProcessRequest(newsockfd);
      exit(0);
   }
   /* Don't close socket here, so that the socket descriptor
      won't get reused
      close(newsockfd);
    */
}

void GetComMode(sockfd, ptr_mode, hostname, ptr_pid)
int  sockfd;
int *ptr_mode;
char hostname[ ];
int *ptr_pid;
{
   int  n, rtn;
   char char_mode [10];
   char inpline   [256];
   char outline[256];

   n = readn(sockfd, inpline, MAXLINE);
   if ( n< 0)
   {
      ErrOut("readn error");
      *ptr_mode = UNDEFINED;
      return;
   }
   inpline[n] = '\0';
   sscanf(inpline, "%s %s %d", char_mode, hostname, ptr_pid);
   if (strcmp(char_mode, "CONCUR") == 0)
   {
      *ptr_mode = CONCURRENT;
      strcpy(outline, "CONCUR\n");
      n = strlen(outline);
      rtn = writen(newsockfd, outline, n);
      if (rtn != n)
      {
         ErrOut("writen error");
         RemoveFromClientList(&first_client, newsockfd);
      }
   }
```

```c
   else if (strcmp(char_mode, "ITERAT") == 0)
   {
      *ptr_mode = ITERATIVE;
      strcpy(outline, "ITERAT\n");
      n = strlen(outline);
      rtn = writen(newsockfd, outline, n);
      if (rtn != n)
      {
         ErrOut("writen error");
         RemoveFromClientList(&first_client, newsockfd);
      }
   }
   return;
}

int ProcessRequest(sockfd)
int sockfd;
{
   int  n, i;
   char *ptr;
   char inpline [MAXLINE];
   char command[MAXLINE];
   char outline[MAXLINE];
   char event_name[40];
   char message[64];
   char text[4096*4];
   char buf[256];
   FILE *pp;
   fd_set ready;
   struct timeval to;
   FD_ZERO(&ready);
   FD_SET(sockfd, &ready);
   to.tv_sec = 0;
   to.tv_usec = 0;
   if (select(sockfd+1, &ready, (fd_set *) 0,  (fd_set *) 0, &to) < 0)
   {
      perror("select");
      return(-1);
   }
   if (!FD_ISSET(sockfd, &ready))
      return(0);   /* data not ready */

   n = readn(sockfd, inpline, MAXLINE);
   if (n == 0)
   {
      fprintf(stdout,"socket %d closed\n", sockfd);
      return(0);  /* connection terminated */
   }
   else if ( n < 0)
   {
      ErrOut("readn error");
      return(-2);
   }
   n = strlen(inpline);
```

```c
    inpline[n-1] = '\0';
    fprintf(stdout,"receive from client:%s\n", inpline);

    ptr = &inpline[0];
    i = 0;
    while ( *ptr != '\0')
    {
        if ( *ptr != ' ')
            command[i] = *ptr;
        else
        {
            command[i] = '\0';
            break;
        }
        ptr++;
        i++;
    }

    while (*ptr == ' ')
        ptr++;
    if (strcmp(command, "broadcast") == 0)
    {
        sscanf(ptr, "%s %s", event_name, message);
        if (strcmp(event_name, "SCALE_CHANGE") == 0)
            BroadcastMessage(ptr, SCALE_CHANGE);
        else if (strcmp(event_name, "COLOR_CHANGE") == 0)
            BroadcastMessage(ptr, COLOR_CHANGE);
        sprintf(outline, "%s\n", inpline);
        n = strlen(outline);
        if (writen(sockfd, outline, n) != n)
        {
            ErrOut("writen error");
            return(-3);
        }
    }
    else if (strcmp(command, "listen") == 0)
    {
        SetEventType(ptr);
        sprintf(outline, "%s\n", inpline);
        n = strlen(outline);
        if (writen(sockfd, outline, n) != n)
        {
            ErrOut("writen error\n");
            return(-3);
        }
    }
    else if (strcmp(command, "query") == 0)
    {
        if ((pp = popen(ptr, "r")) == NULL)
            return(0);
        else
        {
            text[0] = '\0';
            while (fgets(buf, MAXLINE, pp) != NULL)
```

```c
            strcat(text, buf);
            pclose(pp);
        }
        sprintf(outline, "%s\n", inpline);
        n = strlen(outline);
        if (writen(sockfd, outline, n) != n)
        {
            ErrOut("writen error");
            return(-3);
        }
    }
    else
    {
        sprintf(outline, "%s\n", inpline);
        n = strlen(outline);
        if (writen(sockfd, outline, n) != n)
        {
            ErrOut("writen error");
            return(-3);
        }
    }
}

int SetEventType(linebuf)
char *linebuf;
{
    char event_type[20];
    char hostname[64];
    int pid;

    sscanf(linebuf, "%s %s %d", event_type, hostname, &pid);
    SetClientEventType(&first_client, hostname, pid,  event_type);
}

int SetClientEventType(first_client, hostname, pid, event_type)
Client_Info **first_client;
char hostname[ ];
int pid;
char event_type[ ];
{
    Client_Info *tmptr, *ptr;

    tmptr = *first_client;
    if (tmptr->cli_pid == pid &&
        (strcmp(tmptr->cli_hostname, hostname) == 0))
    {
        if (strcmp(event_type, "SCALE_CHANGE") == 0)
            tmptr->event_type = SCALE_CHANGE;
        else if (strcmp(event_type, "COLOR_CHANGE") == 0)
            tmptr->event_type = COLOR_CHANGE;
        return(0);
    }
    tmptr = *first_client;
    while (tmptr != NULL)
    {
```

```
        if (tmptr->cli_pid == pid &&
            (strcmp(tmptr->cli_hostname, hostname) == 0))
        {
            if (strcmp(event_type, "SCALE_CHANGE") == 0)
                tmptr->event_type = SCALE_CHANGE;
            else if (strcmp(event_type, "COLOR_CHANGE") == 0)
                tmptr->event_type = COLOR_CHANGE;
            return(0);
        }
        ptr = tmptr;
        tmptr = tmptr->next;
    }
}
```

Listing 7.16 client_socket.c

```
/*
 * client_socket.c
 */
#include  <stdio.h>
#include  <sys/types.h>
#include  <sys/socket.h>
#include  <sys/select.h>
#include  <sys/time.h>

#define MAX_SOCKET_SIZE  4096
#define MAXLINE          512
#define True             1
/*
 * define communication modes
 */
#define  UNDEFINED    0
#define  CONCURRENT   1
#define  ITERATIVE    2

/*
 * define event types
 */
#define    NO_EVENT      0
#define    SCALE_CHANGE 1
#define    COLOR_CHANGE 2

extern char hostname[64];

main(argc, argv)
int argc;
char *argv[];
{
    int  sockfd;
    int  rtn;
    int  mode;
    char server_name[64];

    if (argc < 2)
    {
        ErrOut("Usage: client server_hostname\n");
```

```c
      exit(-1);
   }
   strcpy(server_name, argv[1]);
   /*
    * Open a TCP socket
    */
   if ((sockfd = OpenSocket()) < 0)
   {
      ErrOut("client: can't open socket");
      exit(1);
   }
   /*
    * Connect to the server
    */
   if (ConnectToServer(sockfd, server_name) < 0)
   {
      ErrOut("client: connection error");
      exit(1);
   }
   /*
    * Set communication mode
    */
   mode = SetComMode(stdin, sockfd);
   RegisterListenEvent(stdin, sockfd);
   while (True)
   {
      if (mode == CONCURRENT || mode == ITERATIVE)
      {
         if ((rtn = SendRequest(stdin, sockfd)) < 0)
            ErrOut("SendRequest error\n");
         else if (rtn == 0)
         {
            /* data not ready */
         }
         else
         {
            rtn = ReceiveResponse(sockfd);
            if (rtn == 1)  /* receive quit request */
               break;
         }
      }
   }
   close(sockfd);
   exit(0);
}

int SetComMode(fp, sockfd)
FILE *fp;
int sockfd;
{
   int  n, i;
   int  event_type;
   char linebuf[MAXLINE+1];
   char sendline[MAXLINE+1], recvline[MAXLINE+1];
```

```c
    gethostname(hostname, sizeof(hostname));

    printf("Please select type of server:\n");
    printf("1: Concurrent\n");
    printf("2: Iterative\n");

    if (fgets(linebuf, MAXLINE, fp) != NULL)
    {
        if (linebuf[0] == '1')
            sprintf(sendline,"CONCUR %s %d\n", hostname,  getpid());
        else if (linebuf[0] == '2')
            sprintf(sendline,"ITERAT %s %d\n", hostname,  getpid());

        n = strlen(sendline);
        if (writen(sockfd, sendline, n) != n)
        {
            ErrOut("SetComMode: writen error");
            return(-1);
        }
    }
    n = readn(sockfd, recvline, MAXLINE);
    if (n < 0)
    {
        ErrOut("SetComMode: readn error");
        return (-1);
    }
    recvline[n] = '\0';
    printf("set server mode to %s\n", recvline);

    if (strcmp(recvline, "CONCUR\n") == 0)
        return (CONCURRENT);
    else if (strcmp(recvline, "ITERAT\n") == 0)
        return(ITERATIVE);
    else
        return(-1);
}

int SendRequest(fp, sockfd)
FILE *fp;
int sockfd;
{
    int n;
    char sendline[MAXLINE];
    char cli_info[128];
    char *ptr;
    fd_set ready;
    struct timeval to;

    FD_ZERO(&ready);
    FD_SET(fileno(fp), &ready);
    to.tv_sec = 0;
    to.tv_usec = 0;
    if (select(fileno(fp)+1, &ready, (fd_set *) 0,  (fd_set *) 0, &to) < 0)
    {
        perror("select");
        return(-1);
```

```c
   }

   if (!FD_ISSET(fileno(fp), &ready))
      return(0); /* data not ready */

   if (fgets(sendline, MAXLINE, fp) != NULL)
   {
      ptr = &sendline[0];
      while (*ptr == ' ')
         ptr++;

      if (strncpy(ptr, "listen", 6) == 0)
      {
         sprintf(cli_info, " %s %d\n", hostname, getpid());
         n = strlen(sendline);
         sendline[n-1] = '\0';
         strcat(sendline, cli_info);
      }

      n = strlen(sendline);
      if (writen(sockfd, sendline, n) != n)
      {
         ErrOut("SendRequest: writen error");
         return(-1);
      }
   }
   return(1);
}

int ReceiveResponse(sockfd)
int sockfd;
{
   int n;
   int i;
   char recvline[MAXLINE+1];
   fd_set ready;
   struct timeval to;
   FD_ZERO(&ready);
   FD_SET(sockfd, &ready);
   to.tv_sec = 0;
   to.tv_usec = 0;
   if (select(sockfd+1, &ready, (fd_set *) 0,  (fd_set *) 0, &to) < 0)
   {
      perror("select");
      return(0);
   }

   /* Is data ready ?  */
   if (!FD_ISSET(sockfd, &ready))
      return(0);
   /*
    * Now read a line from the socket and write it
    * to the standard output
    */

   n = readn(sockfd, recvline, MAXLINE);
```

```
  if (n < 0)
  {
    ErrOut("ReceiveResponse: readn error");
    return(-1);
  }
  recvline[n] ='\0';
  fprintf(stdout,"receive message: %s\n", recvline);
  if (strncmp(recvline, "quit", 4) == 0)
    return(1);
  return(0);
}
```

7.8 PROGRAMMING WITH RPC

The remote procedure call (RPC) is a network programming facility that allows one process (the client process) to have another process (the server process) execute a procedure call as if the client process had executed it in its own address space. Conveniently, the client and the server processes can reside on the same or different host machines.

The RPC facility consists of two protocols that always work hand in hand: the RPC protocol and the external data representation (XDR) protocol. The RPC protocol is a library of procedures that provides the client and the server process a way to communicate. The XDR protocol is a specification for portable data representation.

In an RPC application, you must start the server process before any client processes. Once the server process is started, it immediately goes into a wait state, awaiting the arrival of the client's requests. The client makes a remote procedure call that sends requests to the server as necessary. When the requests arrive at the server side, the server calls a dispatch routine, performs the requested service, and sends back the reply; the remote procedure call then returns to the client process.

7.8.1 Program, Procedure, and Version Numbers

Each RPC server program has a unique program number. The available program numbers for the application programs are given within the range from 0x20000000 to 0x3fffffff. Each procedure within the server program is assigned a procedure number. The combination of the program number and the procedure number uniquely identifies an RPC procedure. Normally, the procedure numbers are numbered from one to the number of procedures the server program may have. Furthermore, a version number is attached to the program number so that you can have two versions of a certain server running at the same time. Version numbers are integers.

7.8.2 Server Programming

The following steps outline the server program, which uses the RPC facility:

1. Get a server transport handle, which is used to receive and send RPC messages (i.e. through svctcp_create()).

2. Call pmap_unset() to remove the mapping associated with the program and version numbers.

3. Associate the program and version numbers through the call to svc_register().

4. Call svc_run(), the remote procedure dispatcher. This function calls the remote procedure in response to the RPC request. Once svc_run() is called, the RPC server process goes into a wait state, awaiting the arrival of RPC requests. After receiving the RPC request, it then calls the proper service routines.

7.8.3 Client Programming

The following steps outline the client program, which uses the RPC facility:

1. Construct the server address structure from the server hostname (i.e., through gethostbyname()).

2. Get the client transport handle from the server address structure (i.e., through the clntcp_create() call).

3. Make a remote procedure call (i.e., clnt_call()).

4. Finally, destroy the client transport handle.

7.8.4 RPC Protocol Functions

The RPC protocol functions are a group of C callable routines that interface to the network programming code developed for the RPC calls. These functions are further divided into two layers: the high-level and low-level RPC function calls. The high-level RPC calls are used when the programmer does not want to worry about the programming details such as choosing the socket and setting the timeout time. The high-level RPC function calls include routines such as registerrpc() and svc_run() on the server side and callrpc() on the client side. The low-level RPC function calls allow the programmer to control network-related parameters. The low-level RPC function calls include routines such as svctcp_create(), svc_register(), svc_getargs(), svc_sendreply(), svc_destroy(), etc. on the server side and clntcp_create(), clnt_call() on the client side.

The following lists all the RPC function calls used later in the examples:

```
/*
 * create a socket and return a TCP RPC transport for that socket
 * return NULL if fails
 */
#include <rpc.h>
SVCXPRT  *svctcp_create(sockfd, sendsz, recvsz)
int sockfd;
int sendsz;
int recvsz;

/*
 * tell the portmap to remove the entry identified by the (prognum, versnum)
 * pair from the registration table
```

```c
 *  return True if succeeds, otherwise False
 */
bool_t pmap_unset(prognum, versnum)
u_long prognum;
u_long versnum;

/*
 * register a dispatch routine of a specified protocol to the portmap
 * return True if succeeds, otherwise False
 */
bool_t svc_register(xprt, prognum, versnum, function, protocol)
SVCXPRT *xprt;
u_long prognum;
u_long versnum;
void        (*function)();
u_long protocol;

/*
 * put the server into an indefinite loop for servicing requests
 * return only if there is an unrecoverable error
 */
void srv_run()

/*
 *    used by the service dispatch routine to reply to the client, pass the
 *    specified data through the specified XDR encoder
 *    return True if succeeds, otherwise False
 */
bool_t svc_sendreply(xprt, outproc, out)
SVCXPRT *xprt;
xdrproc_t      outproc;
char           *out;

/*
 * decode server arguments from XDR from a given data pointer and decode routine
 * return True if succeeds, otherwise False
 */
svc_getargs(xprt, inproc, in)
SVCXPRT  *xprt;
xdrproc_t      inproc;
char           *in;

/*
 * used to report the error that the server does not have the procedure number
 * requested
 */
void svcerr_noproc(xprt)
SVCXPRT  *xprt;

/*
 * create a TCP transport CLIENT handle for the specified program and version
 * number on the server machine
 * return pointer to a CLIENT handle if succeeds, otherwise NULL
 */
CLIENT *clntcp_create(addr, prognum, versnum, sockfdp, sendsz, recvsz)
```

```
struct sockadd_in  *addr;
u_long prognum;
u_long versnum;
int    *sockfdp;
int    sendsz;
int    recvsz;

/*
 * report CLIENT handle creation error
 */
void clnt_pcreateerror(str)
char *str;

/*
 * make call to the remote procedure
 */
enum clnt_stat clnt_call(clnt, procnum, inproc, in, outproc, out, imeout)
CLIENT *clnt;
u_long          procnum;
xdrproc_t       inproc;
char            *in;
xdrproc_t       outproc;
char            *outproc;
struct timeval  timeout;

/*
 * report clnt_call() error
 */
void clnt_perror(clnt, msg)
CLIENT  *clnt;
char         *msg;

/*
 *  deallocate memory associated with the data structure for the named CLIENT
 *  handle and close the socket
 */
void  clnt_destroy(clnt)
CLIENT *clnt;
```

7.8.5 RPC Programming

Listings 7.17 and 7.18 present code listings for a client/server application based on RPC. Listing 7.17 shows the server program code, and Listing 7.18 shows the client program code. In this simple application the server increments each element in an integer array passed from the client by one.

Listing 7.17 server_rpc1.c

```
/*
 * server_rpc1.c
 */
#include <stdio.h>
```

```c
#include <rpc/rpc.h>

#define RADDPROG      0x2000000a
#define RADDVERS      1
#define RADDONEPROC   1
#define RADDTWOPROC   2
#define MAXLEN        1000

typedef struct varintarr {
   int arrlnth;
   int *data;
} vararrtype;

xdr_varintarr (xdrsp, arrp)
XDR *xdrsp;
vararrtype *arrp;
{
   return(xdr_array(xdrsp, &arrp->data, &arrp->arrlnth, MAXLEN,
      sizeof(int), xdr_int));
}

void AddNumber();

main(argc, argv)
int argc;
char *argv[];
{
   SVCXPRT *transp;

   transp = svctcp_create(RPC_ANYSOCK, 0 ,0);
   if (transp == NULL)
   {
      printf("can't create an RPC server handle\n");
      exit(1);
   }

   pmap_unset(RADDPROG, RADDVERS);
   if (!svc_register(transp, RADDPROG, RADDVERS,
         AddNumber, IPPROTO_TCP));
   {
      printf("can't register raddnumber service\n");
      exit(1);
   }
   svc_run();
   printf("RPC server error\n");
}

void AddNumber(reqstp, transp)
struct svc_req *reqstp;
SVCXPRT *transp;
{
   vararrtype *arrvar, *arrres;
   int i;

   arrvar = (vararrtype *)malloc(sizeof(vararrtype));
   arrvar->arrlnth = 200;
```

```
    arrvar->data = (int *)malloc(arrvar->arrlnth *sizeof(int));
    arrres = (vararrtype *)malloc(sizeof(vararrtype));
    arrres->arrlnth = 200;
    arrres->data = (int *)malloc(arrres->arrlnth *sizeof(int));

    switch(reqstp->rq_proc) {
    case NULLPROC:
        if (!svc_sendreply(transp, xdr_void, 0))
            printf("can't reply to RPC call\n");
        break;
    case RADDONEPROC:
        svc_getargs(transp, xdr_varintarr, arrvar);
        for (i=0; i<= 199; i++)
            *(arrres->data + i) = *(arrvar->data + i) + 1;
        if (!svc_sendreply(transp, xdr_varintarr, arrres))
            printf("can't reply to RPC call\n");
        break;
    case RADDTWOPROC:
        svc_getargs(transp, xdr_varintarr, arrvar);
        for (i=0; i<= 199; i++)
            *(arrres->data + i) = *(arrvar->data + i) + 2;
        if (!svc_sendreply(transp, xdr_varintarr, arrres))
            printf("can't reply to RPC call\n");
        break;
    default:
        svcerr_noproc(transp);
        break;
    }
}
```

Listing 7.18 Client_rpc1.c

```
* client_rpc1.c
 */
#include <stdio.h>
#include <rpc/rpc.h>
#include <sys/time.h>
#include <netdb.h>
#include <sys/socket.h>

#define RADDPROG       0x2000000a
#define RADDVERS       1
#define RADDONEPROC    1
#define RADDTWOPROC    2
#define inbufsize      1000
#define outbufsize     1000
#define MAXLEN         1000

typedef struct varintarr {
    int arrlnth;
    int *data;
} vararrtype;

struct hostent *gethostbyname();
```

```c
xdr_varintarr (xdrsp, arrp)
XDR *xdrsp;
vararrtype *arrp;
{
   return(xdr_array(xdrsp, &arrp->data, &arrp->arrlnth, MAXLEN,
      sizeof(int), xdr_int));
}

main(argc, argv)
int argc;
char *argv[];
{
   struct hostent *hp;
   struct timeval total_timeout;
   struct sockaddr_in server_addr;
   int     sock = RPC_ANYSOCK;
   CLIENT *client;
   enum   clnt_stat client_stat;
   int     i;
   vararrtype *cmyarr, *cmyres;

   if (argc < 2)
   {
      printf("Usage: addone hostname\n");
      exit(-1);
   }

   cmyarr = (vararrtype *)malloc(sizeof(vararrtype));
   cmyarr->arrlnth = 200;
   cmyarr->data = (int *)malloc(cmyarr->arrlnth * sizeof(int));

   cmyres = (vararrtype *)malloc(sizeof(vararrtype));
   cmyres->arrlnth = 200;
   cmyres->data = (int *)malloc(cmyres->arrlnth * sizeof(int));
   /* initialize data array */
   for (i=0; i<=199; i++)
      *(cmyarr->data + i) = i;

   if ((hp = gethostbyname(argv[1])) == NULL)
   {
      printf("can't get address for %s\n", argv[1]);
      exit(-1);
   }

   bcopy(hp->h_addr,(caddr_t)&server_addr.sin_addr,hp->h_length);
   server_addr.sin_family = AF_INET;
   server_addr.sin_port = 0;

   if ((client = clntcp_create(&server_addr, RADDPROG, RADDVERS,
         &sock, inbufsize, outbufsize)) == NULL)
   {
      clnt_pcreateerror("clnttcp_create");
      exit(-1);
   }

   total_timeout.tv_sec = 300;
```

```c
      total_timeout.tv_usec = 0;

   client_stat = clnt_call(client, RADDONEPROC, xdr_varintarr,
      cmyarr, xdr_varintarr, cmyres, total_timeout);

   if (client_stat != RPC_SUCCESS)
   {
      clnt_perror(client, "rpc");
      exit(-1);
   }
   /* print partial data, before and after the call */
   printf("   before the call              after the call\n");

   for (i=0; i< 10; i++)
      printf("        %d                        %d\n",
      *(cmyarr->data+i), *(cmyres->data+i));
   clnt_destroy(client);
   exit(0);
}
```

7.8.6 Case Study: A Client/Server Application Based on RPC

This section presents a client/server application that uses the RPC as the communication mechanism. The server in this application accepts system commands from the client through the RPC, and then executes the system command using the popen() system call. The system command's output is sent back to the client application. This kind of service can be very useful because client programs today tend to be larger, due to the X window code inside the client application program. When an application becomes very large, performing a system command within the application program can be very costly in terms of memory and time. Normally, a server program does not contain any X window code, and its program size tends to be small.

So it is advantageous for the client application to allow the server program to perform the system command and have the result sent back to it. For example, during the computation process, the application program may want to know the available disk space in a certain filesystem. In this case, it can request the server to perform a df command on that filesystem, and have the result sent back to it.

Listing 7.19 shows a server program code.

Listing 7.19 server_rpc2.c

```c
/*
 * server_rpc2.c
 */
#include <stdio.h>
#include <rpc/rpc.h>
#define RQUERYPROG    0x2000000b
#define RQUERYVERS    1
#define RQUERYPROC    1
#define MAXOPLEN         80
#define MAXTEXTLEN     20000
```

```c
typedef struct query_struc {
   int    flag;
   char   *op;
   char   *result;
} query_type;

void query();

xdr_query(xdrsp, structp)
XDR *xdrsp;
query_type *structp;
{
   if (!xdr_int(xdrsp, &structp->flag))
       return (0);
   if (!xdr_string(xdrsp, &structp->op, MAXOPLEN))
       return (0);
   if (!xdr_string(xdrsp, &structp->result, MAXTEXTLEN))
       return (0);
   return(1);
}

main(argc, argv)
int   argc;
char *argv[];
{
   SVCXPRT *transp;

   transp = svctcp_create(RPC_ANYSOCK, 0, 0);
   if (transp == NULL)
   {
      printf("can't creat an RPC server\n");
      exit(1);
   }
   pmap_unset(RQUERYPROG, RQUERYVERS);
   if (!svc_register(transp, RQUERYPROG, RQUERYVERS,
         query, IPPROTO_TCP))
   {
      printf("can't register query service\n");
      exit(1);
   }
   svc_run();
   printf("RPC query server error\n");
}

void query(reqstp, transp)
struct svc_req *reqstp;
SVCXPRT *transp;
{
   query_type *in_structp, *out_structp;
   FILE        *pp;
   char        command[128];
   char        text[16384];
   char        buf[256];

   in_structp = (query_type *)malloc(sizeof(query_type));
   in_structp->op = (char *)malloc(MAXOPLEN);
```

```c
    in_structp->result = (char *)malloc(MAXTEXTLEN);

    out_structp = (query_type *)malloc(sizeof(query_type));
    out_structp->op = (char *)malloc(MAXOPLEN);
    out_structp->result = (char *)malloc(MAXTEXTLEN);

    switch (reqstp->rq_proc) {
    case NULLPROC:
       if (!svc_sendreply(transp, xdr_void, 0))
          printf("can't reply to RPC call\n");
       break;
    case RQUERYPROC:
       svc_getargs(transp, xdr_query, in_structp);
       sprintf(command, "%s", in_structp->op);
       if ((pp = popen(command, "r")) == (FILE *) NULL)
          return;
       else
       {
          text[0] = '\0';
          while (fgets(buf, 128, pp) != NULL)
             strcat(text, buf);
          pclose(pp);
       }
       out_structp->flag = 20;
       strcpy(out_structp->op, in_structp->op);
       strcpy(out_structp->result, text);
       if (!svc_sendreply(transp, xdr_query, out_structp))
          printf("RPC reply call error\n");
       break;
    default:
       svcerr_noproc(transp);
       break;
    }
    return;
}
```

Listing 7.20 shows a client program code.

Listing 7.20 client_rpc2.c

```c
/*
 * client_rpc2.c
 */
#include <stdio.h>
#include <rpc/rpc.h>
#include <sys/time.h>
#include <netdb.h>
#include <sys/socket.h>
#include <pwd.h>

#define RQUERYPROG    0x2000000b
#define RQUERYVERS    1
#define RQUERYPROC    1
#define MAXOPLEN      80
```

```c
#define MAXTEXTLEN    14000
#define inbufsize     14000
#define outbufsize    14000
#define True          1

typedef structp query_struc {
   int    flag;
   char   *op;
   char   *result;
} query_type;

xdr_query(xdrsp, structp)
XDR *xdrsp;
query_type *structp;
{
   if (!xdr_int(xdrsp, &structp->flag))
       return (0);
   if (!xdr_string(xdrsp, &structp->op, MAXOPLEN))
       return (0);
   if (!xdr_string(xdrsp, &structp->result, MAXTEXTLEN))
       return (0);
}

main(argc, argv)
int  argc;
char *argv[];
{
   struct hostent *hp;
   struct timeval pertry_timeout, total_timeout;
   struct sockaddr_in server_addr;
   struct passwd *pw;
   query_type *in_struct, *out_structp;
   int     socket = RPC_ANYSOCK;
   CLIENT *client;
   enum    clnt_stat client_stat;
   char    *user_name;
   char    command[256];
   char    cwd[128];
   char    *cwdptr;
   char    linebuf[128];
   int     uid;
   int     n;

   if (argc < 2)
   {
      printf("Usage: rls hostname\n");
      exit(-1);
   }

   uid = getuid();
   if ((pw = getpwuid(uid)) == NULL)
      user_name = "noname";
   else
      user_name = pw->pw_name;

   if ((cwdptr = (char *)getcwd(cwd, 128)) == NULL)
```

```c
{
    printf("can't get current directory\n");
    strcat(cwd, "./");
}

out_structp = (query_type *)malloc(sizeof(query_type));
out_structp->op = (char *)malloc(MAXOPLEN);
out_structp->result = (char *)malloc(MAXTEXTLEN);

/* initialize data */
in_structp = (query_type *)malloc(sizeof(query_type));
in_structp->flag = 10;
in_structp->op = (char *)malloc(MAXOPLEN);
while (True)
{
    fgets(linebuf, 256, stdin);
    n = strlen(linebuf);
    linebuf[n-1] = '\0';
    sprintf(command, "%s ", linebuf);
    strcpy(in_structp->op, command);
    in_structp->result = (char *)malloc(MAXTEXTLEN);
    strcpy(in_structp->result, "NULL");

    if ((hp = gethostbyname(argv[1])) == NULL)
    {
        printf("can't get address for %s\n", argv[1]);
        exit(-1);
    }
    bcopy(hp->h_addr, (caddr_t)&server_addr.sin_addr, hp-> h_length);
    server_addr.sin_family = AF_INET;
    server_addr.sin_port = 0;

    if ((client=clnttcp_create(&server_addr,RQUERYPROG,
            RQUERYVERS, &sock, inbufsize, outbufsize)) == NULL)
    {
        clnt_pcreateerror("clnttcp_create");
        exit(-1);
    }

    total_timeout.tv_sec = 300;
    total_timeout.tv_usec = 0;

    client_stat = clnt_call(client, RQUERYPROC, xdr_query,
        in_structp, xdr_query, out_structp,  total_timeout);
    if (client_stat != RPC_SUCCESS)
    {
        clnt_perror(client, "rpc");
        exit(-1);
    }

    /* print received data */
    printf("%s\n", out_structp->result);
}
clnt_destroy(client);
exit(0);
}
```

7.9 SUMMARY

This chapter featured seven useful UNIX resources (signal, fifo, time/timer, lock, dynamic memory, socket, and RPC) and gave examples showing how to program effectively with each of these resources. The signal, fifo, time/timer, and lock examples are complete and quite simple.

The dynamic memory manager example is very complex; therefore it was used as a case study. The socket programming example belongs to the client/server application category. It, too, was complicated enough to be treated as a case study.

Two examples were given on the RPC, both simple to program, but the reader may find them hard to digest the first time he or she reads them.

Programming with X/Motif

8.1 INTRODUCTION

Almost all applications that run on a computer today use some kind of graphical interface, and X/Motif has become the most popular tool for writing such graphical user interface under the UNIX platform. Generally speaking, it is not easy for a beginner to write graphical user interface using the X/Motif tools in a short period of time, because X/Motif programming uses a different programming style than other programming languages such as C. Also, the amount of material that you must digest before you can use it effectively is enormous. So the only way a beginner can achieve this goal is by using tools or complete examples that can be tailored to suit his or her special applications.

Our major emphasis in this chapter is on Motif programming; X programming examples are given only to supplement those functions Motif does not provide. In the remaining sections of this chapter, we first give a brief outline of the Motif programming model. Then, three complete Motif applications written based on this Motif programming model are presented in three stages. Stage one shows how to implement a text editor with all the basic editing functions. Stage two presents a simple drawing editor. Finally, we show how to build a table editor from the existing Motif widget set.

8.2 MOTIF PROGRAMMING MODEL

An application program that uses the X/Motif to create a graphical user interface must follow the following five basic steps:

1. Initialize the intrinsics, create the application context, and open a display.

The piece of code that does these jobs is

```
XtToolkitInitialize();
app_context = XtCreateApplicationContext();
dpy =  XtOpenDisplay(app_context,   /* application context */
NULL,                  /* display name */
app_name,              /* application name */
app_class,             /* application class */
NULL, 0,               /* xrm options, num_options */
&argc, argv);          /* command line options */
```

2. Create widget trees.

First, a top-level shell widget must be created. This is done by calling function XtAppCreateShell() as follows:

```
n = 0;
top_level = XtAppCreateShell("textTop",   "TextTop",
applicationShellWidgetClass, dpy,  args, n);
```

3. A form or frame widget is created as the child of the top-level widget to hold everything.

```
n = 0;
main_form = XmCreateForm(top_level, "mainForm", args, n);
XtManageChild(main_form);
```

One or more widgets can be created as the children of the form widget. This widget creation process can be continued until no further widget is needed.

4. Register callbacks and event handlers for those widgets within the widget tree.

Here are some examples:

```
XtAddCallback(button[i], XmActivateCallback,
    (XtCallbackProc)  ButtonSelectCB, (XtPointer) i);
```

and

```
XtAddEventHandler(text_widget, ButtonPressMask, False,
    (XtEventHandler)PosChangeEH,   (XtPointer)NULL);
```

The first example says that when the button widget button[i] is pressed, the control goes to the function ButtonSelectCB(), with the integer i passed to it as the second argument. The first argument is always the widget itself. The second example says that when the mouse button is pressed inside the text widget area, the control goes to the event handler function PosChangeEH(), with the NULL value passed to it as the second argument.

5. Realize all widgets by calling XtRealizeWidget(), with the top level widget as the only argument.

```
XtRealizeWidget(top_level);
```

6. Enter the event loop by calling XtAppMainLoop(), with the application context as the only argument.

```
XtAppMainLoop(app_context);
```

8.3 WRITING X/MOTIF PROGRAMS

This section presents a fairly sophisticated X/Motif program using the model outlined in Section 8.2. This program was chosen for case study for two reasons: First, it allows the author to tie all the pieces together in one program. Secondly, it shows how to kick off several application windows in one program. This approach is quite different from others' approaches, which normally concentrate on one widget at a time. Although this is a demo program, it is practical because you can almost always start from this piece of code and tailor it to suit your own application.

This demo program consists of three major applications. The first application is a text editor, which has all the basic editing functions as a professional editor. The second application is a drawing editor in which you can draw lines, rectangles, and text on the drawing area. The third application shows how to construct a simple table editor using existing Motif widgets such as scrolled window, drawing area, text widgets, and pushbutton widgets.

Please keep in mind that this is a three-in-one program: three applications are combined into one executable. When the program initially starts, it brings up a main window for the text editor, which is the first application. This main window has a menubar with four pulldown menus. The first three belong to the text editor, and the fourth serves as a means to start the other two applications.

8.3.1 Case Study: A Text Editor

8.3.1.1 Functional Descriptions

☞ Main window

Figure 8.1 shows the main window for the text editor. This main window consists of a menubar with four pulldown menus, a scrolled text area, and a status label. These four pulldown menus are file, edit, preference, and show.

☞ File menu

The file menu has six options: open, close, save, save as, print, and exit. When the open option is selected, it pops up a file selection dialog box (as Figure 8.2 shows) that allows you to select the text file you want to edit. When the close option is selected, it clears the text window and prompts to save the file (as Figure 8.3 shows) if the file has been edited but not saved yet. The save option saves the file content to the disk file if its content has been modified. The save as option pops up a file selection dialog box similar to Figure 8.2, with the exception that the open pushbutton is changed to the save pushbutton, and the title is changed to save file and prompts for the filename to be saved. If the file to be saved already exists, it pops up a file overwrite window as Figure 8.4 shows. The print option, when selected, pops up a dialog box (as Figure 8.5 shows) that allows the user to specify the printer name and the number of copies to print. When the OK button is selected, the content of the file currently being edited is printed on the specified printer. The exit option terminates this application.

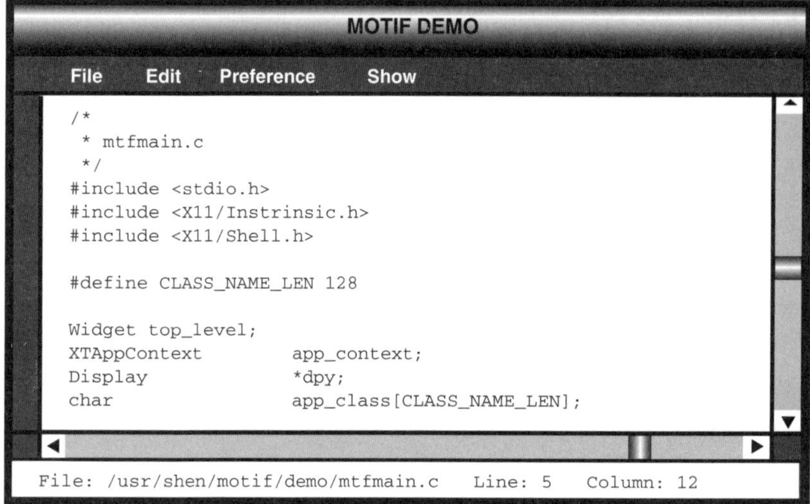

Fig. 8.1 Main Window for the Text Editor

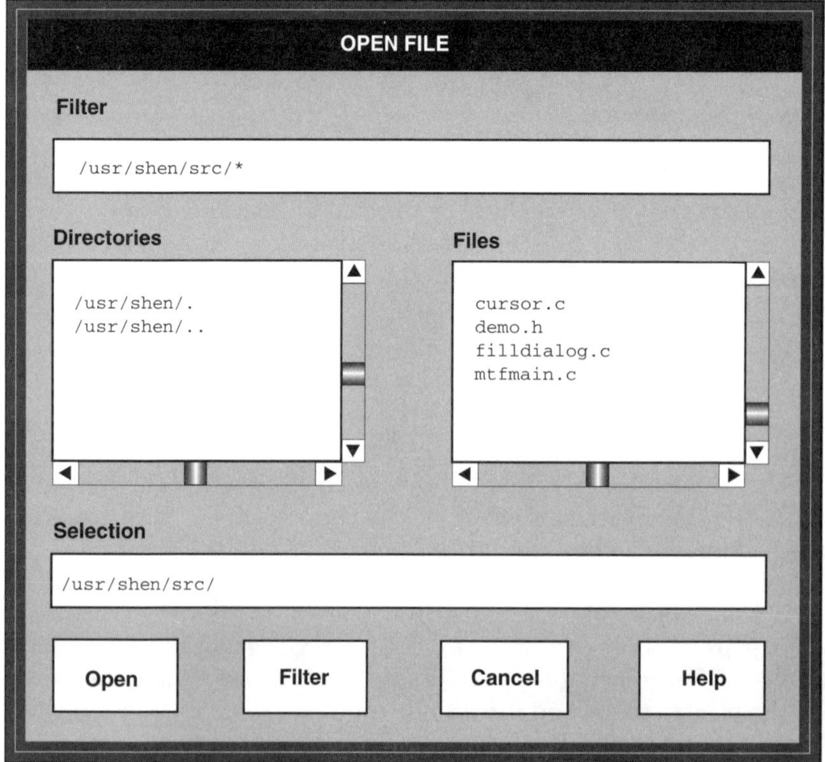

Fig. 8.2 File Selection Box

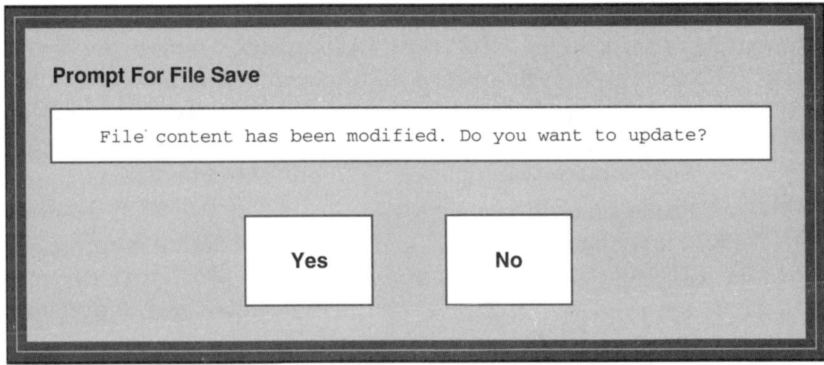

Fig. 8.3 Prompt for File Save

Fig. 8.4 Prompt for File Overwrite

Fig. 8.5 Print Dialog

☞ Edit menu

The edit menu has seven options: cut, copy, paste, delete, search, set mark, and jump to mark. The cut option removes the highlighted text to a scratch area. The copy option copies the highlighted text to the scratch area. The paste option inserts the text saved in the scratch area at the position to which the current cursor location points. The delete option deletes the highlighted text.

The search option pops up a dialog box (as Figure 8.6 shows) that prompts for a search pattern and a replacing string, if so desired. This dialog prompts the user for the text string to search for and, if a match is found, which text string to replace it with. The case sensitive toggle switch, when activated, matches a string only if it has an exact match including the case.

Press the search button to begin searching. When a match is found, press the replace button to replace the matched string with the replacing string. After a matched string is found, the user can press the replace and search button to replace the matched string with the replacing string, and continue the search for the next matched string. The replace all option searches for and replaces all matched strings.

The set mark option saves the current cursor position, and the jump to mark option moves the cursor from the current position to the position saved by the set mark option.

☞ Preference menu

The third pulldown menu is the preference menu, which has two options: color and font. The color option pops up a list of color names (as Figure 8.7 shows) that allows the user to select the foreground and background colors for the text editor window. The font option pops up a list of fonts (as Figure 8.8 shows) that allows the user to select the font for the text in the text window.

Fig. 8.6 Text Search Dialog

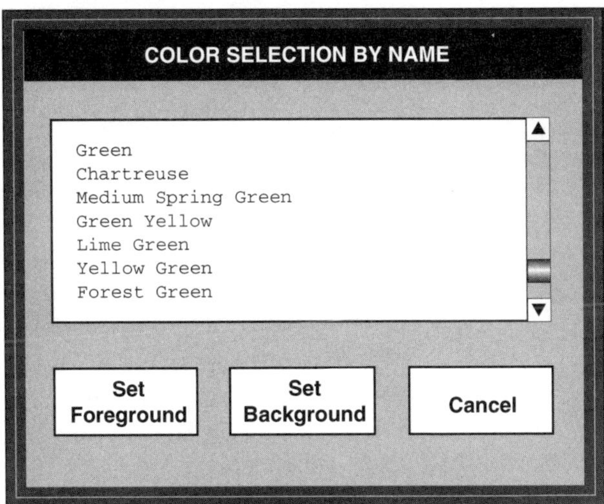

Fig. 8.7 Color Selection Window

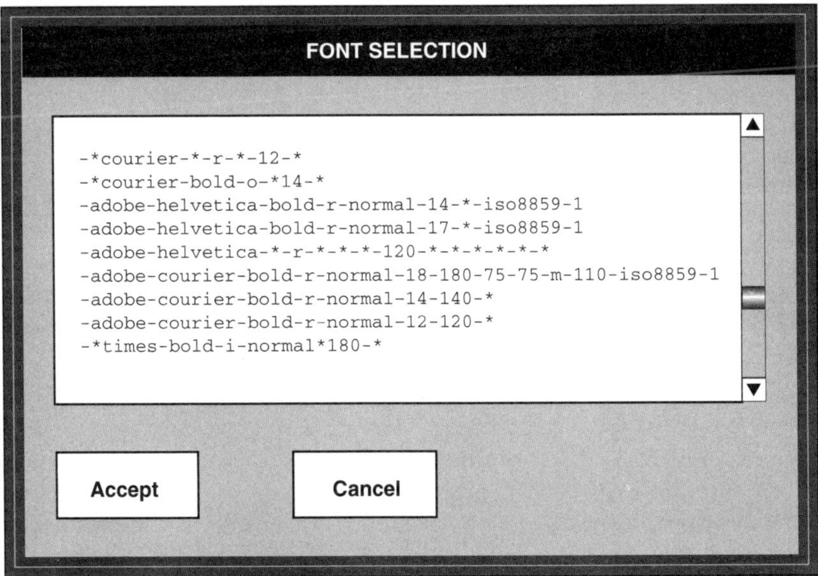

Fig. 8.8 Font Selection Window

☞ Show menu

The fourth pulldown menu is the show menu, which has two options: drawing editor and table editor. Through the show menu, you can start any other application such as drawing editor and table editor.

The scrolled text area, the work area for file editing, is found below the pull-down menu. At the bottom of the main window is the status label, which shows the current open filename and the cursor's position in terms of line number and column number.

8.3.1.2 Program Description

☞ Main program

Look carefully at the coding needed for steps one, five, and six in Section 8.2. The coding within these steps basically is fixed. Therefore, code in these steps is grouped into the main program module. The only other piece of code required in this main program is a call to a function that performs the tasks described in steps two, three, and four. Let us call the function MainMenu(). This results in a common main program as shown in Listing 8.1. The include file demo.h shown in Listing 8.2 includes all the X/Motif headers and some pre-defined constants.

☞ Creating the main window

The code to create the main window is shown in Listing 8.3. MainMenu() is the only function in this program module that is called externally. First, it creates a top-level shell as the root of a new application. It then creates a frame under this top level to show the three-dimensional look. A form widget is created under the frame to hold everything within this application.

The next step is to create a menubar and four pulldown menus, and attach these pulldown menus to the menubar. This constitutes the major part of the work in this function. Creating the menubar is done by calling the function MenuBar(), which takes a parent widget, an array of widgets (with each widget corresponding to a pulldown menu), an array of pulldown menu labels, and a number of pulldown menus as input arguments and returns the menubar widget. The menubar then is attached to the enclosing form widget on all sides except the bottom attachment, which is left open.

Next, it calls function CreateMenuButton() to create all the menu buttons for each pulldown menu. Since it has four pulldown menus, the program calls to the function CreateMenuButton() four times. The function CreateMenuButton() takes seven input arguments, which include a pulldown menu widget, an array of button widgets (with each button corresponding to an option in the menu), an array of option labels, a number of option labels, a callback function, an array of integers that indicate where the separator is needed, and an array of integers that indicate whether an option is a toggle button. For example, if you want to add a separator beneath the ith option, set the array element sep[i] equal to one; otherwise set it to zero. Similarly, if you want the ith option to be a toggle button, set toggle[i] to one; otherwise set it to zero.

After creating the menus and their options, we create a scrolled text area for text display and editing. This is done by calling the function CreateText-WorkArea(), which takes two input arguments: the parent widget, which is a form widget, and the top adjacent widget, which is the menubar widget. It uses the parent widget to create a scrolled text widget, and attaches to the menubar at the top. It adds the callback function TextChangeCB() when the text value is changed. It also adds an event handler function PosChangeEH() when the cursor position moves to track the cursor position instantaneously.

Finally, we create the status label area at the bottom of the main window to show the current filename and current cursor position. This is done by calling the function CreateStatusLabel(). This function also takes two input arguments: the parent widget, which is a form widget, and the top adjacent widget, which is the scrolled text widget. It uses the parent widget to create a frame-form-label widget tree, and attaches the frame widget to the scrolled text widget at the top.

The function SetStatusLabel() at the end of Listing 8.3 is called whenever the cursor position changes or a file is opened or closed. It fills in the filename and the cursor position on the label widget at the bottom of the main window.

☞ Handling the file menu options

The callback function FileMenuCB() handles all the options in the file menu. Whenever an option in the file menu is selected, control goes to this function. Depending on the option selected, this function calls the appropriate routine to perform the required task. For example, if the open option is selected, the control transfers to the callback function FileMenuCB(). It then calls the function CreateOpenWidget() to pop up a file selection box, as shown in Figure 8.2. After the user selects a filename and pushes the open button, control goes to another callback function, FileOpenAcceptCB(). It retrieves the filename that the user has selected and passes it to the ReadFile() routine. This ReadFile() routine opens and reads the file content into a buffer, and sets the text widget to show the buffer content by calling the function SetWorkAreaText().

If the close option is selected, the callback function FileMenuCB() first checks to see if the text has been changed. If so, a dialog, as shown in Figure 8.3, pops up and prompts the user to save the file. After the file has been saved, it calls the function ClearWorkArea() to reset the text area to blank.

If the save option is selected, it calls the function SaveFile() to save the current buffer content into the current working file if the text has been changed; otherwise no action is taken, and control returns to event main loop.

If the save as option is selected, it calls the function CreateSaveWidget() to pop up a file selection box similar to the one shown in Figure 8.2, prompting the user to select a filename. If the saved file name already exists, it prompts the user either to overwrite it or cancel it. This prompt dialog is shown in Figure 8.4.

If the print option is selected, it calls the function CreatePrintWidget() to pop up a dialog box, as shown in Figure 8.5, with the default printer name ps and the default number of print copies set equal to one. The user presses the OK button to start printing or the Cancel button to cancel this dialog.

If the exit option is selected, it calls the function SaveFile() to save the current buffer content into the current working file before it exits the program if the text has been changed; otherwise the program exits immediately.

☞ Handling the edit menu options

The callback function EditMenuCB() handles all the options in the edit menu. Whenever an option in the edit menu is selected, control goes to this function. Depending on the option selected, this function calls the appropriate routine to perform the required task. For example, if the cut option is selected, the control transfers to the callback function EditMenuCB(). It then calls the Motif function XmTextCut() to remove the highlighted text from the text window and move it to a hidden scratch area, which later can be restored to the text widget through the XmTextPaste() call.

If the copy option is selected, the callback function EditMenuCB() calls the Motif function XmTextCopy() to copy the highlighted text within the text window to the hidden scratch area. The highlighted text in the text window remains intact.

If the paste option is selected, the callback function EditMenuCB() calls the Motif function XmTextPaste() to restore the text saved in the hidden scratch area to the text window, starting at the cursor's position. The text in the hidden scratch area remains intact.

If the delete option is selected, the callback function EditMenuCB() calls the Motif function XmTextRemove() to remove the highlighted text from the text window. This deleted text can no longer be retrieved.

If the search option is selected, the callback function EditMenuCB() calls the function CreateFindWidget() to create a pop up dialog shown in Figure 8.6. The function SearchTextCB() is the callback attached to the search button. It first reads the text string to be searched, the case-sensitive flag, and the current cursor location. It then calls the function NextPos(), passing these three variables as arguments to find the next matched string's position. If a matched string is found, it calls SetWorkAreaSelection() to highlight the matched string. ChangeTextCB() is the callback function for both the replace and replace and search buttons. The client_data passed to this function is different from one case to the other. The client_data has a False value if this callback function is called as a result of clicking the replace button. The client_data has a True value if this callback function is called as a result of clicking the replace and search button. In either case, it first gets the replacing text and uses it as an argument to the function ReplaceSelection () to replace the highlighted text. In replace and search's case, two events are generated by calling the X function XSendEvent() to simulate the button press and button release events.

ChangeAllTextCB() is the callback function attached to the change all button. This callback function reads both the search text and replace text. Using the function NextPos(), it then loops through the document searching for the matched string.

☞ Handling the preference menu options

The callback function PreferenceMenuCB() handles all the options in the preference menu. Whenever an option in the preference menu is selected, control goes to this function. Depending on the option selected, this function calls the appropriate routine to perform the required task.

If the color option is selected, the control transfers to the callback function PreferenceMenuCB(). It then calls the function CreateColorList() to create a color selection window, as shown in Figure 8.7. In that example, we want to show all the colors listed in the file rgb.txt. This is done by creating a scrolled list window, with each line in the list corresponding to a line in the rgb.txt file. When a line in the scrolled list is selected, the selection callback function reads the line text. Later, when the set foreground or set background button is pushed, its callback function uses the text just read to get the corresponding pixel for that color through the call to function GetPixelName(). This color pixel then is used to set the color foreground or background of the text widget in the text editor window. The program to implement the color selection window is shown in Listing 8.7. The function CreateColorList() is the main entry point to this module. It creates a new top shell for this demo. Under the top shell, a form widget is created to hold everything inside the window. On the upper part of the window is a scrolled list that occupies 90 percent of the total area. On the bottom of the window is a RowColumn widget that contains the set foreground, set background, and cancel buttons. The function GetColorsFromRGBFile() counts the lines in the file /usr/lib/X11/rgb.txt. The function FillColorArray() fills in the colors array with the actual color text read from the same rgb.txt file. The function ListSelectCB() is the callback function when a line is selected. The function ListControlCB() is the callback when one of the push buttons is selected.

If the font option is selected, it calls the function CreateFontList() to create a font display window shown in Figure 8.8. The function CreateFontList() is the main entry point to this module. It creates a new top shell for this window. Under the top shell, a form widget is created to hold everything inside the window. On the upper part of the window is a scrolled list that occupies 90 percent of the total area. On the bottom of the window is a RowColumn widget that contains accept and cancel buttons. The function GetFontFromFile() counts the number of lines in the file /usr/lib/X11/fonts/75dpi/fonts.dir. The function FillFontArray() fills in the fonts character array with the actual font text read from the fonts.dir file. The function ListSelectCB() is the callback function when a line is selected. The function ListControlCB() is the callback when either of the push buttons is selected.

When a line of the scrolled list is selected, the selection callback function reads the line text that represents a font. Later, when the accept button is pushed, its callback function uses the text just read to load the corresponding font through the function call XLoadQueryFont(). This font then is used to set the font for the text in the scrolled text window.

☞ Handling the show menu options

Technically speaking, the show menu is not a part of the text editor. We use it as a link to other demo applications. A drawing editor and a table editor are the two applications that can be started through the show menu options.

Whenever an option in the show menu is selected, the control goes to the callback function ShowMcnuCB(). It then calls the appropriate routine, depending on the option selected.

Listing 8.1 shows the main program.

Listing 8.1 mtfmain.c

```c
/*
 * mtfmain.c
 */
#include <stdio.h>
#include "demo.h"

/*
 * Global variable
 */
XtAppContext      app_context;
Display           *dpy;
char              *app_name;
char               app_class[80];
Widget             top_level;

/*
 * External functions
 */
Widget            MainMenu();

main(argc, argv)
int  argc;
char *argv[];
{
   /*
    * Set application name and class.
    */
   app_name = argv[0];
   strcpy(app_class, "Demo");

   /*
    * Initialize toolkit, create application context and
    * open global display
    */
   XtToolkitInitialize();

   app_context = XtCreateApplicationContext();

   dpy = XtOpenDisplay(app_context,     /* application context */
      NULL,                             /* display name */
      app_name,                         /* application name */
      app_class,                        /* application class */
      NULL, 0,                          /* xrm options, num_options */
      &argc, argv);                     /* command line options */
   if (!dpy)
   {
```

```
        fprintf(stderr, "Cannot open X Window Display\n");
        exit(-1);
    }
    /*
     * Create main window
     */
    top_level = MainMenu();
    XtRealizeWidget(top_level);
    /*
     * Loop and process events...
     */
    XtAppMainLoop(app_context);

}
```

Listing 8.2 shows the application header file.

Listing 8.2 demo.h

```
/*
 * demo.h
 */
#include <X11/X.h>
#include <X11/Xatom.h>
#include <X11/Xlib.h>
#include <X11/Xos.h>
#include <X11/Xutil.h>
#include <X11/cursorfont.h>
#include <X11/keysym.h>
#include <X11/Intrinsic.h>
#include <X11/Shell.h>
#include <Xm/Xm.h>
#include <Xm/CascadeB.h>
#include <Xm/CascadeBG.h>
#include <Xm/CutPaste.h>
#include <Xm/DialogS.h>
#include <Xm/FileSB.h>
#include <Xm/Form.h>
#include <Xm/Frame.h>
#include <Xm/Label.h>
#include <Xm/LabelG.h>
#include <Xm/PanedW.h>
#include <Xm/PushB.h>
#include <Xm/PushBG.h>
#include <Xm/RowColumn.h>
#include <Xm/ScrollBar.h>
#include <Xm/ScrolledW.h>
#include <Xm/SelectioB.h>
#include <Xm/SeparatoG.h>
#include <Xm/Separator.h>
#include <Xm/Text.h>
#include <Xm/ToggleB.h>
#include <Xm/ToggleBG.h>
```

```c
/*
 * define message type for message box
 */
#define ERROR_MSG_TYPE              0
#define WORKING_MSG_TYPE           1
#define WARNING_MSG_TYPE           2
#define MESSAGE_MSG_TYPE           3
#define INFORMATION_MSG_TYPE       4

/*
 *    define the max number of columns and rows for table
 */
#define K_MAX_COL                  5
#define K_MAX_ROW                  6
/*
 *   define pixmap_data type for pixmap data
 */
typedef struct {
Pixmap        pix;
GC            gc;
Dimension     width, height;
} pixmap_data;

/*
 * define rubber_band_data type for drawing on the window
 */
typedef struct {
int           start_x, start_y, last_x, last_y;
Dimension     width, height;
Pixel         background_color;
GC                  gc;
}   rubber_band_data;
```

Listing 8.3 shows the program to create the main window for the text editor.

Listing 8.3 pdm.c

```c
/*
 * pdm.c
 */
#include "demo.h"

#define MAX_NUM_PULLDOWN           10
#define MAX_OPS                    20

/* Global Data */
static Widget text_top = NULL;
static Widget frame    = NULL;
static Widget main_form;
static Widget menu_bar = NULL;
static Widget status_label = NULL;
static Widget pds[MAX_NUM_PULLDOWN];
Widget text_widget;
Widget save_button;
```

```c
int     text_changed;
extern char     current_open_file[];
extern int      current_line_num;
extern int      current_column_num;
extern Display *dpy;

/* define the main pulldown menu */
char *pd_labels[] = {"File",
    "Edit",
    "Preference",
    "Show"
};

/* File menu */
Widget file_buttons[6];
char *file_ops[] = {"Open",
    "Close",
    "Save",
    "Save As",
    "Print",
    "Exit"
};
/* Edit menu */
Widget edit_buttons[7];
char *edit_ops[] = {"Cut",
    "Copy",
    "Paste",
    "Delete",
    "Search",
    "Set Mark",
    "Jump To Mark"
};

/* preference menu */
Widget preference_buttons[2];
char *preference_ops[] = {
    "Colors",
    "Fonts"
};

/* Show menu */
Widget show_buttons[2];
char *show_ops[] = {
    "Drawing Editor",
    "Table Editor"
};

static char text_override_translations[] =
"<Key>Return:           newline()";

/*
 * External Functions
 */
extern void     FileMenuCB();
extern void     EditMenuCB();
extern void     PreferenceMenuCB();
```

```c
extern void     ShowMenuCB();
extern void     TextChangedCB();
extern void     ConvertToRowCol();
extern void     PosChangeEH();

/*
 *   Internal Functions
 */
static  Widget    CreateTextWorkArea();
static  Widget    CreateStatusLabel();
void    CreateMenuButton();
void    SetStatLabel();
Widget  MainMenu();
Widget  MenuBar();

/*
 * Display the main menu
 */
Widget MainMenu()
{
    int            n;
    Arg            args[16];
    int            toggle[MAX_OPS];
    int            sep[MAX_OPS];

    /*
     * Create the Application Shell as this is to be the root of a new
     * application.
     */

    n = 0;
    text_top = XtAppCreateShell("textTop",  "TextTop", applicationShellWidgetClass,
        dpy, args, n);

    n = 0;
    frame = XmCreateFrame(text_top, "textFrame", args, n);
    XtManageChild (frame);
    /*
     *   Create the Form to hold everything.
     */
    n = 0;
    main_form = (Widget) XmCreateForm(frame, "textForm", args, n);
    XtManageChild (main_form);

    /*
     * Create the Menu Bar.
     */
    menu_bar = (Widget) MenuBar(main_form, pds, pd_labels, XtNumber(pd_labels));
    n = 0;
    XtSetArg (args[n], XmNtopAttachment, XmATTACH_FORM);n++;
    XtSetArg (args[n], XmNleftAttachment, XmATTACH_FORM);n++;
    XtSetArg (args[n], XmNrightAttachment, XmATTACH_FORM);n++;
    XtSetArg (args[n], XmNorientation, XmHORIZONTAL); n++;
    XtSetArg (args[n], XmNspacing, 10); n++;
    XtSetValues(menu_bar, args, n);
```

```c
XtManageChild (menu_bar);

/*
 * Create all the Pulldowns.
 */

for (n=0; n< MAX_OPS; n++)
    toggle[n] = 0;

/*
 * File menu pulldown
 */
for (n=0; n<XtNumber(file_ops); n++)
    sep [n] = 0;

sep[1] = 1;
sep[2] = 1;
sep[4] = 1;
sep[5] = 1;
CreateMenuButton(pds[0], file_buttons,file_ops,XtNumber(file_ops),FileMenuCB,
    sep, toggle);

/*
 *  assign file_buttons[2] to save_button for later use
 */
save_button = file_buttons[2];
/*
 * Edit menu pulldown
 */

for (n=0; n<XtNumber(edit_ops); n++)
    sep [n] = 0;

sep[1] = 1;
sep[3] = 1;
sep[4] = 1;
sep[5] = 1;
CreateMenuButton(pds[1], edit_buttons, edit_ops, XtNumber(edit_ops),
    EditMenuCB, sep, toggle);

/*
 * Preference menu pulldown
 */

for (n=0; n<XtNumber(preference_ops); n++)
    sep [n] = 1;

CreateMenuButton(pds[2],preference_buttons, preference_ops,
    XtNumber(preference_ops), PreferenceMenuCB, sep, toggle);

/*
 * Show menu pulldown
 */

for (n=0; n<XtNumber(show_ops); n++)
    sep [n] = 1;

CreateMenuButton(pds[3],show_buttons, show_ops, XtNumber(show_ops),
```

```c
        ShowMenuCB, sep, toggle);

    /*
     * Create the scrolled text widget
     */
    text_widget = (Widget )CreateTextWorkArea(main_form, menu_bar);

    /*
     * add translation for carriage return
     */
    XtOverrideTranslations(text_widget,
          XtParseTranslationTable(text_override_translations));

    /*
     * Create the status display label widget
     */
    status_label = (Widget) CreateStatusLabel(main_form,  text_widget);

    /*
     *   set the initial status label
     */
    SetStatLabel();

    return(text_top);
}

Widget
MenuBar(parent, pd, pd_label,  npd)
Widget parent;
Widget pd[];
char *pd_label[];
int npd;
{
    Widget menu_bar, cascade;
    Arg arg[8];
    int n;
    register int i;

    /* create a menu bar */
    n = 0;
    menu_bar = XmCreateMenuBar(parent, "MenuBar", arg, n);
    XtManageChild(menu_bar);

    /* create pulldown menus attached to cascade buttons */
    for (i=0; i<npd; i++) {
        n = 0;
        pd[i] = XmCreatePulldownMenu(menu_bar, "PullDownMenu", arg, n);

        n = 0;
        XtSetArg(arg[n], XmNsubMenuId, pd[i]); n++;
        cascade=XtCreateManagedWidget(pd_label[i],xmCascadeButtonWidgetClass,
            menu_bar, arg, n);
        /*
         *  Put Help Buttons on the far right side of the menu bar
         */
        if (strcmp(pd_label[i]," Help")==0)
```

```c
         {
            n=0;
            XtSetArg (arg[n], XmNmenuHelpWidget, cascade);n++;
            XtSetValues (menu_bar, arg, n);
         }
      }
   return(menu_bar);
}

/*
 * pd[] - array of pulldown menus
 * menu_buttons[] - array of menus in each pulldown
 * labels[] - array of menu labels
 * nlabels - number of labels in labels[]
 * callback - menu callback
 * sep[] - array of integer; sep[i] > 0 means after option i there is a separator
 * toggle_indicator - array of flags indicating which option is a toggle button
 */
void
CreateMenuButton(pd, menu_buttons, labels, nlabels, callback, sep,
            toggle_indicator)
Widget pd;
Widget menu_buttons[];
char *labels[];
int nlabels;
XtPointer callback;
int sep[];
int toggle_indicator[];
{
   Arg arg[10];
   int n;
   int i;

   for (i=0; i<nlabels; i++)
   {
      if (sep[i])
      {
         n = 0;
         XtSetArg(arg[n], XmNshadowThickness, 3);n++;
         XtCreateManagedWidget("sep", xmSeparatorWidgetClass, pd, NULL, 0);
      }
      n = 0;

      if (!toggle_indicator[i])
      {
         menu_buttons[i] = XmCreatePushButton(pd, labels[i], arg, n);
         XtAddCallback(menu_buttons[i], XmNactivateCallback, callback,
            (XtPointer) i);
      }
      else
      {
         XtSetArg (arg[n], XmNindicatorOn, True); n++;
         XtSetArg (arg[n], XmNvisibleWhenOff, True); n++;
         XtSetArg (arg[n], XmNfillOnSelect, True); n++;
```

```c
            menu_buttons[i] = XmCreateToggleButton(pd,labels[i],arg, n);
            XtAddCallback(menu_buttons[i], XmNvalueChangedCallback, callback,
                (XtPointer) i);
        }
        XtManageChild(menu_buttons[i]);
    }
}

Widget CreateTextWorkArea(parent, top)
Widget parent;
Widget top;
{
    int i;
    Arg args[15];
    Widget text;

    /*
     * set the resources
     */
    i = 0;
    XtSetArg(args[i], XmNscrollVertical, True); i++;
    XtSetArg(args[i], XmNscrollHorizontal, True); i++;
    XtSetArg(args[i], XmNeditMode, XmMULTI_LINE_EDIT); i++;
    XtSetArg(args[i], XmNcursorPositionVisible, True); i++;
    XtSetArg(args[i], XmNleftAttachment, XmATTACH_FORM); i++;
    XtSetArg(args[i], XmNrightAttachment, XmATTACH_FORM); i++;
    XtSetArg(args[i], XmNbottomAttachment, XmATTACH_POSITION); i++;
    XtSetArg(args[i], XmNbottomPosition, (Position)93); i++;
    XtSetArg(args[i], XmNtopAttachment, XmATTACH_WIDGET); i++;
    XtSetArg(args[i], XmNtopWidget,  top); i++;
    /*
     * create the scrolled text widget
     */
    text = XmCreateScrolledText(parent, "Text", args, i);

    /*
     * add callback for text change
     */
    XtAddCallback(text, XmNvalueChangedCallback,  TextChangedCB,
        (XtPointer) NULL);
    /*
     * add event handler when the cursor position changes
     */
    XtAddEventHandler(text, ButtonPressMask, False, (XtEventHandler)PosChangeEH,
        (XtPointer)NULL);
    XtManageChild(text);
    return(text);
}

Widget CreateStatusLabel(parent, top)
Widget parent;
Widget top;
{
    int  i;
    Arg args[10];
```

```c
    Widget status_frame;
    Widget status_form;
    Widget label;

    /*
     * create a frame for the status area
     */
    i = 0;
    XtSetArg(args[i], XmNtopAttachment, XmATTACH_WIDGET); i++;
    XtSetArg(args[i], XmNtopWidget,  top); i++;
    XtSetArg(args[i], XmNleftAttachment, XmATTACH_FORM); i++;
    XtSetArg(args[i], XmNleftOffset, 2); i++;
    XtSetArg(args[i], XmNrightAttachment, XmATTACH_FORM); i++;
    XtSetArg(args[i], XmNrightOffset, 2); i++;
    XtSetArg(args[i], XmNbottomAttachment, XmATTACH_FORM); i++;
    XtSetArg(args[i], XmNbottomOffset, 2); i++;

    status_frame = XmCreateFrame(parent, "StatusFrame", args, i);
    XtManageChild(status_frame);

    /*
     * create a form for the status area
     */
    i = 0;
    status_form = XmCreateForm(status_frame, "StatusForm", args, i);
    XtManageChild(status_form);

    i = 0;
    XtSetArg(args[i], XmNtopAttachment, XmATTACH_FORM); i++;
    XtSetArg(args[i], XmNleftAttachment, XmATTACH_FORM); i++;
    XtSetArg(args[i], XmNrightAttachment, XmATTACH_FORM); i++;
    XtSetArg(args[i], XmNbottomAttachment, XmATTACH_FORM); i++;
    XtSetArg(args[i], XmNalignment, XmALIGNMENT_BEGINNING); i++;
    label = XmCreateLabel(status_form, "StatusLabel", args, i);
    XtManageChild(label);

    return(label);
}

void SetStatLabel()
{
    int    n;
    Arg args[10];
    XmString xmstring;
    char label_text[256];

    if (status_label == NULL)  return;

    sprintf(label_text, "File: %-60s   Line:  %-10d    Column: %-10d",
        current_open_file, current_line_num, current_column_num);
    xmstring = XmStringCreateLtoR(label_text, XmSTRING_DEFAULT_CHARSET);
    n = 0;
    XtSetArg(args[n], XmNlabelString, xmstring); n++;
    XtSetValues(status_label, args, n);
}
```

Listing 8.4 shows the program to handle the file menu.

Listing 8.4 xfile.c

```
/*
 * xfile.c
 */
#include <stdio.h>
#include <fcntl.h>
#include <sys/stat.h>
#include "demo.h"

#define PRINT_CMD        "lpr -P%s -#%d  %s"

/*
 * Global data
 */
static Widget open_widget = NULL;
static Widget save_widget = NULL;
static Widget print_dialog  = NULL;
static Widget printer_text  =   NULL;
static Widget copies_text  = NULL;
char    *file_buf;
extern char    current_open_file[];
extern int     current_line_num;
extern int     current_column_num;
extern int      text_changed;
extern Widget save_button;

/*
 * Internal Functions
 */
static void OkFileUpdateCB();
static void OkFileSaveCB();
static void NoFileSaveCB();
static void CancelFileSaveCB();
static void HelpFileSaveCB();
static void OverWriteFile();
static void FileOpenAcceptCB();
static void FileHelpCB();
static void FileOpenCancelCB();
static void DoPrint();
static void FileTextPrintCB();
static void CreatePrintDialog();
static void ResetPrintDialogCB();
static void CancelPrintCB();
static void CreateSaveWidget();
static void CreateOpenWidget();
static void ReadFile();
static void SetSaveNeeded();
static void ResetToSave();
static void OkToOverwrite();
static void SaveToFile();
static void SaveFile();
```

```c
Boolean FileExist();
extern char * GetWorkAreaText();

void FileMenuCB(widget, client_data, call_data)
Widget widget;
XtPointer client_data;
XtPointer call_data;
{
    int    selection;
    char   msg[256];

    selection = (int)client_data;
    switch (selection) {
    case 0:
       if (text_changed)
       {
          sprintf(msg,
             "File content has been modified. Do you want to update?");
          PromptSave(widget, msg, "open");
       }
       else
          CreateOpenWidget(widget, client_data, call_data);
       break;
    case 1:
       if (!text_changed)
       {
          ClearWorkArea();
          text_changed = 0;
          ResetToSave();
       }
       else
       {
          sprintf(msg,
             "File content has been modified. Do you want to update?");
          PromptSave(widget, msg, "close");
       }
       break;
    case 2:
       SaveFile(widget);
       break;
    case 3:
       CreateSaveWidget(widget, client_data, call_data);
       break;
    case 4:
       CreatePrintDialog(widget, client_data, call_data);
       break;
    case 5:
       if ( ! text_changed)
          exit(0);
       sprintf(msg,
          "File content has been modified. Do you want to update?");
       PromptSave(widget, msg, "exit");
       break;
    default:
```

```c
      break;
   }
}

void CreateOpenWidget(parent, client_data, call_data)
Widget parent;
XtPointer client_data;
XtPointer call_data;
{
   Arg args[10];
   int   i;

   i = 0;
   XtSetArg(args[i], XmNokLabelString,
      XmStringCreateLtoR("Open",  XmSTRING_DEFAULT_CHARSET)); i++;
   XtSetArg(args[i], XmNdialogTitle,
      XmStringCreateLtoR("Open File", XmSTRING_DEFAULT_CHARSET)); i++;
   open_widget =XmCreateFileSelectionDialog(parent, "FileBox", args, i);
   XtManageChild(open_widget);
   XtAddCallback(open_widget, XmNokCallback, FileOpenAcceptCB, NULL);
   XtAddCallback(open_widget, XmNhelpCallback, FileHelpCB, NULL);
   XtAddCallback(open_widget, XmNcancelCallback, FileOpenCancelCB, NULL);
}

static void FileOpenAcceptCB(w, client_data, call_data)
Widget w;
XtPointer client_data;
XtPointer call_data;
{
   int     n;
   Arg     args[10];
   char *filename;

   /*
    * retrieve the file name
    */
   XmFileSelectionBoxCallbackStruct *fs_info =
      (XmFileSelectionBoxCallbackStruct *) call_data;
   /*
    * convert to ascii string
    */
   XmStringGetLtoR(fs_info->value, XmSTRING_DEFAULT_CHARSET, &filename);
   /*
    * set watch cursor
    */
   ChangeToWatchCursor(w);
   /*
    * read the file into the text widget
    */
   ReadFile(filename);
   text_changed = 0;
   /*
    * reset the Save button label back to Save
    */
   ResetToSave();
```

```c
    /*
     * set the file name label
     */
    strcpy(current_open_file, filename);
    current_line_num =1;
    current_column_num= 1;
    SetStatLabel();
    /*
     * change back to original cursor
     */
    ChangeBackCursor(w);

    XtUnmanageChild(open_widget);
}

void ReadFile(file_name)
char *file_name;
{
    struct stat statbuf;
    int      file_length;
    char   msg[128];
    FILE    *fp;

    if ((fp = fopen(file_name, "r")) == NULL)
    {
        sprintf(msg, "Open file for read error: %s", file_name);
        MsgOut(ERROR_MSG_TYPE, msg);
        return;
    }
    if (stat(file_name, &statbuf) == 0)
        file_length = statbuf.st_size;
    else
        file_length = 80 * 25;

    file_buf = (char *)XtMalloc(file_length+1);
    fread(file_buf, sizeof(char), file_length, fp);
    file_buf[file_length] = '\0';
    fclose(fp);
    /*
     * put the file buffer into the text widget
     */
    SetWorkAreaText(file_buf);
}

static void FileOpenCancelCB(w, client_data, call_data)
Widget w;
XtPointer client_data;
XtPointer call_data;
{
    /*
     *  unmanage the open widget to make it invisible to the user
     */

    XtUnmanageChild(w);
    return;
}
```

```c
static void FileHelpCB(w, client_data, call_data)
Widget w;
XtPointer client_data;
XtPointer call_data;
{
    /*
     *  unmanage the open widget to make it invisible to the user
     */

    XtUnmanageChild(w);

    return;
}

void TextChangedCB(w, client_data, call_data)
Widget w;
XtPointer client_data;
XtPointer call_data;
{
    /*
     *  set the save flag to False to indicate the file needs to be save
     */

    if (!text_changed)
    {
        text_changed = 1;
        SetSaveNeeded();
    }
}

void CreatePrintDialog(w, client_data, call_data)
Widget w;
XtPointer client_data;
XtPointer call_data;
{
    int   n;
    Arg args[10];
    Widget ok_button = NULL;
    Widget cancel_button = NULL;
    Widget row_col, frame;
    Widget print_label, copy_label;

    /*
     *  Create the print dialog
     */

    if (!print_dialog)
    {
        n = 0;
        XtSetArg(args[n], XmNdialogTitle,
            XmStringCreateLtoR("Text Print", XmSTRING_DEFAULT_CHARSET)); n++;
        print_dialog = XmCreateFormDialog (w, "printDialog", args, n);
        XtManageChild(print_dialog);
        /*
         *  create printer name label
         */
```

```c
    n = 0;
    XtSetArg(args[n], XmNtopAttachment, XmATTACH_POSITION); n++;
    XtSetArg(args[n], XmNleftAttachment, XmATTACH_POSITION); n++;
    print_label = XmCreateLabel(print_dialog,  "printerNameLabel", args, n);
    XtManageChild(print_label);

    /*
     *  create printer text field
     */
    n = 0;
    XtSetArg(args[n], XmNtopAttachment, XmATTACH_POSITION); n++;
    XtSetArg(args[n], XmNleftAttachment, XmATTACH_POSITION); n++;
    XtSetArg(args[n], XmNrightAttachment, XmATTACH_POSITION); n++;
    printer_text = XmCreateText(print_dialog, "printerNameText",args, n);
    XtManageChild(printer_text);
    XmTextSetString(printer_text, "ps");

    /*
     *  create copies label
     */

    n = 0;
    XtSetArg(args[n], XmNtopAttachment, XmATTACH_WIDGET); n++;
    XtSetArg(args[n], XmNtopWidget, print_label); n++;
    XtSetArg(args[n], XmNleftAttachment, XmATTACH_POSITION); n++;
    copy_label = XmCreateLabel(print_dialog,  "copiesLabel", args, n);
    XtManageChild(copy_label);

    /*
     *  create copies text field
     */

    n = 0;
    XtSetArg(args[n], XmNtopAttachment, XmATTACH_WIDGET); n++;
    XtSetArg(args[n], XmNtopWidget, printer_text); n++;
    XtSetArg(args[n], XmNleftAttachment, XmATTACH_POSITION); n++;
    copies_text = XmCreateText(print_dialog, "copiesText", args, n);
    XtManageChild(copies_text);
    XmTextSetString(copies_text, "1");

    /*
     *  create the frame for the action buttons
     */

    n = 0;
    XtSetArg (args[n], XmNtopAttachment, XmATTACH_WIDGET); n++;
    XtSetArg (args[n], XmNtopWidget, copy_label); n++;
    XtSetArg (args[n], XmNleftAttachment, XmATTACH_POSITION); n++;
    XtSetArg (args[n], XmNrightAttachment, XmATTACH_POSITION); n++;
    XtSetArg (args[n], XmNbottomAttachment, XmATTACH_POSITION); n++;
    frame = XmCreateFrame(print_dialog, "actionFrame", args, n);
    XtManageChild(frame);

    /*
     *  create the row/col for the action buttons
     */
```

```c
    n = 0;
    XtSetArg(args[n], XmNorientation, XmHORIZONTAL); n++;
    XtSetArg(args[n], XmNpacking, XmPACK_TIGHT); n++;
    row_col = XmCreateRowColumn(frame, "actionRowCol", args, n);
    XtManageChild(row_col);

    /*
     * create the OK button...
     */

    n = 0;
    ok_button = XmCreatePushButton(row_col, "okButton", args, n);
    XtManageChild(ok_button);
    XtAddCallback(ok_button, XmNactivateCallback, FileTextPrintCB, NULL);

    /*
     * create cancel button
     */
    n = 0;
    cancel_button = XmCreatePushButton(row_col, "cancelButton", args, n);
    XtManageChild(cancel_button);
    XtAddCallback(cancel_button, XmNactivateCallback, CancelPrintCB,
        print_dialog);
    }
    if (!XtIsManaged(print_dialog)) XtManageChild(print_dialog);
}

static void CancelPrintCB(w, client_data, call_data)
Widget w;
XtPointer client_data;
XtPointer call_data;
{
    XtUnmanageChild((Widget)client_data);
}

static void FileTextPrintCB(w, client_data, call_data)
Widget w;
XtPointer client_data;
XtPointer call_data;
{
    char *file_buf;
    char *file_name;
    char *printer;
    char *copies_ascii;
    int   copies;
    /*
     * retrieve printer name
     */
    printer = XmTextGetString(printer_text);
    if (!printer) return;
    copies_ascii = XmTextGetString(copies_text);
    if (!copies_ascii) return;
    /*
     * get the file name
     */
```

```c
   file_name = current_open_file;
   /*
    * get the text from text widget
    */
   file_buf = GetWorkAreaText();
   if (!file_buf) return;
   copies = atoi(copies_ascii);
   if (copies <= 1) copies = 1;
   DoPrint(file_name, file_buf, printer, copies);
   XtFree(printer);
   XtFree(copies_ascii);
   XtFree(file_buf);
   XtUnmanageChild(print_dialog);
}

static void DoPrint(file_name, file_buf, printer, copies)
char *file_name;
char *file_buf;
char *printer;
int     copies;
{
   char cmd_buf[256];
   char tmp_file[256];
   char msg[256];
   int     fd;

   sprintf(tmp_file, "%s.tmp", file_name);
   if ((fd = open(tmp_file,  O_WRONLY | O_CREAT | O_TRUNC, 0755)) == -1)
   {
      sprintf(msg, "Unable to open file %s for write", tmp_file);
      MsgOut(ERROR_MSG_TYPE,  msg);
   }
   else
   {
      write(fd, file_buf, strlen(file_buf));
      close(fd);
      sprintf(cmd_buf, PRINT_CMD, printer, copies, tmp_file);
      system(cmd_buf);
      remove(tmp_file);
   }

   return;
}

static void ResetPrintDialogCB(w, client_data, call_data)
Widget w;
XtPointer client_data;
XtPointer call_data;
{
   print_dialog = NULL;
}

void CreateSaveWidget(parent,  client_data, call_data)
Widget parent;
XtPointer client_data;
```

```c
XtPointer call_data;
{
   Arg args[10];
   int   i;

   i = 0;
   XtSetArg(args[i], XmNokLabelString,
      XmStringCreateLtoR("Save",  XmSTRING_DEFAULT_CHARSET)); i++;
   XtSetArg(args[i], XmNdialogTitle,
      XmStringCreateLtoR("Save File", XmSTRING_DEFAULT_CHARSET)); i++;
   save_widget =XmCreateFileSelectionDialog(parent, "FileBox", args, i);
   XtManageChild(save_widget);
   XtAddCallback(save_widget, XmNokCallback, OkFileSaveCB, NULL);
   XtAddCallback(save_widget, XmNhelpCallback, HelpFileSaveCB, NULL);
   XtAddCallback(save_widget, XmNcancelCallback, CancelFileSaveCB, NULL);
}

static void OkFileSaveCB(parent,  client_data, call_data)
Widget parent;
XtPointer client_data;
XtPointer call_data;
{
   XmSelectionBoxCallbackStruct *sb_info =
      (XmSelectionBoxCallbackStruct *) call_data;

   static char *filename;

   /*
    * retrieve file name
    */
   XmStringGetLtoR(sb_info->value, XmSTRING_DEFAULT_CHARSET, &filename);
   if (strlen(filename) <= 0) return;

   if (FileExist(filename))
      OverWriteFile(parent, filename);
   else
      SaveToFile(parent, filename);
}

static void CancelFileSaveCB(parent,  client_data, call_data)
Widget parent;
XtPointer client_data;
XtPointer call_data;
{
   XtUnmanageChild(parent);
}

static void HelpFileSaveCB(parent,  client_data, call_data)
Widget parent;
XtPointer client_data;
XtPointer call_data;
{
   XtUnmanageChild(parent);
}

void SaveFile(widget)
Widget widget;
```

```c
{
   SaveToFile(widget, current_open_file);
}

void SaveToFile(w, filename)
Widget w;
char *filename;
{
   int      fd;
   char   *tempstr;
   char   msg[256];
   XmTextPosition from_pos, to_pos;

   if (tempstr = GetWorkAreaText())
   {
      if ((fd = open(filename, O_WRONLY | O_CREAT | O_TRUNC, 0755)) == -1)
      {
         sprintf(msg, "Can't open file %s", filename);
         MsgOut(ERROR_MSG_TYPE, msg);
         return;
      }
      write(fd, tempstr, strlen(tempstr));
      close(fd);
      to_pos = strlen(tempstr);
      from_pos = 0;
      XtFree(tempstr);
      text_changed = 0;
      ResetToSave();
   }
}

static void OverWriteFile(parent, filename)
Widget parent;
char *filename;
{
   int     n;
   Arg args[15];
   static Widget question = NULL;
   char msg[256];
   char   file_name[256];

   strcpy(file_name, filename);

   n = 0;
   question = (Widget)XmCreateQuestionDialog(parent, "overWrite", args, n);
   XtUnmanageChild((Widget)XmMessageBoxGetChild(question, XmDIALOG_HELP_BUTTON));
   XtAddCallback(question, XmNokCallback, OkToOverwrite, (XtPointer)&file_name);
   sprintf(msg, "File %s exists. Do you want to overwrite it?", filename);
   n = 0;
   XtSetArg(args[n], XmNmessageString,
      XmStringCreateLtoR(msg, XmSTRING_DEFAULT_CHARSET)); n++;
   XtSetValues(question, args, n);

   XtManageChild(question);
}
```

```c
static void OkToOverwrite(w, client_data, call_data)
Widget w;
XtPointer client_data;
XtPointer call_data;
{
    char *filename = (char *) client_data;

    if (strlen(filename) > 0)
    {
        SaveToFile(w, filename);
        XtDestroyWidget(save_widget);
    }
}

void SetSaveNeeded()
{
    int   n;
    Arg   args[2];

    if (save_button)
    {
        n =0;
        XtSetArg(args[n], XmNlabelString, XmStringCreateLtoR("Save (needed)",
            XmSTRING_DEFAULT_CHARSET)); n++;
        XtSetValues(save_button, args, n);
    }
}

void ResetToSave()
{
    int   n;
    Arg   args[2];

    if (save_button)
    {
        n =0;
        XtSetArg(args[n], XmNlabelString, XmStringCreateLtoR("Save",
            XmSTRING_DEFAULT_CHARSET)); n++;
        XtSetValues(save_button, args, n);
    }
}

int PromptSave(Widget parent, char *msg, char *option)
{
    int   n;
    Arg   args[10];
    char question[256];
    static char action[20];
    XmString msg_string;
    Widget question_dialog;

    strcpy(action, option);
    sprintf(question, "%s", msg);
    msg_string = XmStringCreateLtoR(question, XmSTRING_DEFAULT_CHARSET);

    n=0;
```

```c
      XtSetArg (args[n], XmNx, (Position) 0); n++;
      XtSetArg (args[n], XmNy, (Position) 0); n++;
      XtSetArg (args[n], XmNdialogTitle,
         XmStringCreateLtoR("Prompt For File Save", XmSTRING_DEFAULT_CHARSET)); n++;
      XtSetArg (args[n], XmNmessageString, msg_string);n++;
      XtSetArg (args[n], XmNokLabelString,
         XmStringCreateLtoR("Yes", XmSTRING_DEFAULT_CHARSET)); n++;
      XtSetArg (args[n], XmNcancelLabelString,
         XmStringCreateLtoR("No", XmSTRING_DEFAULT_CHARSET)); n++;
      question_dialog = (Widget)XmCreateQuestionDialog(parent, "QuestionDialog",
         args, n);
      XtUnmanageChild((Widget)XmMessageBoxGetChild(question_dialog,
         XmDIALOG_HELP_BUTTON));
      XtManageChild(question_dialog);
      XtAddCallback(question_dialog, XmNokCallback, OkFileUpdateCB,
         (XtPointer)action);
      XtAddCallback(question_dialog,XmNcancelCallback, NoFileSaveCB,
         (XtPointer)action);
}

static void OkFileUpdateCB(w, client_data, call_data)
Widget w;
XtPointer client_data;
XtPointer call_data;
{
   char filename[128];
   char *option;
   option = (char *)client_data;

   strcpy(filename, current_open_file);
   if (strlen(filename) <= 0) return;

   SaveToFile(w, filename);
   ClearWorkArea();
   text_changed = 0;
   ResetToSave();

   if (strcmp(option, "exit")==0)
      exit(0);
   else if (strcmp(option, "open") == 0)
      CreateOpenWidget(w, client_data, call_data);
   else if (strcmp(option, "close") == 0)
      XtDestroyWidget(w);
}

static void NoFileSaveCB(w, client_data, call_data)
Widget w;
XtPointer client_data;
XtPointer call_data;
{
   char *option;

   option = (char *)client_data;
   if (strcmp(option, "exit")==0)
      exit(0);
   else
```

```c
    {
        XtDestroyWidget(w);
        ClearWorkArea();
        text_changed = 0;
        ResetToSave();
    }
}
```

Listing 8.5 shows the program to handle the edit menu.

Listing 8.5 xedit.c

```c
/*
 * xedit.c
 */
#include <stdio.h>
#include <sys/types.h>
#include <fcntl.h>
#include <sys/stat.h>
#include "demo.h"

typedef struct_findStruct
{
    Widget find_widget;
    Widget find_text;
    Widget change_text;
    Widget case_toggle;
} FindStruct, *PTR_FindStruct;

/*
 * Global data
 */
static Widget search_button;
static Time find_time;
static char *search_strg = NULL;
static XmTextPosition mark_file_pos = -1;
static FindStruct finder;
extern Widget text_widget;
extern char      *file_buf;
char    current_open_file[128];
int     current_line_num = 0;
int     current_column_num = 0;

/*
 * Internal functions
 */
static void ConvertToRowCol();
static char *GetWorkAreaSelection();
static void ReplaceSelection();
static void ClearWorkAreaSelection();
static void ReplaceWorkAreaText();
static void CreateFindWidget();
static void ConverToRowCol();
static void ReplaceSelection();
```

```c
static void ToUpperCase();
static XmTextPosition NextPos();
static XmTextPosition GetWorkAreaCursorPos();
static void ChangeTextCB();
static void ChangeAllTextCB();
static void SearchTextCB();
static void QuitSearchCB();
static void SetWorkAreaSelection();
void    SetWorkAreaText();
char    *GetWorkAreaText();

void EditMenuCB(widget, client_data, call_data)
Widget widget;
XtPointer client_data;
XtPointer call_data;
{
    XmAnyCallbackStruct *cb = (XmAnyCallbackStruct *) call_data;

    static int curr_trans = 0;
    static int first = 1;
    XmTextPosition cursor_pos;
    int selection;
    int n;
    Arg args[10];

    selection = (int)client_data;
    switch (selection) {
    case 0:
        XmTextCut(text_widget, cb->event->xbutton.time);
        break;
    case 1:
        XmTextCopy(text_widget, cb->event->xbutton.time);
        break;
    case 2:
        XmTextPaste(text_widget);
        break;

    case 3:
        XmTextRemove(text_widget);
        break;

    case 4:
        if (first)
        {
            first = 0;
            CreateFindWidget(widget);
        }
        find_time = ((XmAnyCallbackStruct *)call_data)->event->xbutton.time;
        XtManageChild(finder.find_widget);
        XmProcessTraversal(finder.find_text, XmTRAVERSE_CURRENT);
        break;

    case 5:
        n = 0;
        XtSetArg(args[n], XmNcursorPosition, &cursor_pos); n++;
        XtGetValues(text_widget, args, n);
```

```
            mark_file_pos = cursor_pos;
            break;

        case 6:
            if (mark_file_pos >= 0)
            {
                n = 0;
                XtSetArg(args[n], XmNcursorPosition, mark_file_pos); n++;
                XtSetValues(text_widget, args, n);
            }
            break;
        default:
            break;
    }
}

void SetWorkAreaText(value)
char *value;
{
    if (text_widget != NULL)
    {
        XmTextSetString(text_widget, value);
        XtManageChild(text_widget);
    }
    return;
}

void ClearWorkArea()
{
    XmTextSetString(text_widget, "");
    return;
}

void CreateFindWidget(parent)
Widget parent;
{
    Arg args[20];
    int    n;
    Widget find_widget;
    Widget find_label;
    Widget case_toggle;
    Widget find_text;
    Widget change_to_label;
    Widget change_text;
    Widget action_rc;
    Widget change_button;
    Widget change_all_button;
    Widget change_search_button;
    Widget quit_button;

    /*
     * create a dialog
     */
    n = 0;
    XtSetArg(args[n], XmNdialogTitle,
```

```c
    XmStringCreateLtoR("Text  Search", XmSTRING_DEFAULT_CHARSET)); n++;
find_widget = XmCreateFormDialog(parent, "findBox", args, n);
XtManageChild(find_widget);

/*
 * create the search for label
 */
n = 0;
XtSetArg(args[n], XmNtopAttachment, XmATTACH_POSITION); n++;
XtSetArg(args[n], XmNleftAttachment, XmATTACH_POSITION); n++;
find_label = XmCreateLabel(find_widget, "findLabel", args, n);
XtManageChild(find_label);

/*
 * create the case toggle
 */
n = 0;
XtSetArg(args[n], XmNtopAttachment, XmATTACH_POSITION); n++;
XtSetArg(args[n], XmNrightAttachment, XmATTACH_POSITION); n++;
XtSetArg(args[n], XmNfillOnSelect, True); n++;
XtSetArg(args[n], XmNvisibleWhenOff, True); n++;
XtSetArg(args[n], XmNindicatorType, XmN_OF_MANY); n++;
case_toggle = XmCreateToggleButton(find_widget, "caseToggle", args, n);
XtManageChild(case_toggle);
XmAddTabGroup(case_toggle);

/*
 * create Find text
 */
n = 0;
XtSetArg(args[n], XmNtopAttachment, XmATTACH_POSITION); n++;
XtSetArg(args[n], XmNleftAttachment, XmATTACH_WIDGET); n++;
XtSetArg(args[n], XmNleftWidget, find_label); n++;
XtSetArg(args[n], XmNrightAttachment, XmATTACH_WIDGET); n++;
XtSetArg(args[n], XmNrightWidget, case_toggle); n++;
XtSetArg(args[n], XmNeditable,TRUE); n++;
find_text = XmCreateText (find_widget, "findText", args, n);
XtManageChild(find_text);
XmAddTabGroup(find_text);

/*
 * create change to label
 */
n = 0;
XtSetArg(args[n], XmNtopAttachment, XmATTACH_WIDGET); n++;
XtSetArg(args[n], XmNtopWidget, find_label); n++;
XtSetArg(args[n], XmNleftAttachment, XmATTACH_POSITION); n++;
change_to_label = XmCreateLabel (find_widget, "changeToLabel", args, n);
XtManageChild(change_to_label);

/*
 * create change to text
 */
n = 0;
XtSetArg(args[n], XmNtopAttachment, XmATTACH_WIDGET); n++;
```

```c
    XtSetArg(args[n], XmNtopWidget, find_text); n++;
    XtSetArg(args[n], XmNleftAttachment, XmATTACH_WIDGET); n++;
    XtSetArg(args[n], XmNleftWidget, change_to_label); n++;
    XtSetArg(args[n], XmNrightAttachment, XmATTACH_POSITION); n++;
    XtSetArg(args[n], XmNeditable, TRUE); n++;
    change_text = XmCreateText (find_widget, "changeText", args, n);
    XtManageChild(change_text);
    XmAddTabGroup(change_text);

    /*
     * create the row column
     */
    n = 0;
    XtSetArg(args[n], XmNtopAttachment, XmATTACH_WIDGET); n++;
    XtSetArg(args[n], XmNtopWidget,change_text); n++;
    XtSetArg(args[n], XmNleftAttachment, XmATTACH_POSITION); n++;
    XtSetArg(args[n], XmNrightAttachment, XmATTACH_POSITION); n++;
    XtSetArg(args[n], XmNbottomAttachment, XmATTACH_POSITION); n++;
    XtSetArg(args[n], XmNbottomPosition, (Position) 95); n++;
    XtSetArg(args[n], XmNorientation, XmHORIZONTAL); n++;
    action_rc  = XmCreateRowColumn (find_widget, "actionBox", args, n);
    XtManageChild(action_rc);

    /*
     * create search button
     */
    n = 0;
    search_button = XmCreatePushButton (action_rc, "searchButton", args, n);
    XtAddCallback(search_button, XmNactivateCallback, SearchTextCB, NULL);
    XtManageChild(search_button);
    XmAddTabGroup(search_button);

    n = 0;
    XtSetArg(args[n], XmNdefaultButton, search_button); n++;
    XtSetArg(args[n], XmNnoResize, True); n++;
    XtSetValues(find_widget, args, n); n++;

    /*
     * create change button
     */
    n = 0;
    change_button = XmCreatePushButton (action_rc, "changeButton", args, n);
    XtAddCallback(change_button, XmNactivateCallback, ChangeTextCB,
            (XtPointer)False);
    XtManageChild(change_button);
    XmAddTabGroup(change_button);

    /*
     * create change  and search button
     */
    n = 0;
    change_search_button = XmCreatePushButton (action_rc, "changeSearchButton",
            args, n);
    XtAddCallback(change_search_button, XmNactivateCallback, ChangeTextCB,
        (XtPointer)True);
```

```c
   XtManageChild(change_search_button);
   XmAddTabGroup(change_search_button);

   /*
    * create changeall button
    */
   n = 0;
   change_all_button = XmCreatePushButton (action_rc, "changeAllButton", args, n);
   XtAddCallback(change_all_button, XmNactivateCallback, ChangeAllTextCB,
      (XtPointer)False);
   XtManageChild(change_all_button);
   XmAddTabGroup(change_all_button);

   /*
    * create quit button
    */
   n = 0;
   quit_button = XmCreatePushButton (action_rc, "quitButton", args, n);
   XtAddCallback(quit_button, XmNactivateCallback, QuitSearchCB,
      find_widget);
   XtManageChild(quit_button);
   XmAddTabGroup(quit_button);

   finder.find_widget  = find_widget;
   finder.find_text    = find_text;
   finder.change_text  = change_text;
   finder.case_toggle  = case_toggle;

   XmProcessTraversal(finder.find_text, XmTRAVERSE_CURRENT);
}

static void SearchTextCB(w, client_data, call_data)
Widget  w;
XtPointer client_data;
XtPointer call_data;
{
   char *msg_buf;
   XmTextPosition cursor_pos, new_pos;
   XmPushButtonCallbackStruct *cd = (XmPushButtonCallbackStruct *) call_data;
   Boolean case_sensitive;
   Arg  args[5];
   int    n;

   if (((XmAnyCallbackStruct *) call_data)->event != NULL)
      find_time = ((XmAnyCallbackStruct *)call_data)->event->xbutton.time;

   if (search_strg != NULL)
   {
      XtFree(search_strg);
      search_strg = NULL;
   }
   search_strg = XmTextGetString(finder.find_text);

   if (strlen(search_strg) <= 0)
   {
      MsgOut(WARNING_MSG_TYPE, "no search string entered");
      return;
```

```c
      }
      else
      {
         cursor_pos = GetWorkAreaCursorPos();
         XtSetArg(args[0], XmNset, &case_sensitive);
         XtGetValues(finder.case_toggle, args, 1);
         if ((new_pos = NextPos(cursor_pos, search_strg, case_sensitive)) < 0)
         {
            msg_buf = (char *)XtMalloc(strlen(search_strg) + 30);
            sprintf(msg_buf, "String [%s] not found.", search_strg);
            MsgOut(WARNING_MSG_TYPE, msg_buf);
            XtFree(msg_buf);
         }
         else
            SetWorkAreaSelection(new_pos, new_pos+strlen(search_strg), find_time);
      }
}

static void ChangeTextCB(w, client_data, call_data)
Widget w;
XtPointer client_data;
XtPointer call_data;
{
   Boolean search_again = (Boolean)client_data;
   Boolean replaced_text = False;
   char *replace_text;
   char *selected_text;
   Time time;
   static XButtonEvent *event1, *event2;
   XtWidgetGeometry preferred, intended;
   extern Display *dpy;

   if (!event1)
   {
      event1 = (XButtonEvent *)calloc(1, sizeof(XButtonEvent));
      event1->type = ButtonPress;
      event1->display = XtDisplay(search_button);
      event1->window = XtWindow(search_button);
      event1->root = RootWindow(dpy, DefaultScreen(dpy));
      XtQueryGeometry(search_button, &intended, &preferred);
      event1->x = preferred.x+preferred.width/2;
      event1->y = preferred.y+preferred.height/2;
      event1->x_root = 0;
      event1->y_root = 0;
      event1->button = Button1;
      event1->same_screen = True;
      event2 = ( XButtonEvent *)calloc(1, sizeof(XButtonEvent));
      *event2 = *event1;
      event2->type = ButtonRelease;
   }
   time = ((XmAnyCallbackStruct *)call_data)->event->xbutton.time;
   if (selected_text = GetWorkAreaSelection())
   {
      if (replace_text = XmTextGetString(finder.change_text))
```

```c
      {
          ReplaceSelection(replace_text, CurrentTime);
          replaced_text = True;
          XtFree(replace_text);
      }
      XtFree(selected_text);
   }

   if (replaced_text && search_again)
   {
      event1->time = CurrentTime;
      XSendEvent(XtDisplay(search_button), XtWindow(search_button), True,
         ButtonPressMask, (XEvent *)event1);

      event2->time = CurrentTime + 1;
      XSendEvent(XtDisplay(search_button), XtWindow(search_button), True,
         ButtonReleaseMask, (XEvent *)event2);
   }
}

static void ChangeAllTextCB(w, client_data, call_data)
Widget w;
XtPointer client_data;
XtPointer call_data;
{
   Boolean replaced_text = False;
   char *search_text = NULL;
   char *replace_text = NULL;
   char *selected_text = NULL;
   Boolean case_sensitive;
   int    n;
   Arg args[5];
   XmTextPosition replace_pos, start_pos;
   Time time;

   /*
    * get the time of the event
    */
   if (((XmAnyCallbackStruct *)call_data)->event != NULL)
      time = ((XmAnyCallbackStruct *)call_data)->event->xbutton.time;

   /*
    * get the value of case toggle
    */
   n = 0;
   XtSetArg(args[n], XmNset, &case_sensitive); n++;
   XtGetValues(finder.case_toggle, args, n);

   if (search_text = XmTextGetString(finder.find_text))
   {
      if (replace_text = XmTextGetString(finder.change_text))
      {
         if (search_text[0] && strcmp(search_text, replace_text))
         {
            /*
             * loop through the text and replace search_text with replace_text
```

```c
                */
               ClearWorkAreaSelection(time);
               replace_pos = NextPos(0, search_text, case_sensitive);
               start_pos = replace_pos + strlen(replace_text);
               while (replace_pos >= 0)
               {
                   /* replace the search string */
                   ReplaceWorkAreaText(replace_pos, replace_pos + strlen(search_text),
                      replace_text);
                   /* get next search string */
                   replace_pos = NextPos(replace_pos + strlen(replace_text),
                      search_text, case_sensitive);
                   if (replace_pos <= start_pos) break;
               }
           }
       }
   }
   if (search_text) XtFree(search_text);
   if (replace_text) XtFree(replace_text);
}

static void QuitSearchCB(w, client_data, call_data)
Widget w;
XtPointer client_data;
XtPointer call_data;
{
   Widget widget = (Widget)client_data;

   XtUnmanageChild(widget);
}

static void ReplaceWorkAreaText(from_pos, to_pos, value)
XmTextPosition from_pos;
XmTextPosition to_pos;
char *value;
{
   XmTextReplace(text_widget, from_pos, to_pos, value);
   XmTextSetTopCharacter(text_widget, 0);
}

static void ClearWorkAreaSelection(time)
Time time;
{
   XmTextClearSelection(text_widget, CurrentTime);
   return;
}

static void ReplaceSelection(replace_text, time)
char *replace_text;
Time time;
{
   XmTextPosition left;
   XmTextPosition right;
   XEvent  event;
```

```c
   XmTextGetSelectionPosition(text_widget, &left, &right);
   XmTextClearSelection(text_widget,time);
   XmTextReplace(text_widget, left, right, replace_text);
   right = left + strlen(replace_text);
   XmTextSetSelection(text_widget, left, right, time);
}

char *GetWorkAreaSelection()
{
   return(XmTextGetSelection(text_widget));
}

XmTextPosition GetWorkAreaCursorPos()
{
   int    n;
   Arg  arg[5];
   XmTextPosition cursor_pos;

   n = 0;
   XtSetArg(arg[n], XmNcursorPosition, &cursor_pos); n++;
   XtGetValues(text_widget, arg, n);

   return(cursor_pos);
}

static void SetWorkAreaSelection(first, last, time)
XmTextPosition first;
XmTextPosition last;
Time time;
{
   XmTextSetSelection(text_widget, first, last, CurrentTime);
   return;
}

XmTextPosition NextPos(cursor_pos, search_strg, case_sensitive)
XmTextPosition cursor_pos;
char *search_strg;
Boolean case_sensitive;
{
   XmTextPosition tmp_pos;
   char *file_buf;
   char *find_string;

   find_string = XtNewString(search_strg);
   if ((file_buf = GetWorkAreaText()) == NULL)
   {
      MsgOut(WARNING_MSG_TYPE, "no text in file");
      tmp_pos = 1;
      return(tmp_pos);
   }
   else
   {
      if (!case_sensitive)
      {
         ToUpperCase(find_string);
         ToUpperCase(file_buf);
```

```c
        }
        if ((tmp_pos = StrPos(&file_buf[cursor_pos], find_string)) <0)
        {
            file_buf[cursor_pos] = '\0';
            tmp_pos = StrPos(file_buf, find_string);
        }
        else
            tmp_pos += cursor_pos;

        XtFree(file_buf);
    }
    XtFree(find_string);
    return(tmp_pos);
}

char *GetWorkAreaText()
{
    return(XmTextGetString(text_widget));
}

StrPos(s1, s2)
char *s1;
char *s2;
{
    int i,j, pos_found;
    int len_s1, len_s2;

    pos_found = 0;
    len_s1 = strlen(s1);
    len_s2 = strlen(s2);
    if (len_s1 >= len_s2)
    {
        for (i=0; !pos_found && i < len_s1 - len_s2 +1; i++)
        {
            pos_found = i+1;
            for (j=0; j<strlen(s2); j++)
            {
                if (s1[i+j] != s2[j])
                {
                    pos_found = 0;
                    break;
                }
            }
        }
    }
    return(pos_found -1);
}

void ToUpperCase(string)
char *string;
{
    int i, length;

    length = strlen(string);
    for (i=0; i< length; i++)
        if (islower(string[i])) string[i] = toupper(string[i]);
```

```c
}

void PosChangeEH()
{
    XmTextPosition cursor_pos;

    cursor_pos = (XmTextPosition) GetWorkAreaCursorPos();
    ConvertToRowCol(cursor_pos, &current_line_num, &current_column_num);
    SetStatLabel();
}

void ConvertToRowCol(offset, pline_num, pcol_num)
int offset;
int *pline_num;
int *pcol_num;
{
    int line_num;
    int col_num;
    int i;

    line_num = 1;
    col_num  = 1;
    i = 0;
    while ( i < offset)
    {
        if (*(file_buf+i) == '\n')
        {
            line_num++;
            col_num = 1;
        }
        else
            col_num++;
        i++;
    }
    *pline_num = line_num;
    *pcol_num  = col_num;
}
```

Listing 8.6 shows the program to handle the preference menu.

Listing 8.6 xpreference.c

```c
/*
 * xpreference.c
 */
#include <stdio.h>
#include "demo.h"

void
PreferenceMenuCB(widget, client_data, call_data)
Widget widget;
XtPointer client_data;
XtPointer call_data;
{
    int selection;
```

```c
   int i,j,n;
   selection = (int)client_data;
   switch (selection) {
   case 0:
      CreateColorList(widget, "text", call_data);
      break;
   case 1: /* show fonts */
      CreateFontList(widget, "text", call_data);
      break;
   default:
      break;
   }
}
```

Listing 8.7 shows the program to handle the show menu.

Listing 8.7 xshow.c

```c
/*
 * xshow.c
 */
#include <stdio.h>
#include "demo.h"

void
ShowMenuCB(widget, client_data, call_data)
Widget widget;
XtPointer client_data;
XtPointer call_data;
{
   int selection;
   int i,j,n;

   selection = (int)client_data;
   switch (selection) {
   case 0: /* show drawing editor */
      CreateDrawArea(widget, client_data, call_data);
      break;
   case 1: /* show table editor */
      CreateTable(widget, client_data, call_data);
      break;
   default:
      break;
   }
}
```

Listing 8.8 shows the program to handle color selections.

Listing 8.8 xcolor.c

```c
/*
 *  xcolor.c
 */
```

```c
#include <stdio.h>
#include "demo.h"

#define K_FOREGROUND           0
#define K_BACKGROUND           1
#define K_CANCEL               2
#define K_NUM_CONTROLS         3

/*
 * Global data
 */
extern Display *dpy;
extern Widget   text_widget;
extern Widget   canvas;
extern pixmap_data pix_data;

Pixel   green;
Pixel   cyan;
Pixel   red;
Pixel   yellow;
Pixel   black;
Pixel   white;
Pixel   blue;
Pixel   grey;
Pixel   selected_fg_color;
Pixel   selected_bg_color;

static char    **colors;
static int     ncolors;
static char    *text;
static Widget top_level;
static Widget form;
static Widget scroll_list;
static Widget controls_pb[K_NUM_CONTROLS];
static Widget controls_box;
static Widget sep;
static char    appl[20];
static char *controls_pb_names[] = {
    "Set Foreground",
    "Set Background",
    "Cancel"
};

/*
 *   Internal functions
 */
Pixel  GetPixelName();
static void ListControlCB();
static void ListSelectCB();

void CreateColorList(w, client_data, call_data)
Widget w;
XtPointer client_data;
XtPointer call_data;
{
    int i;
```

```c
int n;
Arg args[10];
XmString  *xmstr;
char *application = (char *)client_data;

strcpy(appl, application);
top_level = XtAppCreateShell("colorTop", "ColorTop",
   applicationShellWidgetClass,
   dpy, NULL, 0);
n = 0;
form = XmCreateForm(top_level, "listForm", args, n);
XtManageChild (form);

/*
 * compute number of colors in the colors array
 */
ncolors = GetColorsFromRGBFile();
colors = (char **)XtMalloc(sizeof(char *) * ncolors);

FillColorArray(ncolors, colors);
/*
 * convert color names to an array of type XmString
 */
xmstr = (XmString *)XtMalloc(sizeof(XmString) * (ncolors+1));
for (i=0; i< ncolors; i++)
   xmstr[i] = XmStringCreate(colors[i], XmSTRING_DEFAULT_CHARSET);

/*
 * create the scrolled list widget and register callback
 */
n = 0;
XtSetArg(args[n], XmNitems, xmstr); n++;
XtSetArg(args[n], XmNitemCount, ncolors);n++;
XtSetArg(args[n], XmNvisibleItemCount,  20);n++;
XtSetArg(args[n], XmNselectionPolicy, XmSINGLE_SELECT);n++;
XtSetArg(args[n], XmNscrollingPolicy, XmAUTOMATIC);n++;
XtSetArg(args[n], XmNtopAttachment, XmATTACH_FORM); n++;
XtSetArg(args[n], XmNrightAttachment, XmATTACH_FORM); n++;
XtSetArg(args[n], XmNleftAttachment, XmATTACH_FORM); n++;
scroll_list = (Widget)XmCreateScrolledList (form, "List ", args, n);
XtManageChild(scroll_list);
XtAddCallback(scroll_list, XmNsingleSelectionCallback,
   ListSelectCB, (XtPointer)NULL);

/*
 * create control box
 */
n = 0;
XtSetArg(args[n], XmNorientation, XmHORIZONTAL); n++;
XtSetArg(args[n], XmNtopAttachment, XmATTACH_POSITION);n++;
XtSetArg(args[n], XmNtopPosition, (Position)90);n++;
XtSetArg(args[n], XmNrightAttachment, XmATTACH_FORM); n++;
XtSetArg(args[n], XmNleftAttachment, XmATTACH_FORM); n++;
XtSetArg(args[n], XmNbottomAttachment, XmATTACH_FORM);n++;
controls_box = XmCreateRowColumn(form, "listControl", args, n);
```

```c
    XtManageChild(controls_box);

    /*
     * create separator
     */
    n = 0;
    XtSetArg(args[n], XmNshadowThickness,  1);n++;
    XtSetArg(args[n], XmNtopAttachment, XmATTACH_WIDGET); n++;
    XtSetArg(args[n], XmNtopWidget, scroll_list); n++;
    XtSetArg(args[n], XmNrightAttachment, XmATTACH_FORM); n++;
    XtSetArg(args[n], XmNleftAttachment, XmATTACH_FORM); n++;
    XtSetArg(args[n], XmNbottomAttachment, XmATTACH_WIDGET); n++;
    XtSetArg(args[n], XmNbottomWidget, controls_box); n++;
    sep = XmCreateSeparator(form, "Separator", args, n);
    XtManageChild(sep);

    /*
     * create control pushbutton
     */
    n = 0;
    XtSetArg(args[n], XmNpushButtonEnabled, True); n++;

    for (i =0; i < K_NUM_CONTROLS; i++)
    {
        XtSetArg(args[n], XmNlabelString,
          XmStringCreateLtoR(controls_pb_names[i],  XmSTRING_DEFAULT_CHARSET));n++;
        controls_pb[i] = XmCreatePushButton(controls_box,"cntlBtn",  args, n);
        XtManageChild(controls_pb[i]);
        XtAddCallback(controls_pb[i], XmNactivateCallback,
          (XtCallbackProc) ListControlCB, (XtPointer)i);
    }
    XtRealizeWidget(top_level);
}

static void ListSelectCB(w, client_data, call_data)
Widget w;
XtPointer client_data;
XmListCallbackStruct *call_data;
{
    XmStringGetLtoR(call_data->item, XmSTRING_DEFAULT_CHARSET, &text);
}

static void ListControlCB(w,  client_data, call_data)
Widget w;
XtPointer client_data;
XtPointer call_data;
{
    int  control_index = (int) client_data;
    int  n;
    Arg args[10];
    Pixel color;

    if (control_index == K_FOREGROUND)
    {
        selected_fg_color = GetPixelName(w, text);
        if (strcmp(appl, "text") == 0)
```

```c
      {
         n= 0;
         XtSetArg(args[n], XmNforeground, selected_fg_color); n++;
         XtSetValues(text_widget, args, n);
      }
      n = 0;
      XtSetArg(args[n], XmNbackground, selected_fg_color); n++;
      XtSetValues(controls_box, args, n);
   }
   else if (control_index == K_BACKGROUND)
   {
      selected_bg_color = GetPixelName(w, text);
      if (strcmp(appl, "text") == 0)
      {
         n= 0;
         XtSetArg(args[n], XmNbackground, selected_bg_color); n++;
         XtSetValues(text_widget, args, n);
      }
      else if (strcmp(appl, "drawing") == 0)
      {
         n= 0;
         XtSetArg(args[n], XmNbackground, selected_bg_color); n++;
         XtSetValues(canvas, args, n);
         XSetForeground(XtDisplay(w), pix_data.gc, selected_bg_color);
         XFillRectangle(XtDisplay(w), pix_data.pix, pix_data.gc, 0, 0,
            pix_data.width, pix_data.height);
      }
      n= 0;
      XtSetArg(args[n], XmNbackground, selected_bg_color); n++;
      XtSetValues(controls_box, args, n);
   }
   else if (control_index == K_CANCEL)
   {
      XtDestroyWidget(top_level);
   }
}

/*
 *
 * This procedure is used to dynamically allocate color values for
 * name color.
 */
Pixel GetPixelName ( w, colorname)
Widget w;
char    *colorname;
{
   char         message[128];
   Display      *dpy = XtDisplay (w);
   int          scr  = DefaultScreen (dpy);
   Colormap     cmap = DefaultColormap (dpy, scr);
   XColor       color, ignore ;

   if ( XAllocNamedColor (dpy, cmap, colorname, &color, &ignore))
      return (color.pixel);
```

```c
    else
    {
        sprintf(message, "Warning: could not allocate color for %s", colorname);
        MsgOut(WARNING_MSG_TYPE, message);
        return (BlackPixel (dpy, scr));
    }
}

/*
 * count number of lines in the rgb.txt file
 */

int GetColorsFromRGBFile()
{
    FILE   *fp;
    char   linebuf[256];
    int    nlines;

    if ((fp = fopen("/usr/lib/X11/rgb.txt",  "r")) == NULL)
    {
        MsgOut(ERROR_MSG_TYPE, "can't open file /usr/lib/X11/rgb.txt");
        return(0);
    }

    nlines = 0;
    while (fgets(linebuf, 256, fp) != NULL)
        nlines++;

    return(nlines);
}

/*
 * fill in the colors array with the color names in the rgb.txt file
 */
int FillColorArray(ncolors, colors)
int   ncolors;
char *colors[];
{
    FILE   *fp;
    char   linebuf[256];
    int    nlines;
    char   *ptr;

    if ((fp = fopen("/usr/lib/X11/rgb.txt",  "r")) == NULL)
    {
        MsgOut(ERROR_MSG_TYPE, "can't open file /usr/lib/X11/rgb.txt");
        return(0);
    }

    nlines = 0;
    while (fgets(linebuf, 256, fp) != NULL)
    {
        nlines++;
        linebuf[strlen(linebuf)-1] = '\0';
        ptr = &linebuf[0];
        while ( ! isalpha(*ptr))
```

```
        ptr++;
      colors[nlines] = (char *)XtMalloc(strlen(ptr) +1);
      strcpy(colors[nlines], ptr);
   }
   return(nlines);
}

/*
 * initialize some predefine color names
 */
void InitColor(widget)
Widget widget;
{
   /*
    * get the named colors
    */
   green = GetPixelName(widget, "green");
   cyan = GetPixelName(widget, "cyan");
   red = GetPixelName(widget, "red");
   yellow = GetPixelName(widget, "yellow");
   blue = GetPixelName(widget, "blue");
   black = GetPixelName(widget, "black");
   grey = GetPixelName(widget, "grey");
   white = GetPixelName(widget, "white");
}
```

Listing 8.9 shows the program to handle the font selections.

Listing 8.9 xfont.c

```
/*
 * xfont.c
 */
#include <stdio.h>
#include "demo.h"

#define K_NUM_CONTROLS    2
#define K_ACCEPT          0
#define K_CANCEL          1

/*
 * Global data
 */
extern Display *dpy;
extern Widget text_widget;

Font    selected_font = NULL;
XFontStruct    *label_font;
XmFontList     label_font_list;

static Widget top_level;
static Widget form;
static Widget scroll_list;
static Widget controls_pb[K_NUM_CONTROLS];
static Widget controls_box;
```

```c
static Widget sep;
static int    nfonts;
static char   **fonts;
static char   *text;
static char   appl[20];
static char   *controls_pb_names[] = {
   "Accept",
   "Cancel"
};

/*
 *  Internal functions
 */
static void ListControlCB();
static void ListSelectCB();

void CreateFontList(w, client_data, call_data)
Widget w;
XtPointer client_data;
XtPointer call_data;
{
   int    n, i;
   Arg  args[10];
   XmString *xmstr;
   char  *application = (char *)client_data;

   strcpy(appl, application);
   top_level = (Widget)XtAppCreateShell("fontTop", "FontTop",
         applicationShellWidgetClass, dpy, NULL, 0);

   n = 0;
   form = XmCreateForm(top_level, "listForm", args, n);
   XtManageChild (form);

   /*
    * compute number of fonts in the fonts array
    */
   nfonts = GetFontsFromFontFile();

   fonts = (char **)XtMalloc(sizeof(char *) * nfonts);

   /*
    * Fill in the array of font
    */
   FillFontArray(nfonts, fonts);

   /*
    * convert font specifications to an array of type XmString
    */
   xmstr = (XmString *)XtMalloc(sizeof(XmString) *  nfonts);
   for (i=0; i< nfonts-1; i++)
     xmstr[i] = XmStringCreate(fonts[i], XmSTRING_DEFAULT_CHARSET);
   /*
    * create the scrolled list widget and register callback
    */
```

```c
    n = 0;
    XtSetArg(args[n], XmNitems,xmstr); n++;
    XtSetArg(args[n], XmNitemCount,nfonts);n++;
    XtSetArg(args[n], XmNvisibleItemCount,  20);n++;
    XtSetArg(args[n], XmNselectionPolicy, XmSINGLE_SELECT);n++;
    XtSetArg(args[n], XmNscrollingPolicy, XmAUTOMATIC);n++;
    XtSetArg(args[n], XmNtopAttachment, XmATTACH_FORM); n++;
    XtSetArg(args[n], XmNrightAttachment, XmATTACH_FORM); n++;
    XtSetArg(args[n], XmNleftAttachment, XmATTACH_FORM); n++;
    scroll_list = (Widget )XmCreateScrolledList (form, "List ", args, n);
    XtManageChild(scroll_list);
    XtAddCallback(scroll_list, XmNsingleSelectionCallback, ListSelectCB, NULL);
    /*
     * create control box
     */
    n = 0;
    XtSetArg(args[n], XmNorientation, XmHORIZONTAL); n++;
    XtSetArg(args[n], XmNtopAttachment, XmATTACH_POSITION);n++;
    XtSetArg(args[n], XmNtopPosition, (Position)90);n++;
    XtSetArg(args[n], XmNrightAttachment, XmATTACH_FORM); n++;
    XtSetArg(args[n], XmNleftAttachment, XmATTACH_FORM); n++;
    XtSetArg(args[n], XmNbottomAttachment, XmATTACH_FORM);n++;
    controls_box = XmCreateRowColumn(form, "ListControl", args, n);
    XtManageChild(controls_box);

    /*
     * create separator
     */
    n = 0;
    XtSetArg(args[n], XmNshadowThickness,  1);n++;
    XtSetArg(args[n], XmNtopAttachment, XmATTACH_WIDGET); n++;
    XtSetArg(args[n], XmNtopWidget, scroll_list); n++;
    XtSetArg(args[n], XmNrightAttachment, XmATTACH_FORM); n++;
    XtSetArg(args[n], XmNleftAttachment, XmATTACH_FORM); n++;
    XtSetArg(args[n], XmNbottomAttachment, XmATTACH_WIDGET); n++;
    XtSetArg(args[n], XmNbottomWidget, controls_box); n++;
    sep = XmCreateSeparator(form, "Separator", args, n);
    XtManageChild(sep);

    /*
     * create control pushbutton
     */
    n = 0;
    XtSetArg(args[n], XmNpushButtonEnabled, True); n++;

    for (i =0; i < K_NUM_CONTROLS; i++)
    {
       XtSetArg(args[n], XmNlabelString,
          XmStringCreateLtoR(controls_pb_names[i], XmSTRING_DEFAULT_CHARSET));n++;
       controls_pb[i] = XmCreatePushButton(controls_box,"CntlBtn",  args, n);
       XtManageChild(controls_pb[i]);
       XtAddCallback(controls_pb[i], XmNactivateCallback,
          (XtCallbackProc) ListControlCB, (XtPointer)i);
    }
```

```c
       XtRealizeWidget(top_level);
}

static void ListSelectCB(w, client_data, call_data)
Widget w;
XtPointer client_data;
XmListCallbackStruct *call_data;
{
    XmStringGetLtoR(call_data->item, XmSTRING_DEFAULT_CHARSET, &text);
    printf("fonts selected is \n%s\n", text);
}

static void ListControlCB(w,  client_data, call_data)
Widget w;
XtPointer client_data;
XtPointer call_data;
{
    int  control_index = (int) client_data;
    int  n;
    Arg args[10];

    if (control_index == K_ACCEPT)
    {
       selected_font = XLoadFont(XtDisplay(w), text);
       label_font = XLoadQueryFont(XtDisplay(w), text);
       if (label_font == NULL)
          XLoadQueryFont(XtDisplay(w), "9x15");
       label_font_list = XmFontListCreate(label_font, XmSTRING_DEFAULT_CHARSET);
       if (strcmp(appl, "text") == 0)
       {
          n= 0;
          XtSetArg(args[n], XmNfontList,label_font_list); n++;
          XtSetValues(text_widget, args, n);
       }
       XtDestroyWidget(top_level);

    }
    else if (control_index == K_CANCEL)
    {
       XtDestroyWidget(top_level);
    }
}

int GetFontsFromFontFile()
{
    FILE   *fp;
    char   linebuf[256];
    int    nlines;

    if ((fp = fopen("/usr/lib/X11/fonts/75dpi/fonts.dir",  "r")) == NULL)
    {
       MsgOut(ERROR_MSG_TYPE, "can't open file /usr/lib/X11/fonts/75dpi/
           fonts.dir");
       return;
    }
```

```
   nlines = 0;
   while (fgets(linebuf, 256, fp) != NULL)
      nlines++;

   return(nlines);
}

FillFontArray(nfonts, fonts)
int nfonts;
char *fonts[];
{
   FILE *fp;
   char linebuf[256];
   int  nline;
   char *ptr;

   if ((fp = fopen("/usr/lib/X11/fonts/75dpi/fonts.dir", "r")) == NULL)
   {
      MsgOut(ERROR_MSG_TYPE,
          "can't open file /usr/lib/X11/fonts/75dpi/fonts.dir");
      return;
   }

   nline = 0;
   /* skip the line count */
   fgets(linebuf, 256, fp);
   while (fgets(linebuf, 256, fp) != NULL)
   {
      linebuf[strlen(linebuf)-1] = '\0';
      ptr = &linebuf[0];
      while ( (*ptr) != '-')
      ptr++;
      fonts[nline] = (char *)XtMalloc(strlen(ptr)+1);
      strcpy(fonts[nline], ptr);
      nline++;
   }

   return(0);
}
```

Listing 8.10 shows the program to switch between the default cursor and the watch cursor.

Listing 8.10 xcursor.c

```
/*
 * xcursor.c
 */
#include "demo.h"

/*
 * Global data
 */
```

```c
extern Display    *dpy;

/*
 * Internal functions
 */
void ChangeToWatchCursor();
void ChangeBackCursor();
void ChangeCursor();

/*
 *  Change to the watch cursor...
 */
void ChangeToWatchCursor (w)
Widget w;
{
    static Cursor watch = NULL;

    if (!watch) watch = XCreateFontCursor ( dpy, XC_watch);
    ChangeCursor(w,watch);

}   /* end of ChangeToWatchCursor() */

void ChangeBackCursor(w)
Widget w;
{
    ChangeCursor(w, None);
}

void ChangeCursor (w, newCursor)
Widget w;
Cursor newCursor;
{
    Widget tmp_widget;
    Display *display = 0;
    Window  window;

    tmp_widget = w;
    while (!display || !window)
    {
        if (!tmp_widget) break;
        if (XtIsShell(tmp_widget) )
        {
            display = XtDisplay (tmp_widget);
            window  = XtWindow (tmp_widget);
        }
        tmp_widget = XtParent(tmp_widget);
    }

    if (display && window)
    {
        XUndefineCursor (display, window);
        XDefineCursor (display, window, newCursor);
        XFlush(display);
    }
} /* end of ChangeCursor() */
```

8.3.2 A Case Study: A Drawing Editor

8.3.2.1 Functional Descriptions

☞ The main window

Fig. 8.9 shows the main window for the drawing editor, consisting of a menubar and a scrolled window. The menubar has four pulldown menus: file, edit, preference, and draw. Inside the scrolled window is a drawing area where we can draw dots, lines, rectangles, circles, and text. We also have the capability to select colors and fonts for the things we draw.

The file menu has four options: open, close, save, and exit. If the open option is selected, it pops up a file selection box from which you can select an image file. Once the image file is selected, the user clicks on the open button to load the selected image onto the drawing area. If the close option is selected, the drawing area is cleared. If the save option is selected, it pops up a file selection box that prompts the user for the filename to which the image is saved. The exit option terminates this drawing editor.

The edit menu has three operations: cut, copy, and paste. The cut option allows the user to select and remove a part of the drawing, then save it to a hidden area. The selection is done by enclosing that section in a rectangle, drawn by using mouse button two through the rubber-band technique. The copy option allows the user to select a part of a drawing to copy and save to a hidden area through the same rubber-band technique. The paste option restores that image saved in the hidden scratch area to the cursor's location.

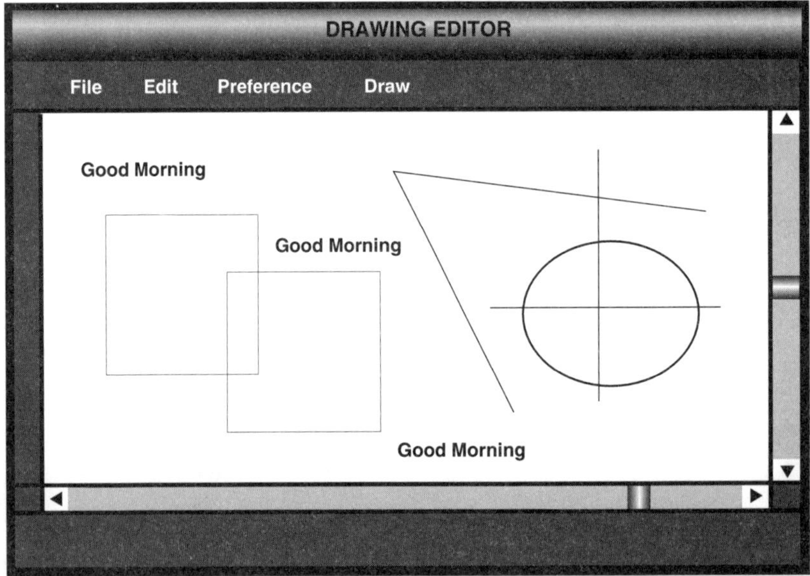

Fig. 8.9 A Drawing Editor

The preference menu has two options: color and font. Selecting the color option pops up a color selection window (as shown in Figure 8.7), through which the user can select both the foreground and background colors for the image he or she draws. Selecting the font option pops up a font selection window (as shown in Figure 8.8), through which the user can select the font for the text drawn on the drawing window.

The draw menu has five options: dot, line, rectangle, circle, and text. The mouse fully controls the drawing capability in this example. To draw a dot, first select the dot option, then position the cursor to where you want to draw and click on mouse button one. To draw a line, select the line option, then hold down mouse button one at the starting point of a line. Move the mouse to the line's endpoint while continuing to hold down mouse button one. When the button is released, a line is drawn. To draw a rectangle, select the rectangle option, then hold down mouse button one at the upper left corner of the rectangle. Then move the mouse toward the lower right corner of the rectangle while continuing to hold down mouse button one. When you release the mouse button, a rectangle is drawn. To draw a circle, select the circle option, then follow the same instructions for the rectangle. To draw a text box, select the text option. It pops up a dialog box (as shown in Figure 8.10) with a text input area. Type in the text string, then click on the accept button. The text entered is saved. Then move the cursor to where you want the text drawn in the drawing area, and click on mouse button three. The text you entered is drawn on the drawing area, starting at the cursor's location.

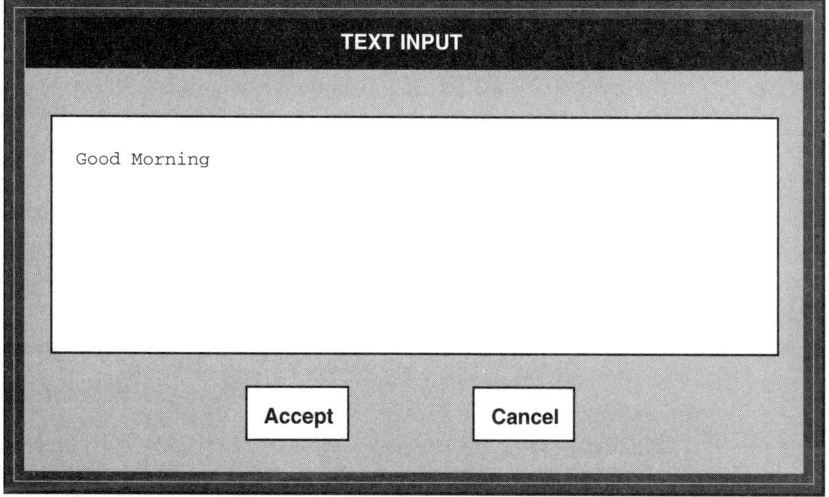

Fig. 8.10 Text Input Dialog

8.3.2.2 Program Description

☞ Creating the main window

The code to create the main window for the drawing editor is shown in Listing 8.11. The function CreateDrawArea() is the only function in this program module that is called externally. First, it creates a top-level shell as the root of a new application. It then creates a form widget under this top-level widget to hold everything within this application. This is initial work required within this function.

The next step is to create a menubar and four pulldown menus. It then attaches these four pulldown menus to the menubar. This constitutes the major portion of the work in this function. Creating the menubar is done by calling the function MenuBar(), as described in Section 8.3.1.2.

Next, it calls function CreateMenuButton() to create all the menu buttons for each pulldown menu. Since it has four pulldown menus, the program calls the CreateMenuButton() function four times. The function CreateMenuButton() was described in Section 8.3.1.2, also.

After creating the menus and their options, we create a scrolled window to house the drawing area. A pixmap the same size as the canvas is created to redisplay the picture after the expose event occurs. Three callbacks are added to the canvas. The StratRubberBand() callback is assigned to the ButtonPressMask event. The TrackRubberBand() callback is assigned to the ButtonMotionMask event. The EndRubberBand() callback is assigned to the ButtonReleaseMask event. These three functions combined result in the rubber-band effect.

Two types of data structure are used to draw pictures on the canvas. The data type rubber_band_data is used to make rubber-band drawings, and the data type pixmap_data is used for non-rubber-band drawings. The key difference between these two data types lies in the graphics context. A graphics context is an internal data structure with all the attributes that determine line widths, foreground and background colors, fill patterns, fonts, and the display function to use when a drawing is made. A graphics context's display function attribute determines how each pixel of a new picture combines with a destination drawable's current contents. The display function's default value is set to GXcopy, in which case the source picture completely replaces the current contents of the drawable's affected region. On the other hand, if the same picture is drawn using the GXxor display function, the pixels of the drawable's affected region are set to the source's logical XOR, with the destination's previous contents. The following derivation shows how we can use GXxor to achieve the rubber-band effect:

Let F be the pixel for the tentative foreground color, and B be the pixel for the tentative background color. Before the picture is drawn, if the display function is set to GXxor and the pixel for the foreground color is set to F XOR B, the resultant color is (F XOR B) XOR B, which is F. Let's assume the picture drawn is a box. The first time the box is drawn, it shows F as the foreground color. When the same box is drawn a second time, the resultant color is (F XOR B) XOR F, which is B. This means drawing the same box the second time erases the previously drawn box. Thus in the rubber_band_data data type, we set the display function of its graphics context to the value GXxor.

The function InitRubberBandData() initializes the data structure for rb_data, which is a rubber_band_data data type. It retrieves the tentative foreground and background colors, then sets the foreground color of the graphics context to be the XOR of these two colors. It also sets the line style attribute to LineOnOffDash, and sets the display function to GXxor.

The function InitPixmapData() initializes the data structure for pix_data, which is a pixmap_data data type. It calls the xlib function XCreatePixmap() to create a pixmap with the same dimensions as the canvas. It also initializes the background color.

☞ Handling the file menu options

The callback function FileMenuCB() handles all the options in the file menu. This FileMenuCB() callback is declared static so that it can be known within the source module draw.c. Whenever an option in this file menu is selected, control goes to this function, which then calls the appropriate routine to perform the required task. For example, if the open option is selected, the control transfers to this function. It then calls the function CreateOpenWidget() to pop up a file selection box as shown in Figure 8.2. After the user selects a filename and clicks the open button, control goes to another callback function, FileOpenAcceptCB(). It retrieves the filename the user selected and passes it to the ReadFile() routine. This ReadFile() routine opens and reads the image file. Two types of data are stored in this image file: The initial 200 bytes of data contain this image data's attributes such as width, height, depth, format, byte_order, bytes_per_line, bits_per_pixel, and so forth. The second part of the data stored in this image file contains the image itself. Thus, two read operations are necessary. The image data's size is computed through the equation

```
nbytes = depth * bytes_per_line * height
```

This image data is displayed in the window through the xlib function XPutImage().

If the save option is selected, it retrieves the image attributes and image data through a function call to XGetImage(). The attribute data is written to the save file first, followed by the image data.

If the close option is selected, it calls function XClearArea() to clear the drawing window. The corresponding pixmap data is cleared by calling the function XFillRectangle() with the selected background color.

If the Exit option is selected, it calls XDestroyWidget() to exit this drawing editor window.

☞ Handling the edit menu options

The callback function EditMenuCB() handles all the options in the edit menu. Whenever an option in the edit menu is selected, control goes to this function, which then calls the appropriate routine to perform the required task. For example, if the cut option is selected, the control transfers to the callback function EditMenuCB(). It then calls the function DrawingCut() to remove the selected portion of the drawing from the drawing window, and move it to a hidden scratch pixmap that later can be restored to the drawing window through the DrawingPaste() call.

If the copy option is selected, the callback function EditMenuCB() calls the function DrawingCopy() to copy the selected portion of the drawing within the drawing window to the hidden scratch pixmap. This selected portion of the drawing in the drawing window remains intact.

If the paste option is selected, the callback function EditMenuCB() calls the function DrawingPaste() to restore the pixmap saved in the hidden scratch pixmap to the drawing window, starting at the cursor's position. The pixmap in the hidden scratch area remains intact.

☞ Handling the preference menu options

The callback function PreferenceMenuCB() handles all the options in the preference menu. Whenever an option in the preference menu is selected, control goes to this function, which then calls the appropriate routine to perform the required task.

If the color option is selected, the control transfers to the callback function PreferenceMenuCB(). It then calls the function CreateColorList() to create a color selection window, as shown in Figure 8.7. A complete description of the function is given in Section 8.3.1.2.

If the font option is selected, it calls the function CreateFontList() to create a font display window, as shown in Figure 8.8. A complete description of the function is given in Section 8.3.1.2, also.

☞ Handling the draw menu options

The callback function DrawMenuCB() sets the value of the variable what_to_draw according to the user's selection. Its value can be set to DOT, LINE, RECTANGLE, CIRCLE, or TEXT. In the case of TEXT, it also calls the function PopUpTextInputBox() to pop up a text input dialog where the user enters the text to be drawn on the drawing window.

☞ Handling the mouse buttons

The mouse buttons actually draw the dots, lines, rectangles, circles, and text strings. The callback function StartRubberBand() handles the ButtonPress-Mask event. When the mouse button one is pressed, it draws a dot, the beginning of a line, a small rectangle, or a small circle. When mouse button two is pressed, it draws a small rectangle with on-off dash lines. When mouse button three is pressed, it draws the text string starting at the mouse pointer position. The xlib function XDrawPoint() is used to draw points; the xlib function XDrawLine() is used to draw lines; the xlib function XDrawRectangle() is used to draw rectangles; the function XDrawArc() is used to draw circles; and the xlib function XDrawImageString() is used to draw text strings.

The callback function TrackRubberBand() handles the ButtonMotionMask event. If mouse button one is pressed, nothing happens when drawing dots and text. For lines, rectangles, and circles, it draws once to clear the previous line, rectangle, or circle. It then draws a second time using the new x and y positions. The same happens if mouse button two is pressed. Nothing happens if mouse button three is pressed.

The callback function EndRubberBand() handles the ButtonReleaseMask event. If mouse button one is pressed, nothing happens for drawing dots and text. For lines, rectangles, and circles, it draws once, to the pixmap only, using the new x and y positions. If mouse button two is pressed, it draws once to the window to erase the last rectangle drawn. Nothing happens if mouse button three is pressed.

☞ Handling the window expose event

The callback function Redisplay() handles the window expose event. It simply copies the image stored in the pixmap back to the window by calling the function XCopyArea().

Listing 8.11 contains all the code needed for the drawing editor.

Listing 8.11 draw.c

```c
/*
 * draw.c
 */
#include "demo.h"

#define     DOT             1
#define     LINE            2
#define     RECTANGLE       3
#define     CIRCLE          4
#define     TEXT            5

/*
 * Global data
 */
extern Display *dpy;
extern Pixel    selected_fg_color;
extern Pixel    selected_bg_color;
extern Pixel    green;
extern Pixel    black;
extern Font     selected_font;
extern XFontStruct  *label_font;

rubber_band_data    rb_data;               /* used to draw image on window */
pixmap_data         pix_data;              /* used to draw image on pixmap */
Widget              canvas;
static int          what_to_draw = 1;
static char         input_text[256];
static char         text_override_translations[] =
"<Key>Return:       newline()";
```

```c
static Widget          draw_form;
static Widget          draw_top;
static Widget          scroll_win;
static Widget          menu_bar;
static Widget          pds[100];
static char            *pd_labels[] = {  "File",
                                         "Edit",
                                         "Preference",
                                         "Draw"
};
static Widget          file_buttons[4];
static char            *file_ops[] = {   "Open",
                                         "Save ",
                                         "Clear",
                                         "Exit"
};
static Widget          edit_buttons[3];
static char            *edit_ops[] = {   "Cut",
                                         "Copy",
                                         "Paste"
};
static Widget          preference_buttons[2];
static char            *preference_ops[] = {
                                         "Color ",
                                         "Font"
};
static Widget          draw_buttons[5];
static char            *draw_ops[] = {   "Dot",
                                         "Line ",
                                         "Rectangle",
                                         "Circle",
                                         "Text"
};

/*
 * Internal functions
 */
static void FileMenuCB();
static void EditMenuCB();
static void PreferenceMenuCB();
static void DrawMenuCB();
static void ReDisplay();
static void InitRubberBandData();
static void InitPixmapData();
static void StartRubberBand();
static void TrackRubberBand();
static void EndRubberBand();
static void PopUpTextInputBox();
static void TextAcceptCB();
static void TextCancelCB();
static int  DrawString();

void CreateDrawArea(widget, client_data, call_data)
Widget widget;
```

```c
XtPointer client_data;
XtPointer call_data;
{
    int             i, n;
    Arg             args[16];
    int             toggle[10];
    int             sep[10];

    /*
     * Create the Application Shell as this is to be the root of a new
     * application.
     */

    n = 0;
    draw_top = XtAppCreateShell("drawEditor", "DrawEditor",
        applicationShellWidgetClass, dpy, args, n);
    /*
     *  Create the Form to hold everything.
     */
    n = 0;
    draw_form = (Widget) XmCreateForm(draw_top, "drawForm", args, n);
    XtManageChild (draw_form);

    /*
     * Create the Menu Bar.
     */
    menu_bar = (Widget) MenuBar(draw_form, pds, pd_labels, XtNumber(pd_labels));
    n = 0;
    XtSetArg (args[n], XmNtopAttachment, XmATTACH_FORM);n++;
    XtSetArg (args[n], XmNleftAttachment, XmATTACH_FORM);n++;
    XtSetArg (args[n], XmNrightAttachment, XmATTACH_FORM);n++;
    XtSetArg (args[n], XmNorientation, XmHORIZONTAL); n++;
    XtSetArg (args[n], XmNspacing, 10); n++;
    XtSetValues(menu_bar, args, n);

    XtManageChild (menu_bar);

    /*
     * Create all the Pulldowns.
     */

    for (n= 0; n< 10; n++)
    {
        sep[n] = 0;
        toggle[n] = 0;
    }

    /*
     * File menu pulldown
     */
    for (n=0; n<XtNumber(file_ops); n++)
        sep [n] = 1;

    CreateMenuButton(pds[0], file_buttons, file_ops,XtNumber(file_ops), FileMenuCB,
        sep, toggle);
```

```c
/*
 * Edit menu pulldown
 */
for (n=0; n<XtNumber(edit_ops); n++)
   sep [n] = 1;

CreateMenuButton(pds[1], edit_buttons,edit_ops,XtNumber(edit_ops), EditMenuCB,
   sep, toggle);

/*
 *  Preference menu pulldown
 */
for (n=0; n<XtNumber(preference_ops); n++)
   sep [n] = 1;

CreateMenuButton(pds[2],
   preference_buttons,preference_ops,XtNumber(preference_ops),
   PreferenceMenuCB,  sep, toggle);

/*
 * Draw menu pulldown
 */
for (n=0; n<XtNumber(draw_ops); n++)
   sep [n] = 1;

CreateMenuButton(pds[3], draw_buttons,draw_ops,XtNumber(draw_ops),
   DrawMenuCB,  sep, toggle);

/*
 * create the scrolled window for drawing area
 */
n=0;
XtSetArg(args[n], XmNscrollingPolicy,   XmAUTOMATIC);    n++;
XtSetArg(args[n], XmNscrollBarDisplayPolicy,   XmSTATIC ); n++;
XtSetArg(args[n], XmNtopAttachment,   XmATTACH_WIDGET);    n++;
XtSetArg(args[n], XmNtopWidget,     menu_bar); n++;
XtSetArg(args[n], XmNleftAttachment, XmATTACH_FORM ); n++;
XtSetArg(args[n], XmNrightAttachment,XmATTACH_FORM); n++;
XtSetArg(args[n], XmNbottomAttachment,XmATTACH_POSITION); n++;
XtSetArg(args[n], XmNbottomPosition, (Position) 93); n++;

scroll_win = XmCreateScrolledWindow(draw_form, "scrollWin", args, n);
XtManageChild(scroll_win);

/*
 * Create the drawing surface
 */
n = 0;
XtSetArg(args[n], XmNresizePolicy,   XmRESIZE_GROW); n++;
XtSetArg(args[n], XmNwidth,          600); n++;
XtSetArg(args[n], XmNheight,         400); n++;
canvas = (Widget)XmCreateDrawingArea(scroll_win, "drawCanvas", args, n);
XtManageChild(canvas);

/*
 *  set the size of pixmap equal to the size of the drawing area
```

```c
    */

   n = 0;
   XtSetArg(args[n], XmNwidth,  &pix_data.width); n++;
   XtSetArg(args[n], XmNheight, &pix_data.height); n++;
   XtGetValues(canvas, args, n);

   XtAddCallback(canvas, XmNexposeCallback, ReDisplay,  &pix_data);

   XtAddEventHandler(canvas, ButtonPressMask,   FALSE, StartRubberBand, &rb_data);
   XtAddEventHandler(canvas, ButtonMotionMask,  FALSE, TrackRubberBand, &rb_data);
   XtAddEventHandler(canvas, ButtonReleaseMask, FALSE, EndRubberBand,   &rb_data);

   /*
    * set default foreground and background colors
    */
   selected_fg_color = GetPixelName(canvas, "black");
   selected_bg_color = GetPixelName(canvas, "grey");

   /*
    *  initialize pix_data and rb_data.
    */
   InitRubberBandData(canvas, &rb_data);
   InitPixmapData(canvas, &pix_data);

   /*
    * initialize input_text
    */
   strcpy(input_text, "");

   XtRealizeWidget(draw_top);
}

void InitRubberBandData (w, data)
Widget                  w;
rubber_band_data  *data;
{
   XGCValues values;
   GC              gc;
   Arg             wargs[10];
   Display         *dsp;

   /*
    * Get the colors used by the widget.
    */
   XtSetArg(wargs[0], XtNforeground, &values.foreground);
   XtSetArg(wargs[1], XtNbackground, &values.background);
   XtGetValues(w, wargs,2);
   /*
    * Set the fg to the XOR of the fg and bg, so if it is
    * XOR'ed with bg, the result will be fg and vice-versa.
    * This effectively achieves inverse video effect.
    */
   values.foreground = values.foreground ^ values.background;
   data->background_color = values.background;
```

```c
    /*
     * Set the rubber band gc to use XOR mode and dOnOffDashraw
     * a dashed line.
     */
    values.line_style = LineOnOffDash;
    values.function   = GXxor;
    dsp = XtDisplay(w);
    data->gc = XCreateGC(XtDisplay(w), DefaultRootWindow(dsp),
        GCForeground | GCBackground | GCFunction | GCLineStyle, &values);
    return;
}

void InitPixmapData (w, data)
Widget              w;
pixmap_data    *data;
{
    Arg                wargs[10];

    /*
     * Get the size of the drawing area.
     */
    XtSetArg(wargs[0], XtNwidth, &data->width);
    XtSetArg(wargs[1], XtNheight, &data->height);
    XtGetValues(w, wargs,2);

    data->gc = XCreateGC(XtDisplay(w), DefaultRootWindow(XtDisplay(w)), NULL,
          NULL);
    /*
     * free the old pixmap and create a new pixmap the size of the window
     */
    if (data->pix)
       XFreePixmap(XtDisplay(w), data->pix);
    data->pix = XCreatePixmap(XtDisplay(w), DefaultRootWindow(XtDisplay(w)),
        data->width, data->height, DefaultDepthOfScreen(XtScreen(w)));
    XSetForeground(XtDisplay(w), data->gc, selected_bg_color);
    XFillRectangle(XtDisplay(w), data->pix, data->gc, 0, 0, data->width,
        data->height);
}

void StartRubberBand(w, data, event)
Widget                  w;
rubber_band_data        *data;
XEvent                  *event;
{
    Display *display = XtDisplay(w);
    Pixel    xor_fg_color;
    char     tmp_text[256];
    char     *ptr, *ptr1;
    int      font_height;
    int      i;

    XSetBackground (display, data->gc, selected_bg_color);
    xor_fg_color = selected_fg_color ^ selected_bg_color;
    XSetForeground (display, data->gc, xor_fg_color);
```

```c
XSetBackground (display, pix_data.gc, selected_bg_color);
XSetForeground (display,  pix_data.gc, selected_fg_color);

/*
 * determine font height
 */
if (label_font == NULL)
   font_height = 12;
else
{
   font_height = label_font->ascent + label_font->descent + 1;
   if (font_height < 8)
      font_height = 12;
}

if (event->xbutton.button == Button1)
{
   XSetLineAttributes(display, data->gc, 1, LineSolid, CapButt, JoinBevel);
   if (what_to_draw == DOT)
   {
      data->last_x  =  data->start_x = event->xbutton.x;
      data->last_y  =  data->start_y = event->xbutton.y;
      XDrawPoint(XtDisplay(w), XtWindow(w),
         data->gc, data->start_x, data->start_y);
      XDrawPoint(XtDisplay(w), pix_data.pix,
         pix_data.gc, data->start_x, data->start_y);

   }
   else if (what_to_draw == LINE)
   {
      data->last_x  =  data->start_x = event->xbutton.x;
      data->last_y  =  data->start_y = event->xbutton.y;
      XDrawLine(XtDisplay(w), XtWindow(w),
         data->gc, data->start_x, data->start_y,
         data->last_x, data->last_y);
   }
   else if (what_to_draw == RECTANGLE)
   {
      data->last_x  =  data->start_x = event->xbutton.x;
      data->last_y  =  data->start_y = event->xbutton.y;

      data->width  = data->last_x  - data->start_x;
      data->height = data->last_y  - data->start_y;

      XDrawRectangle(XtDisplay(w), XtWindow(w),
         data->gc, data->start_x, data->start_y,
         data->width, data->height);
   }
   else if (what_to_draw == CIRCLE)
   {
      data->last_x  =  data->start_x = event->xbutton.x;
      data->last_y  =  data->start_y = event->xbutton.y;

      data->width  = data->last_x  - data->start_x;
      data->height = data->last_y  - data->start_y;
```

```
            XDrawArc(XtDisplay(w), XtWindow(w),
                data->gc, data->start_x, data->start_y,
                data->width, data->height, 0, 64 * 360);
        }
        else if (what_to_draw == TEXT)
        {

        }
    }
    else if (event->xbutton.button == Button2)
    {
        XSetLineAttributes(display, data->gc, 1, LineOnOffDash, CapButt, JoinBevel);
        data->last_x  =  data->start_x = event->xbutton.x;
        data->last_y  =  data->start_y = event->xbutton.y;

        data->height = data->last_y - data->start_y;
        data->width  = data->last_x - data->start_x;

        XDrawRectangle(XtDisplay(w), XtWindow(w),
            data->gc, data->start_x, data->start_y,
            data->width, data->height);
    }
    else if (event->xbutton.button == Button3)
    {
        i = 0;
        strcpy(tmp_text, input_text);
        ptr1 = ptr = &tmp_text[0];
        while ( *ptr != '\0')
        {
            if ( *ptr == '\n')
            {
                *ptr = '\0';
                DrawString(data, event->xbutton.x, event->xbutton.y + i, ptr1);
                ptr++;
                ptr1 = ptr;
                i += font_height;
            }
            else
                ptr++;
        }
        DrawString(data, event->xbutton.x, event->xbutton.y + i,   ptr1);
    }
}

void TrackRubberBand(w, data, event)
Widget                  w;
rubber_band_data        *data;
XEvent                  *event;
{
    Display *display = XtDisplay(w);
    Pixel     xor_fg_color;

    XSetBackground (display, data->gc, selected_bg_color);
    xor_fg_color = selected_fg_color ^ selected_bg_color;
    XSetForeground (display, data->gc, xor_fg_color);
```

```c
XSetBackground (display, pix_data.gc, selected_bg_color);
XSetForeground (display,  pix_data.gc, selected_fg_color);

if (event->xbutton.button == Button3)
{
    if (what_to_draw == DOT)
    {
    }
    else if (what_to_draw == LINE)
    {
        /*
         * Draw once to clear the previous line.
         */
        XDrawLine(XtDisplay(w), XtWindow(w), data->gc,
            data->start_x,data->start_y,
            data->last_x, data->last_y);
        /*
         * Update the endpoints.
         */
        data->last_x  =  event->xbutton.x;
        data->last_y  =  event->xbutton.y;
        /*
         * Draw the new line.
         */
        XDrawLine(XtDisplay(w), XtWindow(w), data->gc,
            data->start_x, data->start_y,
            data->last_x, data->last_y);
    }
    else if (what_to_draw == RECTANGLE)
    {
        /*
         * Draw once to clear the previous box.
         */
        XDrawRectangle(XtDisplay(w), XtWindow(w), data->gc,
            data->start_x,data->start_y,
            data->width, data->height);
        /*
         * Update the endpoints.
         */
        data->last_x  =  event->xbutton.x;
        data->last_y  =  event->xbutton.y;
        /*
         * Draw the new rectangle.
         */
        data->height = data->last_y - data->start_y;
        data->width  = data->last_x - data->start_x;
        XDrawRectangle(XtDisplay(w), XtWindow(w), data->gc,
            data->start_x,data->start_y,
            data->width, data->height);
    }
    else if (what_to_draw == CIRCLE)
    {
        /*
         * Draw once to clear the previous circle.
```

```c
            */
          XDrawArc(XtDisplay(w), XtWindow(w),
             data->gc, data->start_x, data->start_y,
             data->width, data->height, 0, 64 * 360);
          /*
           * Update the endpoints.
           */
          data->last_x = event->xbutton.x;
          data->last_y = event->xbutton.y;
          data->width  = data->last_x  - data->start_x;
          data->height = data->last_y  - data->start_y;
          /*
           * Draw the new circle.
           */
          XDrawArc(XtDisplay(w), XtWindow(w),
             data->gc, data->start_x, data->start_y,
             data->width, data->height, 0, 64 * 360);
      }
      else if (what_to_draw == TEXT)
      {
      }
   }
   else if (event->xbutton.button == Button2)
   {
      XSetLineAttributes(display, data->gc, 1, LineOnOffDash, CapButt, JoinBevel);
      /*
       * Draw once to clear the previous box.
       */
      XDrawRectangle(XtDisplay(w), XtWindow(w), data->gc,
         data->start_x,data->start_y,
         data->width, data->height);
      /*
       * Update the endpoints.
       */
      data->last_x  =  event->xbutton.x;
      data->last_y  =  event->xbutton.y;
      data->height = data->last_y - data->start_y;
      data->width  = data->last_x - data->start_x;
      /*
       * Draw the new box.
       */
      XDrawRectangle(XtDisplay(w), XtWindow(w), data->gc,
         data->start_x,data->start_y,
         data->width, data->height);
   }
}

void EndRubberBand(w, data, event)
Widget              w;
rubber_band_data *data;
XEvent              *event;
{
   Display *display = XtDisplay(w);
```

```c
    Pixel     xor_fg_color;

XSetBackground (display, data->gc, selected_bg_color);
xor_fg_color = selected_fg_color ^ selected_bg_color;
XSetForeground (display, data->gc, xor_fg_color);

XSetBackground (display, pix_data.gc, selected_bg_color);
XSetForeground (display, pix_data.gc, selected_fg_color);

if (event->xbutton.button == Button1 )
{
   XSetLineAttributes(display, data->gc, 1, LineSolid, CapButt, JoinBevel);
   if (what_to_draw == DOT)
   {
   }
   else if (what_to_draw == LINE)
   {
      /*
       * Update the endpoints.
       */
      data->last_x = event->xbutton.x;
      data->last_y = event->xbutton.y;
      data->height = data->last_y - data->start_y;
      data->width  = data->last_x - data->start_x;

      /*
       * draw on pixmap
       */
      XDrawLine(XtDisplay(w), pix_data.pix, pix_data.gc,
         data->start_x, data->start_y,
         data->last_x, data->last_y);
   }
   else if (what_to_draw == RECTANGLE)
   {
      /*
       * Update the endpoints.
       */
      data->last_x = event->xbutton.x;
      data->last_y = event->xbutton.y;
      data->height = data->last_y - data->start_y;
      data->width  = data->last_x - data->start_x;

      /*
       * draw on pixmap
       */
      XDrawRectangle(XtDisplay(w),  pix_data.pix,  pix_data.gc,
         data->start_x,data->start_y,
         data->width, data->height);
   }
   else if (what_to_draw == CIRCLE)
   {
      /*
       * Update the endpoints.
       */
      data->last_x = event->xbutton.x;
```

```c
            data->last_y = event->xbutton.y;
            data->width  = data->last_x  - data->start_x;
            data->height = data->last_y  - data->start_y;
            /*
             * Draw the new circle.
             */

            XDrawArc(XtDisplay(w), pix_data.pix,
                pix_data.gc, data->start_x, data->start_y,
                data->width, data->height, 0, 64 * 360);

        }
        else if (what_to_draw == TEXT)
        {
        }
    }
    else if (event->xbutton.button == Button2)
    {
        XSetLineAttributes(display, data->gc, 1, LineOnOffDash, CapButt, JoinBevel);
        /*
         * Update the endpoints.
         */
        data->last_x = event->xbutton.x;
        data->last_y = event->xbutton.y;
        data->height = data->last_y - data->start_y;
        data->width  = data->last_x - data->start_x;

        XDrawRectangle(XtDisplay(w), XtWindow(w), data->gc,
            data->start_x,data->start_y,
            data->width, data->height);
    }
}

int DrawString(data, x1, y1, textstring)
rubber_band_data *data;
int x1, y1;
char *textstring;
{
    Display *display = XtDisplay(canvas);
    Font font;

    XSetForeground (display, data->gc,selected_fg_color);
    if (selected_font == (Font)NULL)
    {
        font = XLoadFont(display, "9x15");
        XSetFont(display, data->gc, font);
    }
    else
        XSetFont(display, data->gc, selected_font);

    /*
     * draw on window
     */
    XDrawImageString(XtDisplay(canvas),XtWindow(canvas), data->gc,
        x1, y1, textstring, strlen(textstring));
    /*
```

```c
      * draw on pixmap
      */
   XDrawImageString(XtDisplay(canvas),  pix_data.pix, data->gc,
      x1, y1, textstring, strlen(textstring));
}

static void FileMenuCB(widget, client_data, call_data)
Widget widget;
XtPointer client_data;
XtPointer call_data;
{
   int selection;
   int n;
   int fd;
   long nbytes;
   Arg args[10];
   Dimension width, height;
   char filename[128];
   char buf[2000];
   char msg[256];
   XImage *im;
   XImage *xi;

   selection = (int)client_data;
   switch (selection) {
   case 0:
      im = (XImage *) malloc(sizeof(XImage));
      strcpy(filename, "/usr/shen/motif/demo/image.data");
      if ((fd = open(filename, O_RDONLY, 0755)) == -1)
      {
         sprintf(msg, "Open file error: filename %s\n", filename);
         MsgOut(WARNING_MSG_TYPE, msg);
         return;
      }
      read(fd, buf, 200);
      sscanf(buf, "%d %d %d %d %d %d %d %d %d %d %d %d %d %d\n",
         &im->width, &im->height, &im->xoffset, &im->format,
         &im->byte_order, &im->bitmap_unit,
         &im->bitmap_bit_order, &im->bitmap_pad, &im->depth,
         &im->bytes_per_line, &im->bits_per_pixel,
         &im->red_mask, &im->green_mask, &im->blue_mask);
      /*
       * compute size of the image in bytes
       */
      nbytes = im->depth * im->bytes_per_line * im->height;
      im->data = (char *)malloc(nbytes);
      read(fd, im->data, nbytes);
      close(fd);
      XPutImage(XtDisplay(canvas), XtWindow(canvas), pix_data.gc, im,
         0, 0, 0, 0, im->width, im->height);
      /*
       * put image on pixmap
       */
      XPutImage(XtDisplay(canvas),pix_data.pix,  pix_data.gc, im,
```

```c
            0, 0, 0, 0, im->width, im->height);
        break;
    case 1:
        XtSetArg(args[0], XtNwidth, &width);
        XtSetArg(args[1], XtNheight, &height);
        XtGetValues(canvas, args, 2);

        xi = XGetImage(XtDisplay(canvas), XtWindow(canvas), 0, 0,
            width, height, AllPlanes, XYPixmap);
        strcpy(filename, "/usr/shen/motif/demo/image.data");
        if ((fd = open(filename, O_WRONLY| O_CREAT | O_TRUNC, 0755)) == -1)
        {
            sprintf(msg, "Open file error: filename %s\n", filename);
            MsgOut(WARNING_MSG_TYPE, msg);
            return;
        }

        sprintf(buf, "%d %d %d %d %d %d %d %d %d %d %d %d %d %d\n",
            xi->width, xi->height, xi->xoffset, xi->format,
            xi->byte_order, xi->bitmap_unit,
            xi->bitmap_bit_order, xi->bitmap_pad, xi->depth,
            xi->bytes_per_line, xi->bits_per_pixel,
            xi->red_mask, xi->green_mask, xi->blue_mask);
        for (n=strlen(buf); n<200; n++)
            buf[n] = ' ';
        write(fd, buf, 200);
        /*
         * compute size of the image in bytes
         */
        nbytes = xi->depth * xi->bytes_per_line * xi->height;
        write(fd, xi->data, nbytes);
        close(fd);
        break;
    case 2:
        /*
         * Get the size of the drawing area
         */
        XtSetArg(args[0], XtNwidth,  &width);
        XtSetArg(args[1], XtNheight, &height);
        XtGetValues(canvas, args, 2);
        if (XtIsRealized(canvas))
        {
            /*
             * clear the window
             */
            XClearArea(XtDisplay(canvas), XtWindow(canvas), 0,0,
                width, height, TRUE);
            /*
             * clear the pixmap
             */
            XSetForeground(XtDisplay(canvas), pix_data.gc, selected_bg_color);
            XFillRectangle(XtDisplay(canvas), pix_data.pix, pix_data.gc, 0, 0,
                width, height);
        }
```

```c
            break;
        case 3:
            XtDestroyWidget(draw_top);
            break;
        default:
            break;
    }
}

static void
EditMenuCB(widget, client_data, call_data)
Widget widget;
XtPointer client_data;
XtPointer call_data;
{
    int selection;
    int i,j,n;

    selection = (int)client_data;
    switch (selection) {
    case 0:
        break;
    case 1:
        break;
    case 2:
        break;
    default:
        break;
    }
}

static void
PreferenceMenuCB(widget, client_data, call_data)
Widget widget;
XtPointer client_data;
XtPointer call_data;
{
    int selection;

    selection = (int)client_data;
    switch (selection) {
    case 0:
        CreateColorList(widget, "drawing", call_data);
        break;
    case 1:
        CreateFontList(widget, "drawing", call_data);
        break;
    default:
        break;
    }
}

static void
DrawMenuCB(widget, client_data, call_data)
Widget widget;
```

```c
XtPointer client_data;
XtPointer call_data;
{
    int selection;

    selection = (int)client_data;
    switch (selection) {
    case 0:
       what_to_draw = DOT;
       break;
    case 1:
       what_to_draw =LINE;
       break;
    case 2:
       what_to_draw =RECTANGLE;
       break;
    case 3:
       what_to_draw =CIRCLE;
       break;
    case 4:
       what_to_draw = TEXT;
       PopUpTextInputBox(widget);
       break;
    default:
       break;
    }
}

void PopUpTextInputBox(w)
Widget w;
{
    int    n;
    Arg    args[10];
    Widget form = NULL;
    Widget textwidget, frame;
    Widget rc, apply, exit;

    n=0;
    form = XmCreateFormDialog(w, "textInputForm", args, n);

    /*
     *  Create the entry fields
     */
    n=0;
    XtSetArg(args[n], XmNeditMode, XmMULTI_LINE_EDIT);    n++;
    XtSetArg(args[n], XmNrows, 5); n++;
    XtSetArg(args[n], XmNcursorPositionVisible , True); n++;
    XtSetArg(args[n], XmNtopAttachment, XmATTACH_FORM); n++;
    XtSetArg(args[n], XmNleftAttachment, XmATTACH_FORM); n++;
    XtSetArg(args[n], XmNrightAttachment,XmATTACH_FORM); n++;
    textwidget = XmCreateText(form, "Text", args, n);
    XtManageChild(textwidget);
    XtOverrideTranslations(textwidget,
       XtParseTranslationTable(text_override_translations));
```

```c
    /*
     *  Frame...
     */
    n=0;
    XtSetArg(args[n], XmNtopAttachment,   XmATTACH_WIDGET);    n++;
    XtSetArg(args[n], XmNtopWidget, textwidget);n++;
    XtSetArg(args[n], XmNtopOffset,    5);     n++;
    XtSetArg(args[n], XmNleftAttachment, XmATTACH_POSITION);n++;
    XtSetArg(args[n], XmNleftPosition, (Position)5);n++;
    XtSetArg(args[n], XmNrightAttachment, XmATTACH_POSITION);n++;
    XtSetArg(args[n], XmNrightPosition, (Position)95);n++;
    XtSetArg(args[n], XmNbottomAttachment, XmATTACH_POSITION);n++;
    XtSetArg(args[n], XmNbottomPosition, (Position)95);n++;
    frame = (Widget ) XmCreateFrame(form, "fillFrame", args, n);
    XtManageChild(frame);

    /*
     *  row/column...
     */
    n=0;
    XtSetArg(args[n], XmNorientation, XmHORIZONTAL);n++;
    rc = XmCreateRowColumn(frame, "fillRC", args, n);
    XtManageChild(rc);
    /*
     *  apply button
     */
    n=0;
    apply = (Widget)XmCreatePushButton(rc,"textApply", args, n);
    XtAddCallback(apply, XmNactivateCallback, TextAcceptCB, textwidget);
    XtManageChild(apply);

    /*
     *  exit button
     */
    n=0;
    exit =(Widget) XmCreatePushButton(rc,"textExit", args, n);
    XtAddCallback(exit, XmNactivateCallback, TextCancelCB, form);
    XtManageChild(exit);

    XtManageChild(form);
}

static void TextAcceptCB(w, client_data, call_data)
Widget w;
XtPointer client_data;
XtPointer call_data;
{
    char      *strg;
    Widget widget = (Widget) client_data;

    strg = XmTextGetString(widget);
    strcpy(input_text, strg);
    XtUnmanageChild(XtParent(widget));
}

static void TextCancelCB(w, client_data, call_data)
```

```
Widget w;
XtPointer client_data;
XtPointer call_data;
{
   Widget form = (Widget)client_data;

   XtUnmanageChild(form);
}

static void ReDisplay(w, data, call_data)
Widget w;
pixmap_data  *data;
XmDrawingAreaCallbackStruct *call_data;
{
   Arg   wargs[2];
   Dimension widget_width, widget_height;
   int   n;

   /*
    * Get the current size of the widget window
    */
   n = 0;
   XtSetArg(wargs[n], XtNwidth,   &widget_width); n++;
   XtSetArg(wargs[n], XtNheight, &widget_height); n++;
   XtGetValues(w, wargs, n);
   /*
    * copy the contents of the pixmap to the upper
    * left corner of the window
    */
   XCopyArea(XtDisplay(w), data->pix, XtWindow(w), data->gc,
      0, 0, data->width, data->height, 0, 0);
}
```

8.3.3 A Case Study: A Table Editor

8.3.3.1 Functional Descriptions

☞ The main window

Figure 8.11 shows the table editor's main window, consisting of a scrolled window and a row column. Inside the scrolled window is a table that consists of a column annotation, a row annotation, and an array of cells. The column annotation is used to identify the column number, and the row annotation is used to identify the row number. Each cell in the table can store either numeric or alphanumerical data.

☞ Column/row/cell selections

You select a column by clicking mouse button one on the corresponding column annotation button and a row by clicking mouse button one on the corresponding row annotation button. You select a cell by clicking mouse button one on the cell itself. When a column is selected, its color turns red. Clicking the same column annotation button a second time de-selects that column and its color returns to gray. The same events happen when a row is selected. To select

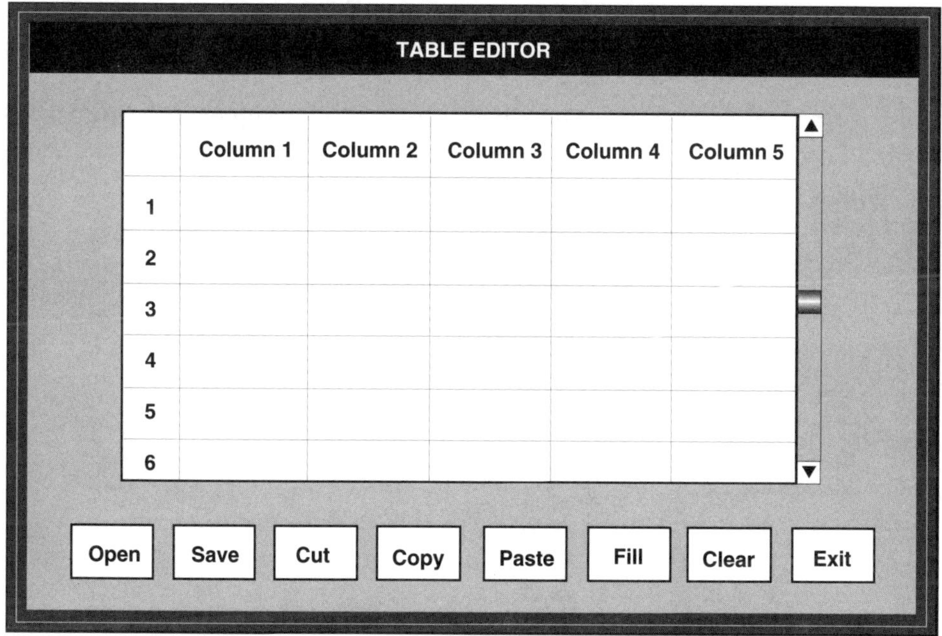

Fig. 8.11 A Table Editor

multiple columns, multiple rows, or multiple cells, you must hold down the shift key while you select the second item.

☞ Table operations

Eight operations can be performed on this table: open, save, cut, copy, paste, fill, clear, and exit. Each operation is selected by clicking the button indicated by the button label.

When the open operation is selected, it pops up a file selection box, which allows the user to select the saved table file. Once a file is selected, its content is loaded into the table.

When the save operation is selected, it pops up a file selection box, which allows the user to select the file to which to save the table content. Once a file is selected, the table content is saved onto the file.

Before the cut operation can be selected, you must first select a column or row. The cut operation then saves the content of the column onto a scratch area, and deletes the column data from the table.

The copy operation performs a similar function as the cut operation, except that it does not delete the column's content.

The paste operation restores the column or row content saved in the scratch area to the selected column or row.

The fill operation allows the user to fill in a column automatically. When the fill operation is selected, it pops up a dialog box that prompts the user for the initial value, the final value, and the increment, as Figure 8.12 shows. Based on these values, a sequence of numbers is generated, and these numbers are then used to fill in the selected column.

The clear operation clears the entire table, and exit operation closes this table editor.

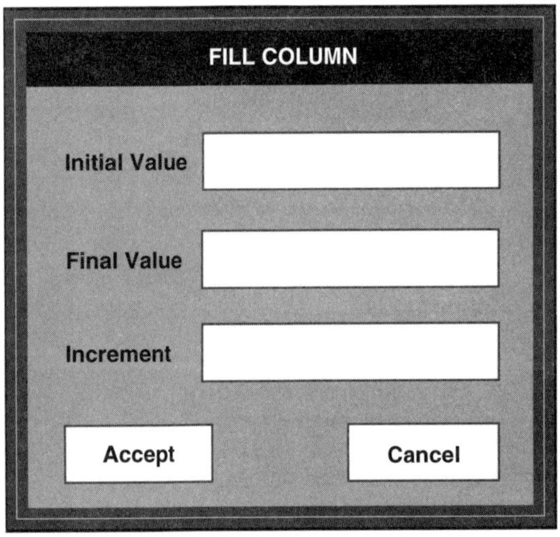

Fig. 8.12 Fill Column Dialog

8.3.3.2 Program Description

☞ Creating the main window

The code to create the main window for the table editor is shown in Listing 8.12. The function CreateTable() creates the main window of this table editor. First, it creates a top-level shell as the root of a new application. It then creates a form widget under this top-level widget to hold everything in this application. This is the initial work required within this function.

The next step is to create a scrolled window that encloses a canvas. Three entities are created on top of the canvas. First, the table entries are created through the function call to CreateTableEntry(). Second, the column annotations are created through the function call to CreateColAnnotation(). Third, the row annotations are created through the function call to CreateRowAnnotation().

In function CreateTableEntry(), a table of dimension K_ROWS multiplied by K_COLUMNS is created as a two-dimensional array of text widgets. Each text widget is created with a width of K_WIDTH and height of K_HEIGHT. The key is to position each text widget so that it aligns vertically and horizontally. Each text widget is assigned to the event handler CellSelectEH() for the event ButtonPressMask.

In function CreateColAnnotation(), the column annotation is created as K_COLUMNS number of pushbuttons. These pushbuttons are labeled as column one through column k, with k set equal to K_COLUMNS. Each pushbutton is created with a width of K_WIDTH and height of 40 pixels. Again, the key is to position each pushbutton so that they align properly. Each pushbutton is assigned to the callback function ColAnnotationCB() for the callback XmNarmCallback.

In function CreateRowAnnotation(), the row annotation is created as K_ROWS number of pushbuttons. These pushbuttons are labeled as row one through row k, with k set equal to K_ROWS. Each pushbutton is created with a width of 50 pixels and height of K_HEIGHT. Again, the key is to position each pushbutton so that they align properly. Each pushbutton is assigned to the callback function RowAnnotationCB() for the callback XmNarmCallback.

Below the canvas, a rowcolumn widget is created to hold eight pushbuttons: open, save, cut, copy, paste, fill, clear, and exit. All the pushbuttons share a common callback function, TableControlCB(). The client_data passed to the callback function TableControlCB() tells which pushbutton has been selected.

☞ Handling the pushbutton commands

For every pushbutton activated, the control goes to the function TableControlCB(), which calls the appropriate function to perform the required function.

If the open pushbutton is selected, it calls the function CreateOpenWidget() to pop up a file selection box (as shown in Figure 8.2) for the user to select the file from which the table data is loaded. After the user selects a filename and clicks the open button, control goes to another callback function, FileOpenAcceptCB(). It retrieves the filename the user has selected and passes it to the ReadFile() routine. This ReadFile() routine opens and reads the table content one row at a time into a two-dimensional data array. It then extracts the column data one column at a time into a column string data array. Later, this column string data array is used to fill in the table column by calling the function SetColText().

If the save pushbutton is selected, it calls the function CreateSaveWidget() to pop up a file selection box, similar to the one shown in Figure 8.2, where the user selects a filename. If the saved filename already exists, it prompts the user either to overwrite it or cancel it, as shown in Figure 8.4.

If the cut pushbutton is selected, it calls the function GetColumnSelected() to determine which column has been selected. If no column is selected, it outputs a warning message. Otherwise, it calls the function GetColumnText() to get the column's data, then stores it in a structure. At the end, it calls ResetColumnToSpace() to clear the column's data.

If the copy pushbutton is selected, it calls the function GetColumnSelected() to determine which column has been selected. If no column is selected, it outputs a warning message. Otherwise, it calls the function GetColumnText() to get the column's data, then stores it in a structure. The column's data stays unchanged.

If the paste pushbutton is selected, it calls the function GetColumnSelected() to determine which column has been selected. If no column is selected, it outputs a warning message. Otherwise, it calls the function SetColText() to set the column's data using the data stored in a pre-defined data structure.

If the fill pushbutton is selected, it calls the function FillCol() to pop up a fill column dialog, as shown in Figure 8.12. After the user enters the initial value, the final value, and the increment, then selects the accept button, it calls function FillColCB() to retrieve these three values and compute an array of numbers. Finally, it calls function FillColumn() to fill a column using the numbers in this array.

If the clear pushbutton is selected, it calls the function ResetColumnToSpace() to clear each column's cell.

If the exit pushbutton is selected, it calls the function XtDestroyWidget() to destroy the table editor.

Listing 8.12 shows the program to create the table editor main window and handle all its callbacks.

Listing 8.12 table.c

```
/*
 * table.c
 */
#include <stdio.h>
#include "demo.h"

#define K_OPEN                          0
#define K_SAVE                          1
#define K_CUT                           2
#define K_COPY                          3
#define K_PASTE                         4
#define K_FILL                          5
#define K_CLEAR                         6
#define K_EXIT                          7
#define K_NUM_CONTROLS                  8
#define K_WIDTH                         95
#define K_HEIGHT                        30
#define X_POS_TABLE                     85
#define Y_POS_TABLE                     95
#define X_POS_HORZ_ANNO                 85
#define Y_POS_HORZ_ANNO                 65
#define X_POS_VERT_ANNO                 25
#define Y_POS_VERT_ANNO                 95
#define K_COLUMNS                       5
#define K_ROWS                          6

typedef struct _SelStruc
{
   char ** cell_array;
   int    col;
   int    row;
   int    ncols;
   int    nrows;
} SelStruc, *PTR_SelStruc;

SelStruc *select_struc;
```

```c
/* Global data */
extern XtAppContext  app_context;
extern Display       *dpy;
extern Pixel         red;
extern Pixel         grey;
extern Pixel         black;

static Widget        table_top;
static Widget        table_form = NULL;
static Widget        scroll_win;
static Widget        canvas;
static Widget        col_annotation_widget[K_MAX_COL];
static Widget        row_annotation_widget[K_MAX_ROW];
static Widget        controls_pb[K_NUM_CONTROLS];
static Widget        controls_box;
static Widget        sep;
static Widget        open_widget;
static Widget        save_widget;
static char          *array_data[K_MAX_ROW][K_MAX_COL];
static char          *controls_pb_names[] = {
                     "Open",
                     "Save",
                     "Cut",
                     "Copy",
                     "Paste",
                     "Fill",
                     "Clear",
                     "Exit"
};

Widget table_text_widget[K_MAX_COL*K_MAX_ROW];
/*
 *   Internal Functions
 */
static void CreateTableOpenWidget();
static void FileOpenAcceptCB();
static void FileOpenCancelCB();
static void ReadFile();
static void CreateOpenWidget();
static void SelectAdditionalCol();
static void SelectAdditionalRow();
static void CreateSaveWidget();
static void FileSaveCB();
static void CancelFileSaveCB();
static void OverWriteFile();
static void SaveToFile();
static void OkToOverWrite();
static void FillRowData();
static void ResetColumnToSpace();
static int FindCellNumberForWidget();
static int FindRowAnnoNum();
static int FindColAnnoNum();
static void SetColumnColor();
static void SetRowColor();
```

```c
static void ColAnnotationCB();
static void RowAnnotationCB();
static void CreateColAnnotation();
static void CreateRowAnnotation();
static void CreateTableEntry();
static char ** GetColumnText();
static void CellSelectEH();
static void TableControlCB();
void SetColText();

static XtActionsRec actions[] = {
   {"SelectAdditionalRow", SelectAdditionalRow},
   {"SelectAdditionalCol", SelectAdditionalCol},
};

static char anno_override_translations[] =
   "Shift<Btn1Down>:   SelectAdditionalRow()  \
   SelectAdditionalCol()";

void CreateTable(widget, client_data, call_data)
Widget widget;
XtPointer client_data;
XtPointer call_data;
{
   int i;
   int n;
   int x_pos, y_pos;
   Arg args[10];

   table_top = XtAppCreateShell("tableTop", "tableTop",
      applicationShellWidgetClass,
      dpy, NULL, 0);
   n = 0;
   table_form = XmCreateForm(table_top, "tableForm", args, n);
   XtManageChild (table_form);

   InitColor(table_form);
   /*
    * create the scrolled window for the table area
    */

   n=0;
   XtSetArg(args[n], XmNscrollingPolicy,   XmAUTOMATIC);   n++;
   XtSetArg(args[n], XmNscrollBarDisplayPolicy,   XmSTATIC ); n++;
   XtSetArg(args[n], XmNtopAttachment,   XmATTACH_FORM);   n++;
   XtSetArg(args[n], XmNleftAttachment,   XmATTACH_FORM ); n++;
   XtSetArg(args[n], XmNrightAttachment,XmATTACH_FORM); n++;
   XtSetArg(args[n], XmNbottomAttachment,XmATTACH_FORM); n++;
   XtSetArg(args[n], XmNbottomOffset, 40); n++;

   scroll_win = XmCreateScrolledWindow(table_form, "scrollWin", args, n);
   XtManageChild(scroll_win);

   /*
    * Create the drawing surface
    */
```

```c
    n = 0;
    XtSetArg(args[n], XmNresizePolicy,  XmRESIZE_GROW); n++;

    canvas = (Widget)XmCreateDrawingArea(scroll_win, "tableCanvas", args, n);
    XtManageChild(canvas);

    /*
     *  create separator
     */
    n = 0;
    XtSetArg(args[n], XmNshadowThickness,  1);n++;
    XtSetArg(args[n], XmNtopAttachment, XmATTACH_WIDGET); n++;
    XtSetArg(args[n], XmNtopWidget, scroll_win); n++;
    XtSetArg(args[n], XmNrightAttachment, XmATTACH_FORM); n++;
    XtSetArg(args[n], XmNleftAttachment, XmATTACH_FORM); n++;

    sep = XmCreateSeparator(table_form, "Separator", args, n);
    XtManageChild(sep);

    /*
     * create control box
     */
    n = 0;
    XtSetArg(args[n], XmNorientation, XmHORIZONTAL); n++;
    XtSetArg(args[n], XmNtopAttachment, XmATTACH_WIDGET);n++;
    XtSetArg(args[n], XmNtopWidget, sep); n++;
    XtSetArg(args[n], XmNrightAttachment, XmATTACH_FORM); n++;
    XtSetArg(args[n], XmNrightOffset, 10); n++;
    XtSetArg(args[n], XmNleftAttachment, XmATTACH_FORM); n++;
    XtSetArg(args[n], XmNbottomAttachment, XmATTACH_FORM);n++;

    controls_box = XmCreateRowColumn(table_form, "Control", args, n);
    XtManageChild(controls_box);

    /* create table entries */
    x_pos = X_POS_TABLE;
    y_pos = Y_POS_TABLE;
    CreateTableEntry(canvas, x_pos, y_pos);
    /* create horizontal annotations */
    x_pos = X_POS_HORZ_ANNO;
    y_pos = Y_POS_HORZ_ANNO;
    CreateColAnnotation(canvas, x_pos, y_pos);
    /*
     * create row annotations
     */
    x_pos = X_POS_VERT_ANNO;
    y_pos = Y_POS_VERT_ANNO;
    CreateRowAnnotation(canvas, x_pos, y_pos);

    /*
     * create control pushbutton
     */
    n = 0;
    XtSetArg(args[n], XmNpushButtonEnabled, True); n++;
    for (i =0; i < K_NUM_CONTROLS; i++)
    {
       XtSetArg(args[n], XmNlabelString,  XmStringCreateLtoR(controls_pb_names[i],
```

```c
                XmSTRING_DEFAULT_CHARSET));n++;
        controls_pb[i] = XmCreatePushButton(controls_box,"CntlBtn",
             args, n);
        XtManageChild(controls_pb[i]);
        XtAddCallback(controls_pb[i], XmNactivateCallback, (XtCallbackProc)
             TableControlCB, (XtPointer)i);
    }

    XtAppAddActions(app_context, actions, XtNumber(actions));
    XtRealizeWidget(table_top);
}

static void TableControlCB(w,   client_data, call_data)
Widget w;
int client_data;
XtPointer call_data;
{
    int control_index = client_data;
    int i,j,k;
    int ncol;
    int cols[K_MAX_COL];
    char message[256];
    char **col_string;
    char *strg;
    int    row, col;
    FILE *fp;

    if (control_index == K_OPEN)
        CreateOpenWidget(w, client_data, call_data);
    else if (control_index == K_SAVE)
    {
        for (row=1; row<=K_ROWS; row++)
        {
            for (col=1; col<= K_COLUMNS; col++)
            {
               k=  col - 1 +(row-1)*K_COLUMNS;
               strg = (char *)XmTextGetString(table_text_widget[k]);
               array_data[row-1][col-1] = (char *)XtMalloc(strlen(strg)+1);
               strcpy(array_data[row-1][col-1], strg);
            }
        }
        CreateSaveWidget(w, client_data, call_data);
    }
    else if (control_index == K_CLEAR)
    {
        for (row=1; row<=K_ROWS; row++)
        ResetColumnToSpace(row);
    }
    else if (control_index == K_EXIT)
    {
        XtDestroyWidget(table_top);
    }
    else if (control_index == K_FILL)
    {
        FillCol(w);
```

```
      }
   else if (control_index == K_COPY)
   {
      GetColumnSelected(&ncol, cols);
      if (ncol == 0)
      {
         sprintf(message, "no columns selected\n");
         MsgOut(WARNING_MSG_TYPE, message);
         return;
      }
      for (i=0; i<ncol; i++)
      {
         col_string = (char **)GetColumnText(cols[i]);
      }
      if (select_struc == NULL)
         select_struc = (PTR_SelStruc)XtMalloc(sizeof(SelStruc));
      select_struc->col = cols[0];
      select_struc->cell_array = col_string;
   }
   else if (control_index == K_CUT)
   {
      GetColumnSelected(&ncol, cols);
      if (ncol == 0)
      {
         sprintf(message, "no columns selected\n");
         MsgOut(WARNING_MSG_TYPE, message);
         return;
      }
      for (i=0; i<ncol; i++)
      {
         col_string = (char **)GetColumnText(cols[i]);
      }
      if (select_struc == NULL)
         select_struc = (PTR_SelStruc)XtMalloc(sizeof(SelStruc));
      select_struc->col = cols[0];
      select_struc->cell_array = col_string;
      ResetColumnToSpace(cols[0]);
   }
   else if (control_index == K_PASTE)
   {
      GetColumnSelected(&ncol, cols);
      if (ncol == 0)
      {
         sprintf(message, "no columns selected\n");
         MsgOut(WARNING_MSG_TYPE, message);
         return;
      }
      SetColText(select_struc->col, select_struc->cell_array);
   }
}

/*
 *  create column annotation
 */
```

```c
static void CreateColAnnotation(w, x_pos, y_pos)
Widget              w;
int     x_pos;
int     y_pos;
{
   int    n;
   Arg    args[10];
   int x;
   int y;
   int i = 0;
   char   col_anno[20];
   x = x_pos;
   y = y_pos;

   for (i=0; i<K_COLUMNS; i++)
   {
      n =0;
      XtSetArg(args[n], XmNx, x); n++;
      XtSetArg(args[n], XmNy, y); n++;
      XtSetArg(args[n], XmNwidth, K_WIDTH); n++;
      XtSetArg(args[n], XmNheight, 40); n++;
      sprintf(col_anno, "Column %d\n", i+1);
      XtSetArg(args[n], XmNlabelString,
         XmStringCreateLtoR(col_anno, XmSTRING_DEFAULT_CHARSET)); n++;
      col_annotation_widget[i] = XmCreatePushButton(w,
         "PushButton", args, n);
      /*
       * Add callbacks.
       */

      XtAddCallback(col_annotation_widget[i], XmNarmCallback,
         ColAnnotationCB, NULL);
      XtManageChild(col_annotation_widget[i]);
      XtOverrideTranslations(col_annotation_widget[i],
         XtParseTranslationTable(anno_override_translations));
      x +=K_WIDTH;
   }
}

/*
 * create row annotation
 */
void CreateRowAnnotation(w, x_pos, y_pos)
Widget              w;
int        x_pos;
int        y_pos;
{
   Widget button;
   int    n;
   Arg    args[10];
   Position x;
   Position y;
   int i =0;
   char   row_anno[20];
```

```c
   x = x_pos;
   y = y_pos;

   for (i=0; i<K_ROWS; i++)
   {
      n =0;
      XtSetArg(args[n], XmNx, x); n++;
      XtSetArg(args[n], XmNy, y); n++;
      XtSetArg(args[n], XmNwidth, 50); n++;
      XtSetArg(args[n], XmNheight,K_HEIGHT); n++;
      sprintf(row_anno, "   %d", i+1);
      XtSetArg(args[n], XmNlabelString,
         XmStringCreateLtoR(row_anno,XmSTRING_DEFAULT_CHARSET)); n++;
      row_annotation_widget[i] = XmCreatePushButton(w,
         "PushButton", args, n);
      /*
       * Add callbacks.
       */
      XtAddCallback(row_annotation_widget[i], XmNarmCallback,
         RowAnnotationCB, NULL);
      XtManageChild(row_annotation_widget[i]);
      XtOverrideTranslations(row_annotation_widget[i],
         XtParseTranslationTable(anno_override_translations));

      y += K_HEIGHT;
   }
}
static void SelectAdditionalCol(w, event, params, num_params)
Widget w;
XButtonEvent *event;
String *params;
Cardinal *num_params;
{
   int    i,j;
   int    n;
   Position x,y;
   Arg args[10];
   Pixel org_color;
   Pixel cur_color;

   i = FindColAnnoNum(w);
   if (i > 0)
      printf("column %d selected\n", i);
   else
      return;

   if (select_struc == NULL)
      select_struc = (PTR_SelStruc)XtMalloc(sizeof(SelStruc));
   select_struc->row = i;
   n =0;
   XtSetArg(args[n], XmNbackground, &cur_color); n++;
   XtGetValues(col_annotation_widget[i-1], args, n);
   if (cur_color == red)
      cur_color = grey;
   else
```

```c
      cur_color = red;

   n = 0;
   XtSetArg(args[n], XmNbackground, cur_color); n++;
   XtSetValues(col_annotation_widget[i-1], args, n);

   SetColumnColor(i, cur_color);
}

static void SelectAdditionalRow(w, event, params, num_params)
Widget w;
XButtonEvent *event;
String *params;
Cardinal *num_params;
{
   int    i,j;
   int    n;
   Position x,y;
   Arg args[10];
   Pixel org_color;
   Pixel cur_color;

   i = FindRowAnnoNum(w);
   if (i > 0)
      printf("row %d selected\n", i);
   else
      return;

   if (select_struc == NULL)
      select_struc = (PTR_SelStruc)XtMalloc(sizeof(SelStruc));
   select_struc->row = i;
   n =0;
   XtSetArg(args[n], XmNbackground, &cur_color); n++;
   XtGetValues(row_annotation_widget[i-1], args, n);
   if (cur_color == red)
      cur_color = grey;
   else
      cur_color = red;
   n = 0;
   XtSetArg(args[n], XmNbackground, cur_color); n++;
   XtSetValues(row_annotation_widget[i-1], args, n);

   SetRowColor(i, cur_color);
}

/*
 * create table text entries
 */
/*
 * create table text entries
 */
static void CreateTableEntry(w, x_pos, y_pos)
Widget                 w;
int    x_pos;
int    y_pos;
{
```

```c
    int    n;
    Arg    args[10];
    Position x;
    Position y;
    int  i,j,k;

    x = x_pos;
    y = y_pos;

    for (i=1; i<= K_ROWS; i++)
    {
       for (j=1; j<= K_COLUMNS; j++)
       {
          k = (j-1) + (i-1)*K_COLUMNS;
          n =0;
          XtSetArg(args[n], XmNx, x); n++;
          XtSetArg(args[n], XmNy, y); n++;
          XtSetArg(args[n], XmNwidth,  K_WIDTH); n++;
          XtSetArg(args[n], XmNheight,  K_HEIGHT); n++;
          XtSetArg (args[n], XmNeditable, TRUE); n++;
          table_text_widget[k] = XmCreateText(w, "cellText",
             args, n);
          /*
           * Add callbacks.
           */
          XtAddEventHandler(table_text_widget[k], ButtonPressMask, False,
             (XtEventHandler) CellSelectEH, (XtPointer)NULL);
          XtManageChild(table_text_widget[k]);
          x +=K_WIDTH;
       }
       x = X_POS_TABLE;
       y += K_HEIGHT;
    }
}

static void SelectadditionalCol()
{
}

/*
 *   table text entry callback
 */
static void CellSelectEH(w, client_data, call_data)
Widget                 w;
XtPointer              client_data;
XmAnyCallbackStruct *call_data;
{
    Arg args[10];
    int n;
    char   *str;
    int i;

    switch(call_data->reason){
    case XmCR_ACTIVATE:
       str = (char *)XmTextGetString(w);
```

```c
      i = FindCellNumberForWidget(w);
      /*
       *   set the cell color to black
       */
      n = 0;
      XtSetArg(args[n], XmNbackground, black); n++;
      XtSetValues(table_text_widget[i], args, n);
      break;
   default:
      break;
   }
}

/*
 *   column annotation callback
 */
static void ColAnnotationCB(w, client_data, call_data)
Widget                 w;
XtPointer              client_data;
XmAnyCallbackStruct    *call_data;
{
   int i, j;
   int n;
   Arg args[10];
   Pixel org_color;
   Pixel cur_color;

   switch(call_data->reason){
   case XmCR_ARM:
      i = FindColAnnoNum(w);
      if (select_struc == NULL)
         select_struc = (PTR_SelStruc)XtMalloc(sizeof(SelStruc));
      select_struc->col = i;

      n = 0;
      XtSetArg(args[n], XmNbackground, &cur_color); n++;
      XtGetValues(col_annotation_widget[i-1], args, n);

      if (cur_color == red)
         cur_color = grey;
      else
         cur_color = red;

      n = 0;
      XtSetArg(args[n], XmNbackground, cur_color); n++;
      XtSetValues(col_annotation_widget[i-1], args, n);
      SetColumnColor(i, cur_color);

      /*
       * set other columns to grey
       */
      for (j=1; j<=K_COLUMNS; j++)
      {
         if ( j != i)
         {
            n = 0;
```

```
                    XtSetArg(args[n], XmNbackground, grey); n++;
                    /*
                     * set column annotation color to grey
                     */
                    XtSetValues(col_annotation_widget[j-1], args, n);

                    /*
                     * set jth column to grey
                     */
                    SetColumnColor(j, grey);
                }
            }
         break;
      default:
         break;
      }
}

/*
 * row annotation callback
 */
static void RowAnnotationCB(w, client_data, call_data)
Widget                 w;
XtPointer              client_data;
XmAnyCallbackStruct *call_data;
{
    int i;
    int n;
    Arg args[10];
    Pixel org_color;
    Pixel cur_color;

    switch(call_data->reason){
    case XmCR_ARM:
       i = FindRowAnnoNum(w);
       if (select_struc == NULL)
          select_struc = (PTR_SelStruc)XtMalloc(sizeof(SelStruc));
       select_struc->row = i;

       n = 0;
       XtSetArg(args[n], XmNbackground, &cur_color); n++;
       XtGetValues(row_annotation_widget[i-1], args, n);

       if (cur_color == red)
          cur_color = grey;
       else
          cur_color = red;
       SetRowColor(i, cur_color);

       n = 0;
       XtSetArg(args[n], XmNbackground, cur_color); n++;
       XtSetValues(row_annotation_widget[i-1], args, n);
       break;
    default:
       break;
    }
```

```c
}

/*
 * find the cell number between 1 to number of table entries for a corresponding
 * cell widget
 */
int FindCellNumberForWidget(w)
Widget w;
{
   int i;

   for (i = 0; i<K_ROWS*K_COLUMNS; i++)
   {
      if (table_text_widget[i] == w)
      {
         return(i+1);
      }
   }
}

/*
 * find the column number for a column annotation widget
 */
int FindColAnnoNum(w)
Widget w;
{
   int i;

   for (i = 0; i< K_COLUMNS; i++)
   {
      if (col_annotation_widget[i] == w)
         return(i+1);
   }
}

/*
 * find the row number for a row annotation widget
 */
int FindRowAnnoNum(w)
Widget w;
{
   int i;

   for (i = 0; i<K_ROWS; i++)
   {
      if (row_annotation_widget[i] == w)
      {
         return(i+1);
      }
   }
}

/*
 * set a column  to a specific color
 */
static void SetColumnColor(col, color)
```

```c
int col;
Pixel color;
{
    int i;
    int n;
    char *strg;
    Arg args[10];

    i = col-1;
    while (i < K_COLUMNS*K_ROWS)
    {
        n = 0;
        XtSetArg(args[n], XmNbackground, color); n++;
        XtSetValues(table_text_widget[i], args, n);
        i+= K_COLUMNS;
    }
}

/*
 * set a row to a specific color
 */
void SetRowColor(row, color)
int row;
Pixel color;
{
    int i;
    int n;
    char *strg;
    Arg args[10];

    i = (row-1)*K_COLUMNS;

    while (i < row*K_COLUMNS)
    {
        n = 0;
        XtSetArg(args[n], XmNbackground, color); n++;
        XtSetValues(table_text_widget[i], args, n);
        i++;
    }
}

/*
 * read column text
 */
char ** GetColumnText(col)
int col;
{
    int i;
    int row;
    char *strg;
    static char *col_string[K_MAX_ROW];

    row =0;
    i = col-1;
    while (i <K_ROWS*K_COLUMNS)
    {
```

```c
        strg = (char *)XmTextGetString(table_text_widget[i]);
        col_string[row] = (char *)malloc(strlen(strg)+1);
        strcpy(col_string[row], strg);
        i+=K_COLUMNS;
        row++;
    }
    return(&col_string[0]);
}

/*
 * set the table column text through an array of text
 */
void SetColText( col, col_string)
int col;
char **col_string;
{
    int i;
    int row;
    char *strg;

    row =0;
    i = col-1;
    while (i <K_ROWS*K_COLUMNS)
    {
        XmTextSetString(table_text_widget[i], col_string[row]);
        i+= K_COLUMNS;
        row++;
    }
    return;
}

/*
 * reset a column to space
 */
static void ResetColumnToSpace(col)
int col;
{
    int i;

    for (i=col-1; i<K_ROWS*K_COLUMNS; i+= K_COLUMNS)
        XmTextSetString(table_text_widget[i], "");
}

/*
 * create the file selection box for file save
 */
void CreateSaveWidget(parent,  client_data, call_data)
Widget parent;
XtPointer client_data;
XtPointer call_data;
{
    Arg args[10];
    int   i;

    i = 0;
    XtSetArg(args[i], XmNokLabelString,
```

```c
            XmStringCreateLtoR("Save",  XmSTRING_DEFAULT_CHARSET)); i++;
   XtSetArg(args[i], XmNdialogTitle,
      XmStringCreateLtoR("Save Table To File", XmSTRING_DEFAULT_CHARSET)); i++;

   save_widget =XmCreateFileSelectionDialog(parent, "FileBox", args, i);
   XtManageChild(save_widget);

   /*
    * remove the help button
    */
   XtUnmanageChild((Widget)XmFileSelectionBoxGetChild(save_widget,
      XmDIALOG_HELP_BUTTON));
   /*
    * add callbacks
    */
   XtAddCallback(save_widget, XmNokCallback, FileSaveCB, NULL);
   XtAddCallback(save_widget, XmNcancelCallback, CancelFileSaveCB, NULL);
}

static void FileSaveCB(parent,  client_data, call_data)
Widget parent;
XtPointer client_data;
XtPointer call_data;
{
   XmSelectionBoxCallbackStruct *sb_info =
      (XmSelectionBoxCallbackStruct *) call_data;

   static char *filename;

   /*
    * retrieve file name
    */
   XmStringGetLtoR(sb_info->value, XmSTRING_DEFAULT_CHARSET, &filename);
   if (strlen(filename) <= 0) return;

   if (FileExist(filename))
      OverWriteFile(parent, filename);
   else
   {
      SaveToFile(parent, filename);
      XtUnmanageChild(parent);
   }
}

static void CancelFileSaveCB(parent,  client_data, call_data)
Widget parent;
XtPointer client_data;
XtPointer call_data;
{
   XtUnmanageChild(parent);
}

static void OverWriteFile(parent, filename)
Widget parent;
char *filename;
{
   int    n;
```

```c
    Arg args[15];
    static Widget question = NULL;
    char msg[256];
    char file_name[256];

    strcpy(file_name, filename);

    /*
     * create the question dialog
     */
    n = 0;
    question =(Widget) XmCreateQuestionDialog(parent, "OverWriteFileQuestion",
        args, n);
    XtUnmanageChild((Widget)XmMessageBoxGetChild(question, XmDIALOG_HELP_BUTTON));
    XtAddCallback(question, XmNokCallback, OkToOverWrite, (XtPointer)&file_name);

    /*
     * fill in message
     */
    sprintf(msg, "File %s exists. Do you want to overwrite it?", filename);
    n = 0;
    XtSetArg(args[n], XmNmessageString,
        XmStringCreateLtoR(msg, XmSTRING_DEFAULT_CHARSET)); n++;
    XtSetValues(question, args, n);

    XtManageChild(question);
}

static void OkToOverWrite(w, client_data, call_data)
Widget w;
XtPointer client_data;
XtPointer call_data;
{
    char *filename = (char *) client_data;

    if (strlen(filename) > 0)
    {
        SaveToFile(w, filename);
        XtDestroyWidget(save_widget);
    }
}

/*
 * save table content to file
 */
static void SaveToFile(w, filename)
Widget w;
char *filename;
{
    FILE *fp;
    int     row, col;

    if ((fp = fopen(filename, "w")) == NULL)
    {
        MsgOut(ERROR_MSG_TYPE, "open file error");
        return;
```

```c
    }
    for (row=1; row<=K_ROWS; row++)
    {
       for (col=1; col<=K_COLUMNS; col++)
          fprintf(fp, "'%s'     ", array_data[row-1][col-1]);
       fprintf(fp, "\n");
    }
    fclose(fp);
}

static void CreateOpenWidget(parent, client_data, call_data)
Widget parent;
XtPointer client_data;
XtPointer call_data;
{
    Arg args[10];
    int   i;

    i = 0;
    XtSetArg(args[i], XmNokLabelString,
       XmStringCreateLtoR("Open",  XmSTRING_DEFAULT_CHARSET)); i++;
    XtSetArg(args[i], XmNdialogTitle,
       XmStringCreateLtoR("Open Table File", XmSTRING_DEFAULT_CHARSET)); i++;
    open_widget =XmCreateFileSelectionDialog(parent, "FileBox", args, i);
    XtManageChild(open_widget);

    /*
     * remove the help button
     */
    XtUnmanageChild((Widget)XmFileSelectionBoxGetChild(open_widget,
       XmDIALOG_HELP_BUTTON));

    XtAddCallback(open_widget, XmNokCallback, FileOpenAcceptCB, NULL);
    XtAddCallback(open_widget, XmNcancelCallback, FileOpenCancelCB, NULL);
}

static void FileOpenAcceptCB(w, client_data, call_data)
Widget w;
XtPointer client_data;
XtPointer call_data;
{
    int     n;

    Arg     args[10];
    char *filename;

    /*
     * retrieve the file name
     */
    XmFileSelectionBoxCallbackStruct *fs_info =
    (XmFileSelectionBoxCallbackStruct *) call_data;
    /*
     * convert to ascii string
     */
    XmStringGetLtoR(fs_info->value, XmSTRING_DEFAULT_CHARSET, &filename);
    /*
```

```c
     * set watch cursor
     */
    ChangeToWatchCursor(w);
    /*
     * read the file into the table text widget
     */
    ReadFile(filename);
    /*
     * change back to original cursor
     */
    ChangeBackCursor(w);

    XtUnmanageChild(open_widget);
}

static void FileOpenCancelCB(w, client_data, call_data)
Widget w;
XtPointer client_data;
XtPointer call_data;
{
    /*
     *  unmanage the open widget to make it invisible to the user
     */

    XtUnmanageChild(w);
    return;
}

static void ReadFile(file_name)
char *file_name;
{
    char    msg[128];
    FILE    *fp;
    char    linebuf[256];
    char    tmpstr[128];
    char    *col_string[K_MAX_ROW];
    int     row, col;

    if ((fp = fopen(file_name, "r")) == NULL)
    {
        sprintf(msg, "Open file for read error: %s", file_name);
        MsgOut(ERROR_MSG_TYPE, msg);
        return;
    }
    row = 0;
    while (fgets(linebuf, 256, fp) != NULL)
    {
        row++;
        FillRowData(row, linebuf);
    }

    for (col =1; col<= K_COLUMNS; col++)
    {
        for (row = 1; row<=K_ROWS; row++)
        {
```

```
            col_string[row-1] = (char *)XtMalloc(strlen(array_data[row-1][col-1])+1);
            strcpy(col_string[row-1], array_data[row-1][col-1]);
        }
        SetColText(col, col_string);
    }

    return;
}

/*
 *  Fill in the row data array from the linebuf
 */
static void FillRowData(row, linebuf)
int   row;
char *linebuf;
{
    char *tmpstr;
    char *start, *ptr, *end;
    int   col = 1;

    tmpstr = (char *)XtMalloc(strlen(linebuf)+1);
    /* make a copy of the buffer string */
    strcpy(tmpstr, linebuf);
    ptr = tmpstr;
    while (*ptr != '\0')
    {
        /* locate the first quote */
        while (*ptr != '\'' && *ptr != '\0')
           ptr++;

        if ( *ptr == '\'')
        {
            start = ptr+1;
            ptr = start;
            /* locate the second quote */
            while ( *ptr != '\'' && *ptr != '\0')
               ptr++;

            if ( *ptr == '\'')
            {
               *ptr = '\0';
               array_data[row-1][col-1] = (char *)XtMalloc(strlen(start)+1);
               strcpy(array_data[row-1][col-1], start);
            }
            col++;
            ptr++;
        }
        else
            return;
    }
}
```

Listing 8.13 shows the program to create an automatic fill column dialog and handle all its callbacks.

Listing 8.13 filldialog.c

```c
/*
 *  filldialog.c
 */
#include <stdio.h>
#include "demo.h"

#define   K_ROWS          6
#define   K_COLUMNS       5

typedef struct _FillStruc
{
    Widget form;
    Widget textwidgets[4];
}  FillStruc, *PTR_FillStruc;

typedef struct _SelStruc
{
    char ** cell_array;
    int   col;
    int   row;
    int   ncols;
    int   nrows;
} SelStruc, *PTR_SelStruc;

/*
 * Global data
 */
extern SelStruc *select_struc;
extern Widget table_text_widget[];
extern Pixel red;

/*
 * Internal functions
 */
static void FillColCB();
static void FillExitCB();
void   GetColumnSelected();

/*
 *  Fill Column Dialog
 */
void FillCol (w)
Widget w;
{
    Arg args[20];
    int   n;
    int   i;
    int   ncol;
    int   cols[100];
    char message[128];

    static char *labels[3] =
    {
        "StartVal",
```

```c
        "EndVal",
        "Inc"
    };

    static PTR_FillStruc  fill_struc;
    static Widget form = NULL;
    static Widget w_save = NULL;

    Widget labelwidgets[3], textwidgets[3], frame;
    Widget rc, apply, exit;
    GetColumnSelected(&ncol, cols);
    if (ncol == 0)
    {
        sprintf(message, "no columns selected\n");
        MsgOut( WARNING_MSG_TYPE, message);
        return;
    }

    if ( w != w_save)
    {
        w_save = w;
        n=0;
        form = XmCreateFormDialog(XtParent(w), "fillForm", args, n);

        /*
         *  Create the entry fields
         */
        n=0;
        XtSetArg(args[n], XmNtopAttachment,   XmATTACH_POSITION);   n++;
        XtSetArg(args[n], XmNtopPosition,     (Position)5); n++;
        XtSetArg(args[n], XmNleftAttachment,  XmATTACH_POSITION); n++;
        XtSetArg(args[n], XmNleftPosition,    (Position) 40); n++;
        XtSetArg(args[n], XmNrightAttachment,XmATTACH_POSITION); n++;
        XtSetArg(args[n], XmNrightPosition,   (Position) 95); n++;
        textwidgets[0] = XmCreateText(form, "Text", args, n);
        XtManageChild(textwidgets[0]);

        n=0;
        XtSetArg(args[n], XmNtopAttachment,   XmATTACH_POSITION);   n++;
        XtSetArg(args[n], XmNleftAttachment,  XmATTACH_FORM); n++;
        XtSetArg(args[n], XmNleftPosition,    (Position) 5); n++;
        XtSetArg(args[n], XmNrightAttachment,XmATTACH_WIDGET); n++;
        XtSetArg(args[n], XmNrightWidget,   textwidgets[0]); n++;
        XtSetArg(args[n], XmNrecomputeSize,   False);
        labelwidgets[0] = XmCreateLabel(form, labels[0], args, n);
        XtManageChild(labelwidgets[0]);

        for (i=1; i < XtNumber(labels); i++)
        {
            n=0;
            XtSetArg(args[n], XmNtopAttachment,   XmATTACH_WIDGET);    n++;
            XtSetArg(args[n], XmNtopWidget,       textwidgets[i-1]); n++;
            XtSetArg(args[n], XmNleftAttachment,  XmATTACH_POSITION); n++;
            XtSetArg(args[n], XmNleftPosition,    (Position) 40); n++;
            XtSetArg(args[n], XmNrightAttachment, XmATTACH_POSITION); n++;
            XtSetArg(args[n], XmNrightPosition,   (Position) 95); n++;
```

```c
      textwidgets[i] = XmCreateText(form, "Text", args, n);
      XtManageChild(textwidgets[i]);

      n=0;
      XtSetArg(args[n], XmNtopAttachment,   XmATTACH_WIDGET);    n++;
      XtSetArg(args[n], XmNtopWidget,        labelwidgets[i-1]);    n++;
      XtSetArg(args[n], XmNleftAttachment, XmATTACH_FORM); n++;
      XtSetArg(args[n], XmNleftPosition,    (Position) 5); n++;
      XtSetArg(args[n], XmNrightAttachment,XmATTACH_WIDGET); n++;
      XtSetArg(args[n], XmNrightWidget,    textwidgets[i]); n++;
      XtSetArg(args[n], XmNrecomputeSize,   False);
      labelwidgets[i] = XmCreateLabelGadget(form, labels[i], args, n);
      XtManageChild(labelwidgets[i]);
}

for (i=0; i < XtNumber(labels); i++)
   XmAddTabGroup(textwidgets[i]);

/*
 *  Frame...
 */
n=0;
XtSetArg(args[n], XmNtopAttachment,   XmATTACH_WIDGET);    n++;
XtSetArg(args[n], XmNtopWidget, textwidgets[2]);n++;
XtSetArg(args[n], XmNtopOffset,    5);    n++;
XtSetArg(args[n], XmNleftAttachment, XmATTACH_POSITION);n++;
XtSetArg(args[n], XmNleftPosition, (Position)5);n++;
XtSetArg(args[n], XmNrightAttachment, XmATTACH_POSITION);n++;
XtSetArg(args[n], XmNrightPosition, (Position)95);n++;
XtSetArg(args[n], XmNbottomAttachment, XmATTACH_POSITION);n++;
XtSetArg(args[n], XmNbottomPosition, (Position)95);n++;
frame = (Widget ) XmCreateFrame(form, "fillFrame", args, n);
XtManageChild(frame);

/*
 *  row/column...
 */
n=0;
XtSetArg(args[n], XmNorientation, XmHORIZONTAL);n++;
rc = XmCreateRowColumn(frame, "fillRC", args, n);
XtManageChild(rc);

/*
 *  apply button
 */
fill_struc = XtNew(FillStruc);
fill_struc->form = form;
for(i=0; i < XtNumber(labels); i++)
  fill_struc->textwidgets[i] = textwidgets[i];

n=0;
apply = (Widget)XmCreatePushButton(rc,"fillApply", args, n);
XtAddCallback(apply, XmNactivateCallback, FillColCB, fill_struc);
XtManageChild(apply);
XmAddTabGroup(apply);
```

```
      /*
       *  exit button
       */
      n=0;
      exit =(Widget) XmCreatePushButton(rc,"fillExit", args, n);
      XtAddCallback(exit, XmNactivateCallback, FillExitCB, form);
      XtManageChild(exit);
      XmAddTabGroup(exit);
   }

   /*
    *  Make the dialog visible...
    */
   XtManageChild(form);
}

static
void FillColCB(w, client_data, call_data)
Widget w;
XtPointer client_data;
XtPointer call_data;
{
   PTR_FillStruc fill_struc = (PTR_FillStruc)client_data;
   int  i, j;
   int  col;
   int  nitems;
   double *items;
   double number[5];
   double init_val;
   double inc_val;
   double last_val;
   double tmp_val;
   char *strg;
   char *ptr;
   char tmpstr[120];
   char message[128];
   char *col_string[100];
   char ch;

   /*
    *  get startVal, endVal, increment...
    */
   for(i=0; i < 3; i++)
   {
      strg = XmTextGetString(fill_struc->textwidgets[i]);
      if (!strg) return;
      ptr = strg;
      while ( *ptr != '\0')
      {
         ch = *ptr;
         if (isdigit(ch) || ch == '.' || ch == '-' || ch == '+')
            ptr++;
         else
         {
            MsgOut(WARNING_MSG_TYPE, "Field value must be numeric\n");
```

```c
                return;
            }
        }
        if (*strg == '\0')
            number[i] = 0.0;
        else
            sscanf(strg,"%lf", &number[i]);
        fprintf(stderr,"Number -- %lf\n",number[i]);
        XtFree(strg);
    }
    init_val = number[0];
    last_val = number[1];
    inc_val  = number[2];
    tmp_val  = init_val;
    nitems   = 0;
    while (tmp_val <= last_val)
    {
        nitems++;
        tmp_val = tmp_val + inc_val;
    }

    items = (double *)malloc(nitems*sizeof(double));
    items[0] = init_val;
    i = 0;
    tmp_val  = init_val;
    while (tmp_val <= last_val)
    {
        items[i] = tmp_val;
        tmp_val = tmp_val + inc_val;
        i++;
    }

    col = select_struc->col;

    j = 0;
    for (i= 1; i<= K_ROWS; i++)
    {
        sprintf(tmpstr, "%lf", items[j]);
        col_string[i-1] = (char *)XtMalloc(sizeof(tmpstr)+1);
        j++;
        if (j <= nitems)
            strcpy(col_string[i-1], tmpstr);
        else
            strcpy(col_string[i-1], "");
    }
    SetColText(col, col_string);

    XtUnmanageChild(fill_struc->form);
}

/*
 *  Close Fill column dialog
 */
static void FillExitCB( Widget w, XtPointer client_data, XtPointer call_data )
{
```

```c
   Widget form = (Widget)client_data;

   XtUnmanageChild(form);
}

void GetColumnSelected( pncol, cols)
int *pncol;
int  cols[];

{
   int  i;
   int  n;
   int  ncol =0;
   Arg  args[10];
   Pixel color;

   i = 0;
   while (i < K_COLUMNS)
   {
      n = 0;
      XtSetArg(args[n], XmNbackground, &color); n++;
      XtGetValues(table_text_widget[i], args, n);
      if (color == red)
      {
         cols[ncol] = i+1;
         ncol++;
      }
      i++;
   }
   *pncol = ncol;
}
```

8.4 Utility Programs

A few functions are commonly used by all applications. These functions are separated from other modules and grouped into two different program modules. The program module msgbox.c (shown in Listing 8.14) and xutil.c (shown in Listing 8.15) are two such examples.

The function MsgOut() in Listing 8.14 which pops up a message dialog that can be called from anywhere in any program. Two utility functions are provided in Listing 8.15: The function GetTopmostAncestor() returns the topmost ancestor widget of a given widget, and the function FileExist() returns true if a given file exists (otherwise it returns false).

Listing 8.14 msgbox.c

```c
/*
 * msgbox.c
 */
#include "demo.h"
```

```c
/*
 * Global data
 */
static Widget msg_top = NULL;
extern Display *dpy;

/*
 * Internal function
 */
void MsgOut();

void
MsgOut(msg_type, msg)
int msg_type;
char *msg;
{
    XmString msg_string;
    Arg args[5];
    int  i;
    static Widget msgbox = NULL;

    if (msg_top == NULL)
    {
        /*
         * create the top level shell for message dialog
         */
        i = 0;
        msg_top = XtAppCreateShell("msgTop", "Message",
        applicationShellWidgetClass, dpy, args, i);

        /*
         * create the message dialog widget
         */
        i=0;
        XtSetArg(args[i], XmNokLabelString,
            XmStringCreateLtoR("Continue", XmSTRING_DEFAULT_CHARSET));i++;
        msgbox = (Widget)XmCreateMessageDialog(msg_top, "msgBox", args, i);

        /*
         * remove the cancel and help button
         */
        XtUnmanageChild((Widget)XmMessageBoxGetChild(msgbox,
            XmDIALOG_CANCEL_BUTTON));
        XtUnmanageChild((Widget)XmMessageBoxGetChild(msgbox,
            XmDIALOG_HELP_BUTTON));
    }
    /*
     * create the compound string
     */
    msg_string = XmStringCreateLtoR(msg, XmSTRING_DEFAULT_CHARSET);

    /*
     * set the message string of the message widget
     */
    i=0;
    XtSetArg(args[i], XmNmessageString, msg_string); i++;
```

```c
    switch(msg_type)
    {
       case ERROR_MSG_TYPE:
           XtSetArg(args[i], XmNdialogType, XmDIALOG_ERROR); i++;
           break;
       case WORKING_MSG_TYPE:
           XtSetArg(args[i], XmNdialogType, XmDIALOG_WORKING);i++;
           break;
       case WARNING_MSG_TYPE:
           XtSetArg(args[i], XmNdialogType, XmDIALOG_WARNING);i++;
           break;
       case MESSAGE_MSG_TYPE:
           XtSetArg(args[i], XmNdialogType, XmDIALOG_INFORMATION);i++;
           break;
       case INFORMATION_MSG_TYPE:
       default:
           XtSetArg(args[i], XmNdialogType, XmDIALOG_INFORMATION);i++;
           break;
    }

    /*
     * set the requested values of the message widget
     */
    XtSetValues(msgbox, args, i);

    /*
     * free the memory used by the compound string
     */
    XmStringFree(msg_string);
    /*
     * make the widget visible to the user
     */
    XtManageChild(msgbox);
    return;
}
```

Listing 8.15 xutil.c

```c
/*  .
 * xutil.c
 */
#include <stdio.h>
#include "demo.h"

Boolean FileExist(filename)
char *filename;
{
    FILE    *fp;

    if (fp = fopen(filename, "r"))
    {
       fclose(fp);
       return(True);
    }
```

```
   else
      return(False);
}

Widget GetTopmostAncestor (Widget w)
{
   Widget w1, w2;

   w1 = w;
   while(w1 != NULL)
   {
      w2 = w1;
      w1 = XtParent(w1);
   }

   return (w2);
}
```

8.5 SETTING THE RESOURCES IN THE RESOURCE FILE

Every X/Motif application program should have a resource file that controls the different settings (e.g. colors, fonts, window's width, and height) for the windows of the application at hand. The resource file's name must be the same as the application class, which is the fourth argument in the function call to XtOpenDisplay(). This resource file usually resides in the directory the environment variable XAPPLRES-DIR points to. The following instructions outline the basic steps to set the resources for your application:

1. Set the default foreground and background colors. Here is an example:

```
        *background          : grey
        *foreground          : black
```

2. Set the default font size.

```
        *fontList       : -adobe-helvetica-bold-r-*-*-12-*-*-*-*-*-iso8859-1
```

3. For each top-level shell, set the resources for geometry, title, and iconName.

```
        *textTop.geometry        : 760x400+100+120
        *textTop.title           : Text Editor
        *textTop.iconName        : TextEditor
```

   This sets the main window to a width of 760 and a height of 400, with the upper left corner position at x = 100 and y = 120.

4. For each menu bar, set the accelerator as

```
        *menuBar*Open.accelerator            : Ctrl<Key>o
        *menuBar*Open.acceleratorText        : Ctrl O
```

   The first line sets the accelerator for the open option to Ctrl o, and the second line sets the accelerator text for the open option to Ctrl O.

5. For each label widget, set the labelString resource.

```
            *findBox*findLabel.labelString      : Search For:
```

6. For each pushbutton widget, set the labelString resource.

```
            *findBox*searchButton.labelString    : Search
```

7. For each text widget, set the columns and maxLength resources.

```
            *findBox*findText.columns            : 35
            *findBox*findText.maxLength           : 35
```

This limits the maximum text input to 35 characters.

8. For each file selection box, set the textColumns resource.

```
            *fileBox*textColumns                 : 32
```

This sets the column width for text input to 32 character spaces.

9. For each popup dialog, set the dialogTitle resource.

```
            *msgBox.dialogTitle                  : Warning Message
```

10. Use topPosition, leftPosition, rightPosition, or bottomPosition resources to position a widget relative to its containing widget (usually a form widget). Use topOffset, leftOffset, rightOffset, or bottonOffset resources to leave space between one widget and an adjacent widget.

```
            *printDialog*printerNameText.topPosition:     10
            *printDialog*printerNameText.leftPosition:    50
            *printDialog*printerNameText.rightPosition:   95
            *printDialog*copiesText.topOffset:            15
            *printDialog*copiesText.leftPosition:         50
```

Listing 8.16 Resource File for Demo

```
!**********************************
!  setting default colors
!**********************************
*background: grey
*foreground: black


!**********************************
! setting default font size
!**********************************
*fontList: -adobe-helvetica-bold-r-*-*-12-*-*-*-*-*-iso8859-1


!**********************************
! setting resources for text editor
!**********************************


*textTop*iconName                    : TextEditor
*textTop.title                       : Text Editor
*textTop.geometry                    : 760x400+100+100
```

```
! setting accelerator for menu bar

*menuBar*Open.accelerator:              Ctrl<Key>o
*menuBar*Close.accelerator:             Ctrl<Key>w
*menuBar*Save.accelerator:              Ctrl<Key>s
*menuBar*Exit.accelerator:              Ctrl<key>e

*menuBar*Open.acceleratorText:          Ctrl O
*menuBar*Close.acceleratorText:         Ctrl W
*menuBar*Save.acceleratorText:          Ctrl S
*menuBar*Exit.acceleratorText:          Ctrl E

!
!   Setting resources for  search dialog
!

*findBox*findLabel.labelString:         Search For:
*findBox*findLabel.topPosition:         5
*findBox*findLabel.leftPosition:        5

*findBox*caseToggle.labelString:        Case Sensitive
*findBox*caseToggle.background:         grey
*findBox*caseToggle.highlightThickness: 2
*findBox*caseToggle.set:                False
*findBox*caseToggle.selectColor:        red
*findBox*caseToggle.topPosition:        3
*findBox*caseToggle.leftOffset:         50

*findBox*findText.topOffset:            5
*findBox*findText.leftPosition:         5
*findBox*findText.rightPosition:        95
*findBox*findText.background:           grey
*findBox*findText.columns:              35

*findBox*changeLabel.labelString:       Replace With:
*findBox*changeLabel.topOffset:         15
*findBox*changeLabel.leftPosition:      5

*findBox*changeText.topOffset:          5
*findBox*changeText.leftPosition:       5
*findBox*changeText.rightPosition:      95
*findBox*changeText.background:         grey
*findBox*changeText.columns:            35

*findBox*actionBox*background:          grey
*findBox*actionBox.topOffset:           15
*findBox*actionBox.leftPosition:        5
*findBox*actionBox.rightPosition:       95

*findBox*searchButton.labelString:      Search
*findBox*changeButton.labelString:      Replace
*findBox*changeSearchButton.labelString: Replace & Search Again
*findBox*changeAllButton.labelString:      Replace All
*findBox*quitButton.labelString:        Exit

! print file dialog
```

```
*printDialog*background:                grey
*printDialog*foreground:                navy

*printDialog*dialogTitle:               Print File
*printDialog*printerNameLabel.labelString:      Printer Name:
*printDialog*printerNameLabel.topPostion:       13
*printDialog*printerNameLabel.leftPosition:     5

*printDialog*printerNameText.topPosition:       10
*printDialog*printerNameText.leftPosition:      50
*printDialog*printerNameText.rightPosition:     95
*printDialog*printerNameText.columns:           10
*printDialog*printerNameText.maxLength:         10

*printDialog*copiesLabel.labelString:           Copies:
*printDialog*copiesLabel.topOffset:             33
*printDialog*copiesLabel.leftPosition:          5

*printDialog*copiesText.topOffset:              15
*printDialog*copiesText.leftPosition:           50
*printDialog*copiesText.columns:                3
*printDialog*copiesText.maxLength:              3

*printDialog*actionFrame.topOffset:             40
*printDialog*actionFrame.leftPosition:          5
*printDialog*actionFrame.rightPosition:         95
*printDialog*actionFrame.bottomPosition:        98

*printDialog*okButton.labelString:              Print
*printDialog*cancelButton.labelString:          Cancel
*printDialog*XmRowColumn*background:            grey
*printDialog*XmText*background:                 grey

! setting resources for file selection box

*fileBox*textColumns:                   32
*fileBox*fontList:              -adobe-helvetica-bold-r-normal--14-*-iso8859-1

!***********************************
! setting resources for drawing editor
!***********************************
*drawEditor.geometry            : 600x400+150+150
*drawEditor.iconName            : DrawEditor
*drawEditor.title               : Drawing Editor

! setting resources for canvas
*drawCanvas.background           : grey
*drawCanvas*width                : 900
*drawCanvas*height               : 600

! setting resources for drawing text input dialog
*textInputForm*dialogTitle              : Text Input
*textInputForm*textApply.labelString    : Apply
*textInputForm*textExit.labelString     : Cancel

!***********************************
! setting resources for table editor
```

```
!*********************************

*tableTop*iconName                      : TableEditor
*tableTop.title                         : Table Editor
*tableTop.geometry                      : 760x400+250+150
*tableCanvas.background                 : grey
*tableCanvas*width                      : 1200
*tableCanvas*height                     : 600

*tableForm*Separator.background         : blue

*fillForm*dialogTitle                   : Auto Fill Column
*fillForm*StartVal.topPosition          : 5
*fillForm*EndVal.topOffset              : 13
*fillForm*Inc.topOffset                 : 13

*fillForm*StartVal.labelString          : Start Value:
*fillForm*EndVAl.labelString            : End Value:
*fillForm*Inc.labelString               : Increment:

*fillForm*fillRC*background             : grey

*fillForm*fillApply.labelString         : Apply
*fillForm*fillExit.labelString          : Cancel

!*********************************************
! setting resources for color selection window
!*********************************************
*colorTop*iconName                      : ColorSelector
*colorTop.title                         : Color Selector
*colorTop.geometry                      : 300x384+250+150

!*********************************************
! setting resources for font selection window
!*********************************************
*fontTop*iconName                       : FontSelector
*fontTop.title                          : Font Selector
*fontTop.geometry                       : 700x385+150+150

!   message box
*msgBox.dialogTitle                     : Message
```

8.6 MAKEFILE

Listing 8.17 shows the makefile to create the executables. Here, we assume that all C
source files and the user include file reside in the directory /usr/shen/motif/demo.
According to this makefile, the .o files and the executable file are created in the same
directory.

Listing 8.17 Makefile

```
SUFFIXES= .a .o .c
.SUFFIXES: $(SUFFIXES)
```

```
COMPILE.c= cc
CFLAGS=  -c -g -I$(SRC_PATH) $(INCLUDES) $(MOTIF_INC) $(X11_INC)
INCLUDES=
MOTIF_INC=  -I/usr/X11R6/include/Xm
X11_INC=    -I/usr/X11R6/include/X11
SRC_PATH=   /usr/shen/src

OBJS= \
   mtfmain.o  \
   pdm.o \
   xfile.o \
   xedit.o \
   xcursor.o \
   xpreference.o \
   xfont.o \
   xcolor.o \
   xshow.o \
   draw.o \
   table.o \
   filldialog.o \
   msgbox.o  \
   xutil.o

LIBS= \
   -L/usr/X11R6/lib  -lm  -lXm -lXt -lX11

.c.o:
   $(COMPILE.c)  $(CFLAGS)   $(SRC_PATH)/$<

editor:  objects
   $(COMPILE.c) -g  $(OBJS)  $(LIBS)  -o editor

objects: $(OBJS)
@echo "$(OBJS) are up-to-date"
```

8.7 SUMMARY

This chapter began with the six-step Motif programming model. The first step is an initialization step that initializes the intrinsics, creates the application context, and opens a display. The second step is a widget creation step that began by creating a top-level shell widget. A frame widget or form widget is usually created immediately under the top-shell widget to contain everything. Afterwards, any number of widgets can be created as the children of this form widget or frame widget. This widget creation process can continue until no further widget is needed. The fourth step is the callback registration for those widgets that need it. The fifth step is the realization step—if this step is skipped, no window is shown on the screen. The last step enters the process into the event loop, which allows the application program to enter into a state ready to accept any event.

The rest of the chapter was a case study, which can be broken into three separate case studies. Case study one required implementing a text editor. Case study two required implementing a drawing editor. Case study three required implementing a table editor. The important topics covered within these exercises included creating pulldown menus, using a file selection box, selecting fonts and colors, setting/resetting the watch cursor, creating the drawing area, and the rubber-band technique.

Finally, we gave a step-by-step procedure to set resources in a resource file.

Bibliography

Ferguson, Paula M., and Davis Brennan. *Motif Reference Manual.* Sebastopol, CA: O'Reilly & Associates, Inc., 1994.

Heller, Dan, and Paula M. Ferguson. *Motif Programming Manual.* Sebastopol, CA: O'Reilly & Associates, Inc., 1994.

IBM. *IBM TCP/IP Programmer's Reference.* SC31-6087-0. Research Triangle Park, NC: IBM Corp., 1991.

Jones, Oliver. *Introduction to the X Window System.* Englewood Cliffs, NJ: Prentice Hall, 1989.

Kernighan, Brian W., and Rob Pike. *The UNIX Programming Environment.* Englewood Cliffs, NJ: Prentice Hall, 1984.

Muster, John, and Peter Birns. *UNIX Power Utilities.* Portland,, OR: MIS, Inc., 1989.

Nye, Adrian. *Xlib Reference Manual.* Sebastopol, CA: O'Reilly & Associates, Inc., 1990.

Nye, Adrian, and Tim O'Reilly. *X Toolkit Intrinsics Programming Manual.* Sebastopol, CA: O'Reilly & Associates, Inc., 1990.

Prata, Stephen. *Advanced UNIX—A Programmer's Guide.* Indianapolis, IN: Howard W. Sams & Co., Inc., 1988.

Rochkind, Marc J. *Advanced UNIX Programming.* Englewood Cliffs, NJ: Prentice Hall, 1985.

Schreiner, Axel T., and H. George Friedman, Jr. *Introduction to Compiler Construction with UNIX.* Englewood Cliffs, NJ: Prentice Hall, 1985.

Stevens, W. Richard. *UNIX Network Programming.* Englewood Cliffs, NJ: Prentice Hall, 1990.

Sun. *Debugging Tools.* Part Number: 800-4948-10. Mountain View, CA: Sun Microsystems, Inc., 1991.

Sun. *Network Programming Guide.* Part Number: 800-3850-10. Mountain View, CA: Sun Microsystems, Inc., 1990.

Sun. *Programming Utilities & Libraries.* Part Number: 800-3847-10. Mountain View, CA: Sun Microsystems, Inc., 1990.

Wirth, Niklaus. *Algorithms + Data Structures = Programs.* Englewood Cliffs, NJ: Prentice Hall, 1990.

Young, Douglas A. *The X Window System: Programming and Application with Xt.* Englewood Cliffs, NJ: Prentice Hall, 1990.

A

accelerator, 364, 366

action-file, 15

address
   domain, 220
   family, 223
   host, 220, 228
   Internet, 3, 218, 219, 220, 223
   IP, 223
   network, 218
   socket, 218, 219, 221

adjacent
   region, 197
   widget, 260, 261, 365

admin, 6, 33, 53, 54, 55, 56

AF_INET, 218, 219, 220, 223, 225, 226, 246, 251

AF_UNIX, 218, 223

AIX, 5, 35, 197, 198, 203, 205

alarm, 172, 173, 185, 191, 192

alias, 2, 166, 167, 168

annotation
   column, 332, 334, 341
   row, 332, 334, 342

ascent, 321

associativity
   left-associative operator, 84
   non-associative operator, 84
   right-associative operator, 84
   rule, 90

attachment
   bottom attachment, 260

attribute
   data, 313
   image, 313
   line style, 313

AVL-tree, 199, 202

awk, 15, 16, 51, 52

B

background color, 258, 312, 313, 319

backslash, 65, 66

Backus-Naur, 83

bind, 217, 218, 220, 223

BNF, 83, 84, 92

Bourne, 1–4, 7, 16, 31, 62

braces, 67

bracket, 4, 6, 66, 88, 93

breakpoint, 165, 167, 168, 170

broadcast, 224

BSD, 172, 217

byte_order, 313, 327, 328

bzero, 225, 226

C

calculator, 94
call-by-reference, 200
callrpc, 241
canvas, 312, 318, 334, 335, 339, 367
cascade, 270
case sensitive, 258, 262
checkin, 32, 33, 42
checkout, 32, 33, 39
chmod, 3, 53, 54, 55
circle, 310, 311, 314, 321
client, 170, 179, 223, 224
clnt_call, 241, 243, 247, 251
clnt_destroy, 243, 247, 251
clnt_pcreateerror, 243
clnt_perror, 243, 247, 251
clnt_stat, 243, 246, 250
clntcp_create, 241, 242, 246
close, 176, 180, 222, 224, 231
colormap, 302
configuration, 89
conflict
   shift/reduce, 83, 89
   reduce/reduce, 90
connect, 221, 224, 226
coredumpsize, 169
csd, 170
.cshrc, 2, 165
ctime, 57, 86

D

datagram, 218
dbx, 108, 165
.dbxinit, 166
DefaultColorMap, 302
DefaultDepthOfScreen, 320

DefaultRootWindow, 320
DefaultScreen, 292
delta, 32, 43
dependency, 19
derivation, 312
descent, 321
directive, 18, 84
display, 254
dollar sign, 66
domain, 218, 220
dot, 310, 314

E

editor, 253, 332, 333
enum, 243, 246, 250
environment, 364
escape sequence, 65
etext, 197, 198
execl, 80
export, 2, 34, 37
expose, 312, 315
extxt, 197

F

fcntl, 59, 178
FIFO, 177, 178, 179, 180
find, 12, 13, 14
finger, 219
finite-state, 85
flock, 57, 193
font, 258, 259, 263
fork, 80, 169, 170, 176, 223, 232
form widget, 254, 260, 261
formulation, 84, 85, 86
frame, 260, 261, 268

T

Y